Tide's Ending

TIDE'S ENDING

TIDE'S ENDING

by

'B. B.'

Illustrated by

D. J. WATKINS-PITCHFORD
F.R.S.A., A.R.C.A.

COLT BOOKS
Cambridge

White Lion Books
an imprint of
COLT BOOKS LTD
9 Clarendon Road
Cambridge CB2 2BH
tel: 01223 357047   fax: 01223 365866

First published by Hollis & Carter 1950

This edition first published by
White Lion Books 1999

Copyright © 1950 'BB'
and © 1999 The Estate of D. J. Watkins-Pitchford
Illustrations © 1950 Denys Watkins-Pitchford
and © 1999 The Estate of D. J. Watkins-Pitchford

ISBN 1 874762 46 5

British Library Cataloguing in Publication Data
A catalogue record for this book is available from the
British Library

Printed and bound in Great Britain by
Biddles Ltd, Guildford and King's Lynn

DEDICATED TO

MAJOR CHARLES OAKEY, M.C.

Companion of many wanderings

by Shore and Loch

Introduction

I HAVE wanted to write this book for years because it deals with a subject which is very dear to me—wildfowl and wild-fowling. I can say without hesitation that some of the happiest times of my life have been spent on the saltings and by the estuaries, sometimes with the gun and glasses, sometimes with glasses alone.

By nature I am a lone watcher and hunter; I prefer it that way. On one's own you see more and enjoy better sport. Wild-fowling, to get the full savour of it, *must* be enjoyed by the solitary man. A companion means distraction; half the magic has gone for me if I know there is a fellow hunter close at hand.

But I would hasten to say that when I return from that magic land of sand, saltings, and stars, I like to meet a companion with whom I can exchange experiences round a roaring fire (if possible over a pint of 'old and mild').

This is one of the things I look forward to after the day (or night) is done. The country where one hunts the grey geese is spacious, there are still places where one may walk the whole of a short winter's day and never meet with another gunner; there is room for two, or even three, fowlers to enjoy themselves without interfering with each other's sport.

I like to start out for flight in the darkness of a dawn with a friend at my side. I look forward to our meeting when I at last return, but once the happy hunting grounds are reached—give me solitude, give me isolation.

While I have been writing this book, which has been such a labour of love, I have been in spirit far out on the wind-swept, tide-washed saltings, or among the winter reed beds, with the sound of the surf and storm in my ears, and with the far clamour of the skeins in the background. I have been out once more on the frosty shore, with a full moon riding behind fleecy clouds, and all about me the luminous darkness has been alive with wings and the voices of wildfowl.

I am hoping (and it may be a vain hope) that something of this enjoyment of the inner spirit has found an echo in these pages.

To hear and see the wild geese flying and to roam the lovely lands they fly over, that is my life, my joy.

Northamptonshire, 1949   'BB'

Acknowledgements

Grateful thanks are due to Eyre and Spottiswoode Ltd. for the extract from the *Countryman's Bedside Book* (Shooting Geese at Night) and for the three extracts from the *Shooting Man's Bedside Book*, which appeared as essays entitled 'One Autumn Day', 'Flighting Wigeon on Kirkconnon Bay', and 'The First Star'.

Contents

'TIDE'S ENDING'

See where those leaning poplars stand
Along the far sea wall?
That is the outpost of the land,
There is the end of all,
Geese in skein, and the sound again
Of their clanging bugles blending,
Samphire scent, and a great content
In the place I call Tide's Ending.

Follow the sheep tracks' winding thread,
Draw deep the dawn wind blowing,
All the world is still and dead,
Only the tide is flowing,
Curlews call from the dim sea wall,
We'll take what the gods are sending,
The first gulls come, the flight's begun
In the place I call Tide's Ending.

Mark yon wheel of the Bar Point light
Uneasy in the gloaming,
Timid spark in the womb of night,
Guide for a curlew's homing,
Whistle of wings and ghostly things
Beyond all comprehending,
Tang of the sea, and a soul set free
In the place I call Tide's Ending.

'BB'

1. 'Back Again'

IHAVE often wondered whether I should have so great a love for wildfowl and 'fowling if I lived 'on the spot'.

I suppose I should. I have friends who are more fortunately placed than myself, living within a mile or two of 'goose country', who seem to be as keen as I am. But there is something to be said for dwelling far from the tidal ways; one keenly relishes expeditions to the coast, winter by winter; one looks forward to them for half the year.

Over many seasons the experienced longshore gunner, if he is enterprising and adventurous, comes to know many differing localities; each favourite haunt of duck, geese, and waders; he seeks out the very path through the reeds which he trod the year before, and looks for the same landmarks, or rather, marsh marks; the old rusty buoy in the mud of the dyke, the rotting timbers of the old crab boat, hull down in the sea lavender.

I have in my mind many such places and sometimes in high summer, when the meadows of my midland county are golden with buttercups and elms heavy in leaf, I look forward to the first morning's flight when winter is again upon the land. I dwell lovingly in my mind on the stack yard where I shall leave the car or cycle. How warm that stack smells on a black frosty morning, when the feet crackle on the ice of the cart track puddles! There will be a light burning in a window of the farm house, one of those old-fashioned oil lamps with an opaque glass globe, which smells so cosily on a winter's evening, when curtains are drawn and the logs blaze high.

Down the lane I tramp, and once clear of the farm buildings I feel the keen frost. Peewits call thinly somewhere out on the fields, and from the saltings there breaks upon the ear the babel of geese. What a moment that is to look forward to! It is perhaps a twelvemonth since last you heard it. That sound has as much magic for me as the first call of the cuckoo in spring, or the falling scales of the willow warbler in an April coppice.

Nothing seems to have changed since last I was here, nothing at all. There are the same loose strands of barbed wire which have to be negotiated in the darkness, the barbs of which invariably catch on the crutch of my trousers.

I know the path along the sea bank as intimately as a rabbit knows its run, every twist, every turn; the spot where care is necessary lest I slip down into the dyke which gurgles loudly in the quiet of dawn. Just beyond the dyke I must be careful of the thorn bush which bars the way, even the same brambles (but longer and more spiny) arch over to catch at me in the darkness.

Higher up the sea wall are many thick thorns wherein the newly arrived redwings roost, and sometimes the big fieldfares also. Their clucking notes are part of winter just as much as the call of the wild geese. As I make my way among the thickets these roosting birds are disturbed, bustling noisily among the branches so that I think the geese must surely hear me.

On a still frosty morning sounds carry a tremendous distance. The wildfowl on the sandbars and among the reeds fall silent as if they were listening, many hundreds of sharp ears are strained to catch the sinister rustle on the bank top, the anxious 'quip! whip!' of uneasy redwings.

I often picture to myself the fear the geese must have of these dark landward forests and the thorn-crowned sea wall. At dead of night, perhaps, they are less vigilant, but as they feel the dawn stealing on them, before even the east has paled, and the form of the mountains has grown dimly out of the darkness, ears and eyes become more alert. The snap of twig or rustle of reeds spells fear and danger, and as the light grows the geese draw clear of the merse edge, walking slowly out if the tide is at the ebb, their paddles 'plickplacking' on the sticky mud. As they go they leave a defined spoor.

When day has come and the flight is over, the longshore gunner can read in the mud all the doings of the night. Here among the short reeds the prints of webbed paddles wind in and out, a perfect maze. Where the short outermost reeds have been laid by wind and tide, forming a mattress which is both warm and dry, the vigilant eye may see where the big grey fowl have been sleeping. The reeds are pressed flat, pyramids of dung are here and there where the geese have evacuated in their sleep, one dropping piled upon another. Grey feathers also show where they have preened.

In actual fact, these short reeds give snug shelter, especially on windy nights. You have only to lie full length among them on a night when an icy nor'easter is blowing to find how cosy you can be. The wind cutting across the flats passes overhead; the reeds form a windshield.

The fieldfares inland know this; they wisely choose the tussocky pastures to roost in, or even long stubble; they know how much warmer it is there than perched up in the thickest thorn bush which lets the wind through like a sieve.

I grope along the bank foot, the thorns now and again plucking at my Balaclava until I come to an opening in the reeds.

Close by, there should be an old oil drum. At any rate, you remember it was there last season. Yes, there it is, still wedged under the roots of the hawthorn, close to the same rabbit hole.

Other fowlers have used this path on other mornings, their footmarks are visible in the black mud. All is frozen hard, the rubber boot slips on the black ice. A good thing it *is* hard or the sucking 'draw' of the 'gutty' boots in the mud would put every fowl on wing.

It is queer, too, how the frost remains down among these reeds. In the darkness the faint white glimmer of the track can be seen as it winds about among the brittle forests.

But the morning is too still, we need a wind to rustle the reeds. Even on the iron hard surface it is not easy to walk in silence. Now and again the boot breaks through the ice with a loud wheezing crack and into the black mud below goes the boot. You sink to above the calf, and when you struggle to draw out your foot there is a squelching 'thock' which must be heard by any goose within two hundred yards of you.

And so it happens. You hear a sudden threshing of big wings and an outburst of hoarse cackling which tells you a party of greylags, roosting in the 'plickplack'—the short reeds of the marsh edge—have heard your stealthy approach and have departed to the sand bars. The noise of their wings and their strident cacklings die away and you wish again this first morning's flight had been windy.

And then, very soon, there appears a faint dull grey glimmer which is the sea. The tall reeds cease and between you and the open muds is a hundred yards of short stuff: short, that is, if you are standing up, but long enough if you have the courage to get down and go 'like a worm upon your belly'.

On an 'open' morning this does indeed require a certain moral courage for the mud is icy cold and very soft, and as you crawl along your hands are buried. What a miserable business that is, crawling in soft half-frozen mud! In one hand you have to hold your gun, you progress upon your knees, aided by your other hand, and in time the water gets over the tops of your 'gutty' boots and your right hand becomes devoid of feeling.

Then you have to change over. With your slimy 'wooden' right you grasp the gun, and your left, hitherto warm and dry, has to take its share until it, too, is devoid of feeling.

But this morning the 'plickplack' is hard and will bear your weight. It feels firm under your knees, the hand does not penetrate the ice.

At last even the short reeds show signs of growing sparse and the time has come to choose your flight position.

This is not so easy. Somewhere here, I seem to remember, there should be a small dyke, a natural drain, about three feet deep and just wide enough to take my legs. Its bottom will be soft mud into which my feet will sink, giving me another useful six inches.

Yes, here it is, a little to the right, the same old dyke from which last year I slew my first greylag of the season.

The big waterproof goose bag is unslung from the back. Within is a deflated air cushion. This is quickly filled with air and placed again inside the bag, and putting this on the edge of the dyke I sit down. It is queer how warm I am with my exertions— even those furtive controlled exertions—and how good it is to sit down at last in a normal position and rest my aching back!

You can now enjoy the unfolding of the dawn, and even if you never have a shot there will be the magic of the waking wildfowl. Geese you will surely see, though whether they pass your way is quite another matter.

At such moments you can understand why wildfowling appeals to some men. No other form of sport can show such mysterious wonder, the wonder of the slow coming dawn, the waking of sleeping fowl.

You have transported your body many hundreds of miles to this spot where you now sit; all yesterday you were travelling, all for this moment.

These very still frosty mornings of midwinter are not conducive to big bags: you will be lucky if you have a shot at a goose. Duck there are in plenty. They whistled over from the dim dark fields just as the first glim of dawn began to show. From all sides came the stuttering quacks, but it was still too dark to make them out. Only a few late-comers were seen, wingless, headless bodies, passing over like jet-propelled planes, bound for the sand banks out in the sea.

But there *are* times when the greylags move on such a morning. Not big skeins, but odd birds, two or three, will sometimes take it into their heads to fly up the 'plickplack'. Why they do this I have no idea, but they may be seeking their fellows, or simply taking exercise. They usually make a good deal of noise, too, which advertises their coming. Moreover, they fly low, within easy shot, albeit as they go they zig-zag like gigantic snipe.

If you are lucky they may pass within range: on occasion, indeed, I have had them pass directly overhead, which is profitable to the bag.

But this morning they will not oblige. Geese there are in plenty out on the muds for you can see their dark blobby forms as the light grows over the hills, but none are in range and no bird is on wing.

They know they are secure, these wise birds! They are still drowsy. They sit with intucked heads, unapproachable by punt or crawling gunner. And they know it. Yet, it is fascinating to watch them.

As the light grows steadily they are easily seen, though as yet without detail or colour: black cut-out birds, absolutely motionless. And then one draws forth its head and in the bad light the neck seems to dwindle to a thread. You see the large blob of the body and above it the tiny blob of the head, the connecting neck is lost against the dazzle of shining muds.

This bird gives a croak and the others (there are five of them) untuck their heads also. Very slowly they walk away across the muds. As they go they seem to roll, it is difficult to see if they are approaching or retreating; all the birds appear very large and much nearer than they really are. Distances over mud, water, or sand are very deceptive. Sometimes even the redshanks seem to be as big as curlews.

I have often fired at geese over mud and later, when I have paced the range, I have found they had been ninety yards away when I could have sworn they were a scant fifty. It is a good dodge to stick some object in the mud opposite your birds as a range-finder, and I frequently do this.

Very quickly the shadows drain away and the sun peeps over the mountains across the estuary. With the coming of day the geese begin to move about in strings and bunches, but all are far out over the river. A few skeins swing inwards to the land. These are bound for some quiet pasture they know of where they can feed in peace. They are the hungry ones, but the big lots are full fed. On moonlight nights they feed in the short reeds, or even on the fields, though the greylag does not care for night feeding so much as the pink-footed goose.

I do not have a shot and at approximately 10 a.m. I get up from my gully and walk slowly back to the shore. In the bright sunlight the red berries of the haws gleam like coral. Upon them feast the redwings and fieldfares and an odd pigeon or two. And what an appetite one has for one's own breakfast!

Of course, the wildfowler, whether longshore gunner or punts-man, who lives on the spot has an immense advantage over the 'once a year' fowler. The puntsman, above all others, must take advantage of the weather.

There come days after prolonged frost when a milder air-stream forms fog over the waters, fog and a flat oily calm. Such times are good for the punter and he must away. Wild coarse weather would sink his craft, nor do the fowl 'sit' when the sea is boisterous. But the puntsman does not concern us in this book, he does not come within the category of the longshore gunner.

Your true longshore gunner is of a very definite calibre, very much a 'marsh lubber', he haunts the high sea mark, its marshes and reed beds; he is adept at camouflage and his wits are ever on the alert. All edible fowl are fair game; redshanks, curlew, plover, all are legitimate quarry, though duck and geese are his chief aim in life. If you want to understand what sort of man he is read the books of Abel Chapman. Chapman was the king of longshore gunners, though it is true he loved his punting also, and was a very good puntsman into the bargain. Chapman was able to identify every bird he saw, wader, duck, or goose, and, what is more, he knew the seasonal plumage changes which can be so confusing to the amateur.

Pot-hunting pure and simple is not the chief aim. I do not worry overmuch if the flight is a blank—which it usually is. I can never remember a single morning or evening flight which I found dull or boring; always there is something to watch, and there are other creatures in the wild places besides fowl.

Your true wildfowler has much of the patience of the coarse fisherman; indeed, fowling can sometimes be very similar; there is the same long wait with nothing stirring and when things do happen the excitement is usually over very quickly. In a week's fowling on an average marsh you will be lucky to secure a couple of geese; sometimes I have had only one, and that after much hard work. On one or two occasions I have had a fortnight with not a single goose to show for my trouble, and that in a locality where they abound.

Much depends on the weather. Those still frosty dawns I spoke of are seldom fruitful. Nor have I found arctic conditions particularly beneficial, as wild geese tend to go elsewhere when all their feeding grounds are frozen up. The answer to the fowler's prayer is wind, as strong a wind as possible, blowing along, or inshore. That wind can be as cold as you like as long as it is strong. Driving rain is also good and the onset of a snowstorm is sometimes excellent.

All these conditions the man on the spot can take advantage of, the 'once a year fowler' who books his digs months before must take pot luck. He may strike a still frosty week with glorious sun every day (and we get many such days in midwinter in the far north) and all his efforts on the shore will be in vain. Notice I say 'on the shore'. If he can find where the geese are feeding inland, then he will speedily fill the bag (if he has any wit about him), but inland shooting is poor sport to shooting on the shore. I would rather shoot a single goose on the wild saltings than fifty on an inland field. But there are times when inland shooting can be very good fun indeed, especially at night when geese are feeding under the moon.

The best chance for the shore is when the moon is young or when there is no moon at all. Then the geese will not feed in the hours of darkness but will either be sleeping in the reeds or out on the high sands, coming out at dawn. There are few certainties in wildfowling, but at such phases of the moon there is the consolation that if the geese are using the river, estuary, loch, or moss as sleeping quarters, *come in they will whatever the weather*. They may not come over you, they may be blown three miles up or down river, but at one point or points they will assuredly come. This is where the weatherwise fowler lays his plans. According to which way the wind blows (and at what strength it blows) he will decide upon the location for his hide at morning flight and again in the evening.

Perhaps the small diagram on page 10 may help the reader to understand what I mean.

That is to say, if you can locate where geese are sitting just at dawn, and you can take into account not only strength of wind but its direction, and also the state of the tide at 'lifting time'—that is, when the geese rise off the banks—then you can make a fairly shrewd guess where your best chance of a shot will be.

Geese will 'lift' between 8 and 9 a.m. on a January morning.

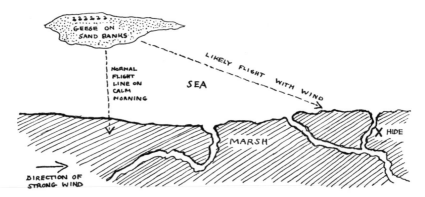

They seldom move in the early dawn, though if they are hungry I have known them to do so.

I remember one occasion at the new moon going to flight in complete darkness and hearing geese moving at about 7.30 a.m. One of us, farther down the sea wall, had one lot over his head and brought one down, a runner, which gave him a long exhausting chase across a ploughed field—no easy matter in the darkness. These geese must have been very hungry to 'lift' in the dark.

On an average I have found them come out surprisingly late; indeed, on calm mild mornings, little parties will keep coming off the banks from sun-up to nearly midday. On a very rough morning, however, they often come off all together in one wild ragged mob. Three or four shots and all may be over, every goose will have gone inland.

2. *Beginner's Gun*

THERE have been many books published in recent years which describe the habits of wildfowl, what guns and ammunition should be used, etc. I do not intend to deal with these matters at any length. Nevertheless, in over a quarter of a century, one learns a good deal for oneself in the hard school of practical fowling. It may be of some value if I touch on the question of firearms, though I deal more fully with this in a later chapter.

The beginner who wishes to slay geese will nearly always favour guns of large calibre, eight-bores, or even fours.

The reason is, I think, that when one first starts upon the long trail of the grey geese one begins by using an ordinary game gun, twelve-bore. You very soon learn that a shot which would crumple up a pigeon merely makes an old greylag fly a little faster. You hear the shot clap on his feathers and you are left with the feeling that your weapon is no longer lethal. The only time I should use a twelve-bore game gun on geese is at night when the birds are coming in low overhead to their feeding grounds.

But for the usual shots at geese which fall to the lot of the long-shore fowler something heavier is required, either an eight-bore or the three-inch twelve.

For the indifferent shot an eight-bore is a good gun for geese, though its weight is, of course, its great drawback. I have never favoured a double-eight because I have found it so unwieldy and cumbersome, and it needs a large, brawny individual to handle this heavy artillery. Indeed, I have only once in my life used a double-eight, and that was when I borrowed one from a friend. It weighed something in the region of fifteen pounds. Though an old under-lever, it was beautifully kept and the condition of the barrels was as good as the day it was made.

I had a shot at a high skein which was passing over a stubble field and the bird I fired at appeared unscathed. It flew on with the rest, but luckily I kept my eyes upon it and when it was half a mile distant it suddenly collapsed in the air and fell into a farm-yard among a flock of chickens. It was stone dead when I picked it up.

For fifteen years or so I did all my goose shooting with a single eight-bore. This gun I bought from a Birmingham firm. The price I paid for it was about four pounds ten shillings; a real old 'Bank' gun which had done duty for half a century on the Wash and Humber.

The length of its barrel is thirty-nine inches and its weight seven pounds, an unusually light weight for an eight-bore. It handles as well as a twelve, but owing to its lack of weight it kicks like a mule every time I fire it, and nearly always the recoil makes my nose bleed. I never troubled to have it proved for nitro powders until a friend, who knows more about ballistics than I do, advised me in no uncertain terms to have it sent to the Birmingham Proof House. It passed with flying colours, and I still use it on occasion.

I have memories of some wonderfully high shots at geese with this antique weapon, though high shots at geese are not to be boasted about; far too many shots are taken at the very limit of range, and this only means wounded birds which go off to die a lingering death.

There are times, however, when a big gun pays handsome dividends. Perhaps the best shot I ever made with my old 'Belching Bess' took place some years ago on an estuary in the far north.

Curiously enough, it was the first morning of my trip, a blustery cold dawn in 'open' weather.

As soon as I reached the sea wall I heard the sound of geese at full sea mark, and from the noise they were making it seemed to me that the 'grand army' was well into the 'plickplack'. One usually finds on most estuaries that the greylags keep together in a big lot, or 'grand army' in fowlers' parlance.

This is especially so when they gather at their roosting places. The tide that morning was on the ebb. It had been a fairly big one, which meant the birds had not slept on the sand-banks in mid-sea but had been floated into the short reeds in the early hours of night.

Greylags do not like to sleep on the water; they prefer solid ground on which to rest, whether it be sand-bank or merse edge. There was sufficient wind to make a rustling in the reeds, enough to drown the sound of my approach, and I soon began to realize that if only I took my time I was in for a 'big' shot.

I got through the tall reeds and reached the 'plickplack' where I adopted my usual tactics of 'bellying' to the fowl, a very un-pleasant job as there had been no frost. The gabbling and 'gungling' seemed very loud, but now and again every bird would fall silent as though listening for the approach of an enemy.

Each time this occurred I lay low and only continued my grisly crawl when they began to chatter afresh.

This sound of a large body of geese heard at close quarters is very curious. All the while there is an underlying buzz which has a curious effect on the ear drums. I have noticed this same 'buzz' when stalking feeding barnacle geese.

For the first part of my stalk I could progress on hands and knees, but as I got farther out I had to lie full length and roll myself along, pushing the eight-bore in front of me, always making sure that the muzzle was clear of the mud. Many an accident has happened through an incautious fowler neglecting this precaution. Mud down the barrel can very easily cause a burst.

By now the light was beginning to grow, though I had begun my stalk in darkness, and I feared that at any moment the geese would begin to walk out. But they still maintained their animated buzz of conversation, with the occasional pause to listen.

Up to now I had not dared to lift my head to see exactly where my quarry was, but now they sounded so close I judged them to be well within range.

But sounds over water are deceptive. Though I could hear the plack of their paddles in the mud and the sloshing sound of the birds tearing at the reed roots on which they feed, I found they were still over eighty yards away, as near as I could judge. So I rolled on my way, and at each wallow the icy water was creeping into my 'gutty' boots.

I had taken the precaution to 'mud' my face well on the cheeks, a wise move if you would stalk geese. Pale flesh shows up very vividly against the sombre tones of the marsh.

When next I raised my head and peered into the dimness I at last made out a mass of large blobs, right ahead of me. They seemed to be in range. Nearer I dare not go, as any moment they might see or wind me, though I do not believe that wildfowl have any great sense of smell.

I pulled back the big hammer and rose on one knee, and at that moment the whole pack saw me and lifted. I fired at once and for a moment did not know what had been the effect of over two ounces of BB shot whistling amongst them.

When I jumped to my feet and ran forward I found three geese were lying dead, while another lay a little way out on the mud. It was certainly the best shot I have ever made with my old Bank gun. It had been a puntsman's shot though, of course, not so murderous. The skill had lain in the stalking and not so much in the firing, though pulling the trigger at the chosen moment had been well judged.

This fortunate start to a fortnight's goose hunting was well maintained, because after gathering my birds I went back to the tall reeds and a little later three greylags passed up the shore and I brought the leader down, making a fifth goose.

To show the uncertainties of fowling, though I spent another thirteen days in the locality, I only managed to bring to bag another couple of geese. My luck had been in that morning, and I have never equalled that record for a first morning's flight.

Needless to say, never again while I was there did the geese come near that particular section of marsh. The wise birds have retentive memories and once 'shot up' are careful to give the scene of past disasters a wide berth.

By going to one particular haunt season after season one gets to know the ways of wildfowl and how they will react under various types of weather and tide. One gets to know the best places to choose an ambush, the shortest way there, and how to tackle a stalk if opportunity offers. How useful that knowledge is!

How can the casual fowler, strange to a locality, expect to meet with any measure of success without local knowledge? Some employ professional fowlers, but I have found such men, naturally, do not show you the best places, it is against their interests to do so, and it is always best to gain what knowledge you can for yourself. I have picked up useful tips from non-fowlers in the tap room of the 'local'. Living in the district all their lives they are bound to get to know where the 'canny laddies' go and they do not mind imparting information, especially if a free pint or two is in the offing. The non-shooting publican can very often put one wise, especially if he caters for the fowling fraternity.

But not many village pubs on the coast *will* cater for fowlers, who are a dirty, unpunctual race. I have always found the best quarters in rooms at the village shop or croft. Before the war the business of accommodation was not the problem it is to-day when everyone earns good money and will not be bothered to take in 'lodgers'.

The stalking of geese is an art in itself. No other wild creature is so hard to approach save the Highland stag and some maintain, very rightly in my opinion, that stalking a stag is easier than stalking a goose.

The stag is usually in broken ground where heather and hill give cover. The goose has to be stalked, invariably, over a flat terrain with very little cover, and you have to approach far closer. They are usually too cunning to feed near 'dead' ground, nor will they usually feed within range of a dyke.

I once saw that fine goose hunter, S. W. P. Freeme, 'belly' to a goose over flat grass marsh on the Solway (in broad daylight), but this was an exception.

It was also, perhaps, the best stalk I have ever witnessed. We had noticed the goose (or geese, I seem to remember that there were two of them) pitch on the flat merse while we were walking along an adjacent road.

Freeme immediately decided to stalk and he set off. When first we saw them pitch they must have been three hundred yards away, possibly more, and it took Freeme about half an hour to get within shooting distance, creeping perfectly flat on his stomach with his head down. For some reason the geese never flew, though they had seen him almost from the start of his stalk. It may have been that they were inquisitive.

Freeme took his shot at about eighty yards and knocked one of the greylags over. He certainly deserved his bird, but all the next day he suffered agonies from stomach cramp.

This stalk took place on the marshes near a little village called Glencaple on the Nith. Glencaple was, in the old days, a most delightful spot for fowlers and at times the shooting was good, especially in wild weather. The pub was excellent and mine host catered for wildfowlers and knew their little ways.

I shall never forget my first introduction to Glencaple. We arrived one January night in a snowstorm and as we got out of the car weary with travel (we had motored over three hundred miles), we heard the greylags calling in the darkness from the marsh over the water.

I heard them at intervals through the night and next morning we were up for flight and were ferried over the Nith by a professional fowler.

Two other guns were staying at the inn and we lined the gullies just as it began to get light. I had one shot with my old Bank gun which knocked me backwards into a deep dyke and I was *hors de combat* for the rest of the flight. But Freeme brought down a very high greylag and I saw the other gun, a youth armed with (I regret to say) an American pump gun, bring down four wigeon one after the other out of a pack which went over his head.

I have been to Glencaple many times since, but I have never seen the greylags there in force as they were on that first visit. In any case the Solway, though it always has its population of ducks and geese in great variety, is now so overshot that it is hardly worth a trial. I shall nevertheless describe later some of my early adventures there, for I like to think of it as it was in the good old days when one hardly saw another fowler in a week's creek crawling.

3. *The Joy of the Game*

WILDFOWLING does not appeal to everyone; you have to be of a certain temperament really to enjoy it. A love of solitude and of natural history are necessary. The strange thing is that many of the men I know who are keen fowlers are able to paint and draw quite well. Even the old hard-baked coastal natives who go out after ducks and geese seem to have a liking for artistic work in their spare time, and on the walls of their cottages you will most likely see the inevitable Peter Scott print alongside their own crude daubs.

Though your good longshore gunner prefers to hunt his game alone he likes a chat about it afterwards with his pals. When I go on my expeditions I always take a well-tried friend with me, many of them public schoolboys. In every big school there are one or two really keen individuals who have the makings of good fowlers, and for many years I took a boy with me from Rugby. It was enjoyable for him and also for me, for I delighted to see the keenness of youth which one rarely finds in the middle-aged, an enthusiasm which is infectious even to the adult. It is a melancholy fact that as we grow older we lose much of the thrill we got out of shooting as boys.

Every moment of the trip was enjoyable, from the setting out on the long journey to the arrival at our fowling quarters, which was usually in the early hours of the morning.

During the war years when petrol was restricted we had to take our bicycles with us, and I have many memories of disem-barking from the stuffy train at the terminus, and setting off on our cycles on the fourteen-mile ride to the little village where we always stayed. What a relief it was to draw deep breaths of that icy northern air after the stale atmosphere of the railway carriage, and all sense of travel weariness was banished.

Nothing but the low crackling of our tyres on the frosty road and all about us the smell of the pine woods, black and ghostly under the moon.

And then at last the woods dropped away as we reached the flat lands, the real goose country, and every year, if the moon was full, we stopped at a certain spot to listen for the first call of geese. It was amazing how, on these moonlight nights, we nearly always heard that far-up magic music from the hounds of heaven, the only audible sound in a world of greenish moonlight. Away to the north the mountain ranges were clearly visible, gleaming dully white with snow, and over them glowed quiet stars. Even the singing of the telegraph wires was stilled, not a dog barked, not a light shone save from the moon and stars.

I remember some years when snow lay on the road and bitter winds blew, but we never had to face that long ride in rain and we usually had the wind behind us.

At long last we neared the village and saw the rise in the ground and the little oak spinney on the right of the road.

Our digs were always at the village shop and ideal quarters they proved to be, with a large room where we could spread ourselves and always a grand roaring fire to greet us. As our arrival took place at two or three in the morning the whole village would be wrapped in slumber, but we would always see a glow from the upper window of our room which overlooked the street. The dear little lady who looked after us would soon come shuffling down to let us in, and what a joy it was to see once again the old familiar quarters, the same pictures on the wall and the Christmas decorations not yet taken down, holly on the mantel shelf; a new calendar hanging in the chimney corner being the only fresh note. There, too, would be a tide-table cut out of the local paper propped up by the clock. Miss Tares always cut this out for us and put it ready, and it was one of the first things we looked at.

Then followed a quick meal and we would turn in for a brief snatch of sleep before morning flight. It seemed hardly a moment before the alarm clock was summoning us to action, though neither my companion nor myself slept very soundly with the prospect of our first morning's flight before us.

A gulp from the Thermos flask, a sandwich or two, and we would don our fowling gear, the high 'gutty' boots with their newspaper soles (no 'sock' is so good as that made of several layers of paper), the leather waistcoat lined with fleece, and finally the stout waterproof shooting coat on top. Then down the dark stairway and a fumbling at the door catch and we would step out into the darkness, wondering what the first morning's flight had in store for us.

There was a steep hill just outside the village with several sharp bends, and when the weather was frosty and snow lay on the ground the descent of this hill was a nerve-wracking experience on a bicycle, burdened as we were with heavy guns and ammunition.

It took us about twenty minutes to reach the farm-yard where we left our cycles under the stack and another ten minutes to reach the sea wall.

The numbers of fowl varied from year to year. When I first began to visit the estuary regularly the geese were far more plentiful, especially the pink-footed geese. But the war wrought great changes. The favourite feeding grounds of the pinks were the flat green meadows within two miles of the sea, but these were taken over by the Air Ministry. A large aerodrome was built, and this drove the pinks away. They still frequent the locality but rarely feed on the old grounds. They forage farther afield over the mountains, returning every day or so to the estuary for a wash and rest.

The return of the whole Pink army to the estuary is usually a fascinating sight. It occurs sometimes during the afternoons when the tide is at the ebb and the sand-banks are exposed. It may well be that they have been disturbed on their feeding grounds over the hills, or that they have need of grit and a bathe. I have noticed that they rarely arrive in force when the tide is at full flood, though I have seen them come when the tide is flowing, and then they never stay long on the sand-banks because they are pushed off by the flow. It is amusing to see them arranged in their military order on the exposed sand bars when the tide is flowing strongly. The bars nearest the sea are, of course, flooded first and party after party rise up to join their companions higher up the estuary. They fly low, 'clawing along', as old Chapman used to say, in serpentine lines, making a beautiful musical clamour. When they reach their brethren there is a great outburst of cackling. The geese which are already settled stretch their necks, gabbling at the new-comers, giving them a great welcome. Then they fall silent save for an occasional old gander who calls 'quink! link! quink! wink!' These two words exactly express the call of the pink-footed goose.

Many writers talk of the 'honking' of wild geese. The only goose which 'honks' is the Canada goose which, in this country, is not really a wild goose, though there are signs that it may one day become truly wild as small parties roam the country, haunting large sheets of water both inland and near the coast. The Canada goose, however, is much more an inland species; one rarely sees it on the sea, save at Holkham, in Norfolk, where they frequently resort to the private marshes on Lord Leicester's estate.

But to return to the pinks. As the tide pushes higher and with greater force the long black line, which may be composed of some two thousand birds, at last takes the air, not all at once, but in three or four big lots, and away they go, climbing all the time, and pass from sight over the mountains. They may be heading for some lonely loch or, if early in the afternoon, they will have another feed before dusk, that is, if there is no moon.

I believe that the pinks are more sagacious than the greylags and they keep much more together. In a greylag locality you will often notice three or four birds, or even single birds, flying in to the fields, and they do not always take the trouble to climb out of gunshot range, as the pinks always do, but will flop in low over hedges and stacks.

But the greylag is a cunning bird and unless ill or wounded will never pitch straightway upon his chosen field. He circles it in a maddening fashion for several minutes to see if the coast is clear before setting his wings and dropping his paddles to alight.

And when he does come down it is invariably in the very centre of the field.

The coastwise pastures are usually devoid of cover, no hedges to speak of, and the boundaries between field and field are post and wire fences: indeed, one of the characteristics of 'goose country' is the spindly fence posts and interminable wire, and the only cover will be an occasional dyke or burn.

Sometimes it happens that a shot may be obtained from the cover of a burn. I have in mind one particular burn which I know very well and from whose shelter I have in the past accounted for several greylags.

Greylags are very particular in their feeding grounds. They will resort year after year to one special field and will never alight on other pastures which to us appear identical.

There was one field where I always used to expect sport, season after season. It was not large and curiously enough was a dangerous feeding ground for geese because on the north side was the course of the burn, its banks thickly grown with alders. The banks were so steep and deep they afforded excellent cover. If you saw greylags on the pasture and could once reach the shelter of the burn without them spotting you, the chances of a shot were fairly certain.

My method was to creep up this bank until I was opposite the feeding birds and then lie in wait, just as an old fox does when he is stalking mallard.

In time the greylags would wander closer and closer to the burn; they never fed in the opposite direction because there was a footpath there along the top of a sea wall.

The wait was probably a long one, sometimes a couple of hours or more, but if I was patient and did not show myself, one bird would at last come within a long gunshot of my ambush and with my three-inch case Magnum twelve, loaded with BB shot, I could often knock it over.

I remember waiting thus the whole of a winter's afternoon. Snow was on the ground but the geese had scraped a clear place in the centre of the field exposing the sweet grass underneath (greylags eat a lot of grass). Six geese were on the field and after a while they began to feed my way. Occasionally the creak of a distant farm cart or the barking of a dog would cause them to raise their heads, but after a while they would go on quietly plucking the grass. It is very interesting to watch wild geese when they are at feed. There will always be one bird with its head up, though there is no systematic sentry changing, no guard mounting, as some naturalists have averred. One goose will remain standing very still with its head turning from side to side for three minutes or so and then will begin to graze and another bird, by some mysterious instinct, will take its turn to watch.

Their eyesight is perhaps the keenest of any wild creature and their range of vision is long. They are extremely quick to spot the tiniest movement or suspicious object and the half-glimpsed pale spot of a man's face is instantly detected. When this occurs the sentry will utter several low croaks, which puts every goose on its guard. All heads are raised. If you bob down again they will remain watching for six or seven minutes, and may, or may not, go on with their feed. Usually, however, when anything suspicious has been seen, they will begin to walk slowly away from the suspected danger and with a sudden running and cackling take wing.

This particular afternoon I lay behind the bole of an alder. There was plenty to interest me. Vast flocks of foreign wood pigeons had lately come in, and these were feeding round some oat stacks on the far side of the field. A mile or so to the west were some big fir plantations in the Castle grounds, and all that afternoon streams of pigeon came flying from these woods, settling first in the alders up the burn, close to where I was lying in wait; some actually came and perched above me and never saw me.

Fieldfares also kept me occupied. I like these handsome winter thrushes and never cease to wonder at their wariness. In the vast pine forests of the Baltic it is unlikely they are disturbed by man or molested in any way, yet they are as cunning almost as geese and will rarely allow you to get within range, save in very hard weather. Incidentally, they are excellent eating, as good as golden plover.

There was nothing to disturb the geese that afternoon, no men were working on the fields near their chosen pasturage, and for an hour or so they fed undisturbed.

I knew my only chance lay in waiting where I was in the hope they would come in range, and when it got dusk I intended to 'belly' along the bank to the sea wall and get between them and the estuary, as greylags will always flight out low at dusk. They remain on the ground until it is late dusk and will then come in, offering an easy shot, if you happen to be under them.

There was one very big gander who fed a little apart from the rest and he seemed to be the chief lookout man. But I was glad to see that he was slowly feeding my way. He would stop now and then and have a prolonged scrutiny of the bank behind which I lay, but he had seen nothing suspicious, and after a long time he had come within ninety yards of me and I began to see the details of his plumage clearly.

There was a minor excitement at about four o'clock when another party of eight greylags came over the alders of the burn above me and joined those already at feed. I thought at one time I might get a shot at them, for I had heard them coming and had glimpsed them flying towards my ambush.

But in the uncanny way they have, they had altered course and dropped in wide.

The arrival of the newcomers seemed to ease the mind of my old gander who became bolder and advanced another twenty yards in my direction. I was afraid that at any moment something would put them up, as farm labourers sometimes took the path along the sea wall on their way home from work and it was now about the time when labour was ending for the day. So I decided to risk a shot at about eighty yards with a long case of AA shot.

I edged the gun up and cuddled my face down to the stock and the old gander saw me at that moment and jumped. But I lifted the gun and shot high and saw he was hit. All the other geese arose, of course, with a deafening clamour, and my old goose followed after them. But he was flying low and I knew he was hit. He cleared the sea wall and dropped from sight. I ran across the snow, climbed the fence and dashed down through the reed beds. When I reached the 'plickplack' I could see no sign of any goose and concluded he had dropped in the tall reeds or had made the estuary. The tide was out and with my glasses I scanned the muds.

And then far out near the tide line I made out a 'lump', with two crows sitting by. It might have been my goose or a clot of sea wrack, but I determined to see what it was and set off over the muds. It was heavy walking for there had not been enough frost to 'set' the surface, but I reached the object and found indeed it was my bird, a magnificent old gander with a snowy white stern.

It is always wise to follow a bird you think is hit. Many will reach the tide and be swept away, but it sometimes happens that they drop before they reach the water.

4. *Field Work*

THE alarm clock was buzzing hideously, grinding out its harsh summons as though some little devil was winding a handle. I awoke with a start and realized how much I wanted to turn over and have another sleep. Moreover, the night before had been Hogmanay and, as every Englishman knows, the Scots let themselves go on that night of nights in all the year. Our digs had been invaded by First Footers in the last stages of inebriation and one had tried to force an entry into my room. He was, I think, urgently seeking an apartment other than a bedroom. I had pushed him out and shut and locked the door, but the noise had continued well into the small hours. At 3 a.m. I heard distant singing of 'Auld Lang Syne' and breathed a prayer that all would now be quiet and that we could get a little sleep before flight. But no, not a bit of it! In a moment or two all the row started up again, people rushing up and down the stairs and other folk making merry in the frosty street.

At last, however, merciful quiet had come, the revellers had staggered away to their homes.

Even old Jim Jagoe, our fowler friend who lived in the little cottage on the burn, had, I knew, been making preparations for

27

Hogmanay. Like everyone else he let himself go on this occasion. The Scots may be a dour race for three hundred and sixty-four days in the year but on the three hundred and sixty-fifth they make up for it!

Even Jim would be incapable this morning, bay the geese never so loudly outside his cottage door.

I envied 'J.J.' his cottage. It was to my mind an ideal fowler's house, built right on the banks of the burn which ran into the estuary, sheltered from the north by a swelling bank topped with thorns, and from the westerly gales by a row of tall trees which lined the sea wall. His punt was tied up almost by his front door, his cabbage patch went down to the brown crinkling water from which he won himself many a breakfast of sea trout.

To-day, Jim's cottage is no longer standing. When I last visited the district I was aghast to see it burnt to the ground and nothing but charred wood and corrugated iron heaped up among the weeds. Poking about in the rubble I had found Jim's fork, one of those old-fashioned, very sharp, two-pronged forks like a pitchfork. I brought it away as a memento, even though the wrinkled stag-horn handle was half-burnt through. I wanted it because I imagined all the appetizing meals he had eaten with it, many a succulent goose's breast had felt its sharp tines.

It appeared that old 'J.J.' himself had set fire to the cottage when he came home one Hogmanay night the worse for wear (he lived alone and was a bachelor). Both he and his Springer spaniel had been lucky to escape with their lives. Nothing could be done to save the cottage. In an hour or two Jim was without a roof. Apparently an oil stove had been his undoing. While trying to light it he had overturned the whole contraption and the flaming oil had run all over the wooden floor. Jim, in his inebriated state, had been unable to cope. He had staggered down to the burn with a bucket and had fallen in. Luckily he wasn't drowned, because the water and mud were deep when the tide was flowing. As it was he managed to get out, much sobered down but still very fuddled. He had poured water on the hungry flames and, of course, had only spread the conflagration.

Nobody knows where Jim went after the disastrous Hogmanay. Rumour had it that he went to Glasgow to live with an aged brother. There, by all report, he died. And no wonder: Jim Jagoe, living in a great city far away from his beloved marshes and the sound of the geese he hunted with such persistency!

Scrabbling about the pitiful ruins I came upon a heap of goose bones and a quantity of feathers—enough to stuff a sofa—under a gooseberry bush. This was evidently the place where Jim plucked his geese and where he threw away the bones after he had subtracted the gravy and marrow and Jess, his Springer, had had her share.

But to return to my narrative.

That year my shooting companions were Douglas Mcdougal and Angus McCance, the latter a boy still at Rugby and a keen wildfowler. Douglas Mcdougal, or 'Mac', also an incurable devotee of goose hunting, had arrived the day before and had brought with him his massive packing case, a sort of Pandora's Box, which contained four or five stuffed geese. Mac is a keen decoyman and will never be separated from his 'coys', though I have never had very great faith in this method of attracting geese.

That was a war winter and, therefore, we had no petrol; journeys had to be done by cycles, and it was a very different matter to the palmy days of peace-time fowling when one threw everything into the boot of the car.

We gulped down our coffee from the tall Thermos flask and pulled on our 'gutty' boots. Angus, peeping through the window curtains, pronounced the morning to be dry and frosty. A moment later we were thumping down the stairs, guided by the beam of an electric torch.

We opened the door and stepped out into the garden, and I

reflected that, in all probability, we were the only sober mortals in the village that morning. The crofts seemed wrapped in a Sabbath calm, not a light showed anywhere.

Mac went on ahead, his precious stuffed decoys slung across his back. In the dim light he looked like Herne the Hunter and seemed possessed of horns.

Perhaps of all the fowlers it has been my good fortune to meet, both professional and 'gentleman' fowlers, Mac is the keenest of them all. I flatter myself I am enthusiastic where geese are concerned, but the energy of Mac is inexhaustible. Once on the long trail of the grey geese the matter of bodily comfort, dry clothes, and meals are of no import to Mac and he will gladly stay out all day long, and all night too, if there is a chance of a successful shot at a goose.

Our destination that January dawn was not the coastwise marshes (in any case it was not a good morning for the creeks as it was so still and frosty).

We had in mind a certain stubble field well inland, about two miles distant from the village, where we had of late noted considerable activity. We certainly had that field 'under observation' and had already scouted the ground and obtained permission from the owner to try for the geese which were using it in considerable numbers. In size it was about twenty acres, a stubble field which had been cut by combine. A long 'straw' had been left on the field and much of it lay about in loose bundles all over the surface.

On its southern and northern sides it was bounded by deep dykes, one full of unwadable water, the other more or less dry. The latter had a certain amount of cover from small thorn bushes growing along the steep slopes of the dyke bank.

The geese, of course, came nowhere near these dykes but kept religiously to the very centre of the field, though they did on occasion fly within range of the ditches.

For the last three days increasing numbers of both greys and pinks had been using this stubble and all day long from daybreak to dusk we had seen small and large parties going back and forth to the estuary.

Leaving our cycles behind some stacks we walked out to the centre of the field. It was still quite dark, though a faint greyness to the east showed that dawn would not be long in coming.

Mac was bent on using his decoys and this being so we set to work to make a hide in the middle of the field, though it was against my better judgement. By the time it was finished it resembled a miniature blockhouse and my doubts were now increased.

The decoys were set out head to wind and Angus and I took up our station in the dykes, while Mac retired into his citadel to await the arrival of the geese.

They began coming in very early. The first thing I knew was a low croak and a party of six greylags appeared out of the gloom and circled the field. They saw the blockhouse and the decoys, and after a little conversation they decided they did not like the look of things and beat off for the estuary again.

Another party arriving half an hour later, just when the moun-tains were sharp against the dawn, did the same thing. They also departed hastily. It was then an idea was born in my mind.

To get a start at all the blockhouse must go. I knew that at this rate we should get no geese all day. I therefore ran over to Mac and told him my plan. It was this. The hide was to be obliterated and one gunner at a time was to go out to the field centre, lie down flat on his back, while his companions covered him with loose straw. When the gunner was concealed, then the other two were to retire to the dyke banks and remain hidden. They were to blow a blast on a whistle when geese were seen approaching the field.

Having thought of this simple scheme myself, I elected to be the first man down. Mac was therefore winkled out of his blockhouse and packed off to the dyke plus his decoys, having covered me over before he left.

I lay stretched out on the frosty stubble with the gun between my knees, staring up at the grey sky through the interstices of the straw. I had my twelve-bore with me, the three-inch case gun, loaded with BB shot, and I must say I felt very confident. I defied any goose in the world to spot me, and provided Angus and Mac kept their heads down and did their stuff, I was sure of a shot.

The minutes passed. Some dumpy golden plover went over, plaintively piping, and after a while a little party of larks came dipping and twittering right over my head. One pitched within a foot of my face and never saw me. I felt more confident than ever. Occasionally a gull flew over with steady wing beat, for it was the time of day when they were leaving the sea for their inland foraging.

Then I heard Mac's blast on the whistle and my numb fingers felt for the trigger. I lay quite still. My plan was to wait until I heard the thresh of wings and then jump to my feet.

Then I heard a croak, very close. A goose must have passed within a few feet of me because I heard a 'wish wish' of broad pinions. But it had come and gone so suddenly I had not stirred. I knew, however, that it was, in all probability, circling, and in this conjecture I was correct. By raising my head a little I just glimpsed it turning about ninety yards away and round he came, directly for me, with his paddles down, just like a plane with retractable undercarriage lowered. I would have been a perfect mug to have missed.

I waited a second, then got up deliberately. By then the goose was almost on top of me. He braked with all his might and started to turn, but I dropped him twenty-five yards out and he never moved a paddle.

It was now Mac's turn, and he had his eight-bore. He had not long to wait, no more than ten minutes. By that time it was quite light and the sun was coming up over the snow-clad hills.

A party of about ten greys hove in sight. Through the glasses

I could see them almost as soon as they left the sea, a little bundle of black blobs against the dawn sky.

I gave a blast on the whistle and lay flat. The geese came in over Angus who was in the far dyke but he, good lad, never showed himself and they made a circle of the field. Then they swung away for the sea and I thought they had spotted Mac, but no! round they circled once more to set their wings and to glide directly over the hidden gunner. I saw the straw stir, as Mac hoisted himself up, his great gun swinging.

The startled geese, croaking frantically, scattered, coming directly for my dyke. The big gun went off with a double thunder-clap. One goose fell dead on the field, another came tumbling over the dyke to hit the pasture twenty yards behind me, a right and left. I had two forlorn shots at the rest of the skein as they banked round and should, I think, have had another. My plan was working well.

Angus then took his turn and now we had a longer wait.

The next skein which came was a big one, all pink-footed geese. These circled the field but did not give Angus a chance; they seemed suspicious of something and went off for the hills. A single goose soon after gave Angus a long shot but he failed to connect, and then we decided to go home for breakfast.

We ambushed the field the following morning, and I had another couple of geese and Mac a single, after which no more came, nor did they again resort to that field. In some way they had grown wise to the danger, as geese always do, but that night we had some splendid fun with mallard which came on to the stubble just at darkling.

Though this particular example of field work was exciting enough, other days spent on inland pastures have been dull, uneventful vigils. Ambushes in dyke or hide with decoys set out on the feeding ground sometimes offer shots, but there is not the interest one finds on the coast, there is not the movement and excitement of the tidal ways. From a marsh dyke or ambush in the reeds one can always see something of interest, the small waders flitting up and down high sea mark, and an occasional duck, though on the particular estuary I have in mind the duck shooting is uncertain and only on very wild mornings or evenings can any appreciable sport be enjoyed. The estuary is so vast and the flight lines of the mallard are so undefined that one may go out for a fortnight and never get a shot at duck. It must be remembered, however, that when one is goose hunting the duck takes second place, all one's energies are concentrated on geese.

On numberless occasions, while waiting for geese to lift at dawn, mallard have come swimming down the gutter close to my hide, and nearly every morning I could have bagged a mallard or two just as it was getting light. One may shoot mallard inland at home, but the average fowler shoots nothing but geese when the latter are in the vicinity.

Some people like shooting on the fields and even prefer it to marsh shooting. Early in the season when the geese have just arrived and are, as yet, unversed in the 'drill', big bags are sometimes made from field ambushes. On one or two occasions I have had some amusing times stalking them. Once, I remember, another good sportsman, Major Charles Oakey, M.C., and myself had an amusing experience. Geese, greylags, had been using a grass field about a mile from the sea and we had built a hide against a fence, setting out decoys in front. We had got under cover at dawn and had spent a fruitless three hours with nothing stirring. It was a cold cheerless morning, and after waiting until after 10 a.m. we decided to go home for breakfast. When we returned we found a small party of greys feeding among the decoys, a most unusual occurrence, as wild geese are usually very quick to notice that the stuffed birds *are* decoys.

I will close this chapter on field work by describing one more ambush, this at night, on a field in Angus. This account has already appeared in my book *The Countryman's Bedside Book*, published by Eyre and Spottiswoode, who have kindly given permission for me to reprint it here.

It gives a true picture of moonlight field work, and this particular night was perhaps the best I have ever enjoyed inland, though I do not greatly relish killing a large number of geese. A bag of six or seven for a fortnight's fowling is ample reward for any sports-man. But every good fowler likes one 'big' night in his career.

I do not know that I want to repeat the experience.

After a week of mild weather, in which we got several geese, a hard frost set in and the marshes were frozen. All the geese in the river seemed to go away and the night before the frost I saw skein after skein heading away north over the hills. Wherever one looked one could see little black bundles hung in the sky, bundles which constantly changed shape, bunching one moment, attenuated the next.

The following morning not a goose was to be heard or seen, so there was nothing to do but consult our old friend Bob Kennedy. We were at his little cottage bright and early and found him just finishing his breakfast with his spaniel sitting waiting for scraps.

"I know what you've come for," said Bob; "no geese on the river, eh?"

"Not a goose, Bob."

"Ah, that means they'll be awa' over the hills. I know where we'll find 'em. There's only one thing to do. We must chase 'em. It's coming full moon now and they will be feeding at night when the men have left the fields. The best thing for us to do is to go and see the grieve."

So an hour or two later my friend and I, plus Bob and his spaniel, were speeding up the mountain road. It was a wonderful morning, so wonderful I can see now the pale wintry sunlight flooding the tawny bracken on the hillsides and the white frost on the shadowed banks. We reached the summit of the pass and dropped down the other side.

Once we saw a lovely sight. On our right a humped field of golden brown plough, beyond was a birch wood, the stems silver in the sunlight, and wheeling round and round over the field with their blue shadows under them, was a skein of about fifty pink-footed geese.

Though we were fairly close, not more than a hundred yards or so, the geese ignored us, and with a graceful sweep they all came to rest on the centre of the field. After looking at them for some time we continued on our way. In the fresh light of the morning the country was spread out below us; the far fir woods and scattered plantations, the wide fields and little farms, each with its cluster of conical ricks, and far in the distance more blue mountains on the horizon. In places where the sun had not reached the road, care was necessary, for overnight there had been about an inch of snow on this high ground and the twists and turns were dangerous.

Soon we were down on the flat fertile plain and after several winding roads we eventually drew up opposite the farm. We found the grieve at his lunch (it was eleven o'clock) and he came down the garden to meet us.

He was a man of about five foot eleven with dark hair and a face like an eagle. There was something almost Welsh in his appearance. His fine dark eyes, looking out from beneath bushy brows, reminded me of some hawk or falcon. He had an almost gipsyish, wild look about him. When he talked he looked you straight in the eyes.

"Och yes to be sure the geese were using the fields right enough, there's no mistake aboot that."

He had seen them the day before, he had heard them all night long; indeed, they had made so much noise they had disturbed his sleep!

"They may be there now, doon on the far field, that's where they come, on the last field on the edge of the farm, near the fir wood."

We walked down the lane by the big ricks. A bitter wind blew out of the north but it was a morning of glitter and sunlight. Our boots crunched and squeaked on the thin snow covering and cracked hollowly on the ice skins over the cattle pocks. Below the farm the fields sloped away; it was hard to tell which was stubble and which arable, all was hidden under the white covering. Here and there I could see a long potato or swede clamp; in one field a lot of sheep were feeding round some hay dumps. But I could see no goose.

To the north the hills stood out sharply against the hard pale blue sky. Right overhead an aeroplane passed, its wings a transparent yellow against the bright light. It must have been cold work flying up there!

The grieve raised his dark eyes until they fastened on the 'plane.

"Those are the things that skere the geese, they hate 'em. If they are feeding and an aeroplane comes along, up they get and go back to the river."

I took out my glasses and scanned the fields.

In a distant meadow, close to a hayrick, a hare was sitting up in the sun washing itself, its shadow blue behind it. Beyond I could see the dark fir wood and grey specks floating in front of it, pigeons no doubt.

I lifted the glasses to the hills. The edges were very hard and white against the sky behind. As I watched, a tiny bundle of specks topped the higher ridge. I looked and looked. For some time that little cluster of black dots hung there, in the centre of a V mark between two peaks. Then another rose behind them, another black cluster. They hung in the air like kites. Then it dawned on me what they were; geese, coming off the river! It was hard to believe they were moving at all, but I suddenly sensed that they were driving onwards at a great speed. Through my glasses

I was looking at the skein head-on. Now, with a sweep of the binoculars, I saw other clusters, all rising over the ridge, one, two, three, four, five more. It was a wonderful sight. The clear bright morning, the snowclad landscape and the biting air, the blue shadows and the homely smell of the farm. And those rising skeins bearing down upon us over the sunlit valley. A picture to remember always.

As they topped the ridge they dropped, and with set wings came gliding over the fields, wheeling this way and that, now with a gentle wing beat, now with rigid pinions. They were gliding boats, floating smoothly on a gentle current, occasionally dipping an oar to help themselves along. And very faintly I heard their bugling cries, seeming to come to us from an immense distance, wonderfully musical and sweet.

As they drew nearer they ceased to move their wings and wheeled round in long lines, gliding lower and lower over the snow. Then a clump of trees hid them from view and we thought they were down, but no, in a second they reappeared, wings beating slowly now, circling over a distant meadow. For some reason however, they did not alight. Perhaps there were men in the field or it may have been another aeroplane which made its appearance, taking advantage of the lovely flying weather. The skeins now began to climb again, some going away westwards and the others turning and heading back for the hills.

"They will no feed the noo," said the grieve; "there's some one down there nae doot. They'll be back to-night though. If ye were to come ye might get a shot."

So we went back over the hills and resolved to try for them when the moon rose.

At four o'clock in the afternoon we were back again. The sun was setting behind the fir wood, a rose red globe, magnified by the evening mists; above, the sky was a pale green and in this light the snow seemed a deep violet. Bob Kennedy had his dog with him so I left Busy in the car, whining piteously with her front paws on the back of the driver's seat.

It was a long walk down to the last field. On the way we passed a multitude of green goose droppings on the snow and a maze of criss-cross paddle marks. There was no doubt that the gaggles had been there the night before and I was all for staying in that place, but Bob knew better and said we should get more shots in the field beyond.

When we got there, perspiring despite the bitter evening, for we had come well wrapped up, I was inclined to agree with him. I had never seen such a mass of droppings and webbed footmarks. They were all over the centre of the field and here and there were little piles of dung where the geese, fed to repletion, had sat down and gone to sleep.

We spread out at intervals of about sixty yards, lying down on the snow at full length. I felt very conspicuous, but Kennedy swore that the geese would come in to us as they had not been disturbed.

By this time the 'red eye of day' had dipped down behind the firs, leaving a wonderful sky of green and gold in the west. There was all the promise of a still, clear, frosty night.

To the east the moon was already getting up, full and pale yellow. It would not be long before the geese would come, for the grieve had told us up at the farm that they had not been back during the day. The dark blobs of Kennedy and Charles (my shooting comrade) seemed very black against the snow. Behind Kennedy was another dark spot, the spaniel.

Not very far away was a stream, half frozen; as it grew darker I heard a mallard pass over and alight in the bed of the burn. It would have been a good stalk, but we were out for nobler game.

Lying there, looking up at the sky, I could see the trembling stars brightening every moment. Over the hills the moon grew brighter also as she climbed the sky. The cold grew more intense, the gun barrels seemed almost to sear the fingers. I could feel my outer skin of garments cold also, though I was warm enough within, for we had all had a tot of rum before we started.

One or two plover flew overhead, they must have seen us on the white background for they called as they passed, a very lonely little sound.

Without any warning I suddenly heard a goose call, quite close. I had been scanning the sky over the mountains and had seen nothing. I could see nothing now though I looked about on all sides.

Then I saw a woolly blur against the stars. It was passing to the right of us and circling round. We lay still, hoping it would come within gunshot, but it passed away, still calling, towards the farm. I was willing to bet then that it had pitched on the other field where we had seen so much goose 'sign'. For a long time nothing happened.

By now the sun had long gone and the moonlight was flooding the field. It seemed as light as day. I was sure that the geese had seen us and in this conjecture I was probably right. Wild geese have sharp eyes and we must have been conspicuous against the snowy field.

Far away, in the fir woods, I heard the owls hooting and once, the bark of a fox. And then the moonlight dimmed. Clouds, with astonishing rapidity, came flocking over the hills. Our shadows on the snow dwindled and vanished; instead of the clear moonlight everything became misty and obscure. Was it rain on the way? Surely not, for it was freezing hard. Something brushed my ear, then another, and there were faint tickings against my 'mac'. It was snow.

Still we lay, even though the flakes thickened and the moon was a mere luminosity behind the banks of cloud.

Kennedy and Charles appeared no longer as black blobs. They were as white as the field.

There was no feeling in my limbs and my fingers ached. I must get up and stretch my legs. Apparently Charles felt the same, for when I next looked that way he was up and walking about. After a while Kennedy got up too and we met and talked. "They'll be here any moment now," said Kennedy. "This snow is just what we want." We talked a while and the flask was passed round. Then we went back to our places and sat down again.

I looked at my wrist watch. It was after eight o'clock. If the geese were coming they should be on their way. Then I felt that tingling sensation of expectation. From over the hills I heard a faint clamour. It was the geese in full cry. I lay full length and made sure the catch was pulled from safety. Strange as it may seem, I have been often caught in this way and missed a good chance through overlooking this simple fact.

The noise grew. I sensed that towards us, from across the valley, a mighty host was heading in our direction. Louder, louder, and still no sight of them. Then I could hear, in addition to the calling geese, the swish of their wings. When you can hear that sound you know that they are getting nicely in range. Then I saw them, indeed the whole sky seemed a moving mass or carpet of black spots. They were coming on set wings. Geese always glide in to their feeding grounds. There was no doubt that they were within range, they could not be more than forty feet up. There could be no question of missing. It seemed unbelievable that these great birds, which we had seen so often from afar, were really so close, right overhead. There were so many that it was difficult to choose one's target. I was just swinging nicely on to mine when four reports rang out to right and left of me.

The dark spots shot upwards as I fired at one bird on the right. It fell to my shot. At the same time two heavy thumps close behind me told of success. At such times things 'happen very quickly'. It is the same with all tense and exciting moments in life.

I was just going to run across the snow and get my goose when I heard again the clamour of more geese heading in for us. So I lay where I was and slipped another cartridge in the right barrel. My fingers were so numbed with cold and shaking with excitement that I could hardly push it home. Again I saw a gliding mass of shapes heading in for us. But instead of passing over, they all lifted their wings and pitched on the field in front. I could not judge the range, for as soon as they had landed they were invisible.

Then I heard Kennedy's dog rushing out on my left. The geese were still on the ground. I then heard the 'lift' of forty or so wings and I fired both barrels 'into the brown'. It was perhaps an unsporting shot but I was so excited I did not know what I was doing.

My shots were followed by a bump, however, and the dog went back to Kennedy with my goose. The latter was swearing. "Why the hell did you want to fire? I was sending the dog out to put them up."

As however I knew the geese would turn downwind I judged I had done the right thing.

I am not going to recount in detail the rest of that flight. Suffice it to say that when they stopped coming the snow was littered with geese. In the dusky half-darkness they might have been sacks scattered on the snow.

Fourteen was the total bag when we stumbled round counting them, fourteen pinkfeet as fat as butter.

It was indeed a load which we carried back to the farm, a load worth the bottle of whisky (pre-war price) which we presented to the grieve.

Everyone of those geese was used. We sent most of them away next day to friends in the south and the one I kept for myself was the best I have ever tasted.

5. Night Work

I HAVE said that the period of the full moon is unfavourable for hunting geese on the shore. Many birds feed on the fields and seem to return to the estuary, or go forth from it, at all hours of the day and night. This certainly holds true for dawn and evening flighting, but in some localities good sport may be enjoyed with the greys under the moon, if the feeding grounds can be located on the marshes.

The greylag geese are not such wanderers as the pinks; they do not forage at great distances from the sea but obtain most of their grazing close at hand, within a mile or two of the estuary or river. It is, of course, from the greylag that our domestic farmyard goose has descended. They are heavier, larger birds than the pinks and tend to roll slightly when they walk. The more feminine pink has a very erect carriage and they are restless spirits, never feeding long in one locality even where they are undisturbed. They love to roam the hills, seeking out a favourite pasture here and some lonely loch there, and on the latter they sleep for nights together and resort to it during the day. Fresh water is visited by wild geese more commonly than many people suppose and where a burn runs into the sands such a place is much frequented, especially round about dawn.

Many and many a morning I have lain in ambush watching from my favourite creek or reed bed the habits of these lovely fowl. When they have walked out from the shore (I am speaking of both greys and pinks) they will often repair to these freshwater burns and for half an hour, between 8.30 and 9 a.m. on a winter's morning, there will they bathe and gambol to their hearts' content. The loud beating of their wings as they throw the water over their backs carries a great distance on a calm morning, a sort of 'clap, clap, clap', and now and again there is an outburst of joyful cackling.

A party of bathing geese will attract others which may be flying up and down the estuary. These set their wings and alight amongst them and those already on the banks of the burn stretch out their necks and give a chiming welcome.

The morning wash and preen completed, the birds then leave in little parties for their chosen feeding grounds for the day. I am speaking, of course, of a calm morning when the weather is more or less open. But on a wild dawn of perhaps snow and wind there is no morning preen. As soon as the geese awake they are off to the land; they dislike having to sit out a rough sea. At such times, when the weather is coarse, even the greys may go far inland, and the chances of sport on the shore are greatly enhanced, for the big birds rarely gain any altitude when they lift from the sand bars.

Where there is ample food in the shape of reed tubers, such as abound on some of our northern estuaries, the greys (and sometimes the pinks) will spend many of the moonlight hours at feed at high sea mark. Then are the chances for the keen gunner fairly good, though shooting under the moon is difficult work and one can only achieve success after long practice. You do not want a clear moon riding a cloudless sky, a light film of cloud is best, as it forms a sort of milky background. On such nights—and we usually get three or four at the period of the full moon—geese and even duck show up very clearly against the clouds. But against a clear sky, even if the birds are low, they are invisible, even when they are within easy range.

My usual practice on favourable nights, that is to say when the moon is full with a good background of cloud and wind, is to set forth two hours before midnight and stay out on the marshes well into the early hours. Geese tend to move about much more in the early part of the night.

In a moment I will describe one such typical night which I enjoyed on a certain northern estuary in the winter of 1947.

The weather on that trip had been still and calm with some hard frost but in the main fairly mild, indeed some days it had been almost spring-like with thrushes in full song and a warm sun— 'butterfly weather', as old Colonel Hawker termed it.

The morning flights, from the very beginning, had been unproductive. I had had occasional shots at geese without success and my only chance now lay in 'night work'.

By day I had located where the greylags had been feeding by the paddle marks in the 'plickplack'; the numerous droppings and feathers showed that the 'grand army' had been frequenting a certain section of the marsh for several nights in succession. There had been no high tides to wash the traces away; indeed, they had barely reached the verge of the 'plickplack'. Nor to my knowledge had the geese been disturbed by local fowlers; in any case there were few gunners on that lonely section of coast.

D. M. and I had been several days at our wildfowling H.Q. and neither of us had yet killed a goose, and as the days went on we began to get restless and more than ever determined to break our spell of bad luck, though, as I say, it was really the weather which was to blame and not our own lack of skill.

I spoke just now of the 'grand army' and the tyro may perhaps wonder what I mean by that term.

On every goose-haunted estuary, greys, pinks, and white-fronts tend to move around in one big lot which may be composed of anything from two hundred to a thousand birds in the case of the whitefront and pinks, and from one hundred to two hundred in the case of the greylag. Of all the wild geese the greys tend to keep very much together in one big lot, though there will always be small parties of from three to six birds which seem to keep apart. These are probably birds of the year, for one notices two larger parent birds with them and the rest are immature.

When greys are feeding on the reed tubers they will resort to one particular place on the coast for three or four nights in succession and will then change their feeding ground, going in some cases a mile or two above or below their original pitch.

But to return to my narrative.

The night was very cold but fine. A stiff wind from the east was useful in that it made a considerable rustling in the reed beds, which was just what we wanted. Absolutely calm nights are not good for stalking geese for they can hear you hundreds of yards away as their hearing is as keen as their sight.

We reached the sea wall soon after ten o'clock. Farms and cottages were in darkness for the rustic population retires early to bed in the country, where work has to begin at dawn. There was a fair amount of cloud which again was favourable though at times the moon, which was one day past the full, rode clear and bright, gleaming on the silvery path of the estuary.

As soon as we reached the sea wall we knew the geese were there in force, in fact, from the clamour it seemed that there were two parties, one above the long breakwater and one below, on the 'plickplack' where I had noticed the spoor. Again this was as good as it could be for it meant we could separate, D. M. going down river and I upstream. But for the first stage of our stalk we were together and followed the same path by the stone dyke. This track in the moonlight appeared like a long corridor with the tall reeds, seven and eight feet high, rising up on either hand to form parallel walls. No moonlight could illuminate that dark narrow passage.

There was no need to crawl; we could walk for the first hundred yards in the normal way, though we were careful to negotiate the boggy spots with care. Though there was a frost and most of the muds were rock hard there were places where the path was lightly skimmed with ice and the feet broke through. When this occurred the big 'gutty' boots sank well in to the calf and it was necessary to lean forward and carefully *draw* the foot out, otherwise there was a noise like a giant's kiss which even the wind could not mask.

At last we reached the end of the corridor where the tall reeds ceased and the short stuff began. These short reeds were about three feet high, very thick and tangled, splendid cover, though the mud below was soft. This band of shorter growth extended out into the estuary for a width of perhaps a hundred yards, becoming shorter and more sparse until the 'plickplack' was reached. Here the reed clumps grew in bunches with wide spaces of liquid mud in between and it was in this area that the geese were feeding.

It was now a matter of getting down on all fours and crawling, but before we did this we crouched for quite ten minutes trying to locate where the geese actually were. This is a most difficult thing to do. I judged my party, which appeared to be the bulk of the 'grand army', was quite two hundred yards to the west of me. D. M.'s lot were a little closer, perhaps.

Wishing each other good hunting, we set off. I saw D. M.'s head sink down into the short stuff and I had told him to take special care in crossing the stone dyke which was about four feet high at that point.

I crawled for about one hundred yards and then lay flat and listened. The geese were making a tremendous noise, I could hear them splattering about in the semi-liquid mud and occasionally

47

heard them fighting. Geese at feed are as quarrelsome as starlings in a meadow.

But they were evidently hungry and unsuspicious and I soon began to hear the 'buzz' which I have described in an earlier chapter. It is rather curious that geese make such a commotion when feeding at night. One would think that so wary a bird would have learnt wisdom down the centuries. On a still night a gaggle of feeding wild geese can be heard from a considerable distance, a mile or more.

Soon after midnight the moon became filmed with cloud and it began to snow. It was a perfect sky for shooting and I hoped that even if I did not succeed in stalking the geese in front, I might get some odd birds dropping in from down river. I began to get very cold and my fingers numb and 'wooden'. I was obliged to put them down into the mud as I crawled along and every now and again I had to stop and thaw them out.

There is a solemn beauty about the marshes during the hours of darkness. One realizes how busy all the bird population is in the small hours of a moonlight night. I could hear the oyster catchers piping on the tideway and the whistling of innumerable curlews, some of which passed low over my head as I lay in the short reeds.

The wind had died with the coming of the snow and the noise made by the feeding geese sounded very close. Now and then I would hear one run at another, a scuffle, and a splattering in the mud, followed by a sharp complaint and guzzling noises.

After thawing out I made another thirty yards before I had to thaw out once more. My hands were now so numb they had no feeling in them. The snow was beginning to lie on the tops of the reeds and my head and shoulders were white. I imagined I must be very close to my quarry, and once I fancied a goose was within six feet of me, though, of course, it was quite invisible. Even when their heads were up they were hidden, as they were now well into the 'plickplack'.

Just after 1 a.m. I heard a single shot to the east of me, and judged it to be D. M. The gabbling in front of me was cut short as if by a knife. All was deathly still, uncannily so. I feared the whole pack might rise and that my stalk was all in vain.

Rather foolishly that night I had taken my single eight-bore (Belching Bess) and because of its length of barrel it was difficult to keep it clear of the mud. I lay quite still, full length on my stomach, hardly daring to breathe. It was hard to imagine that I had within shot a whole army of geese which a moment ago had been making such a noise.

Then with a stupendous uproar the whole pack was up. The noise made by an uprising pack of greylags, numbering perhaps three or four hundred birds, is quite awe-inspiring. They do not cackle as they rise, it is the thunder of their wings which is so impressive.

I rose on one knee with the gun at my shoulder, but they had been farther off than I had judged, and I only glimpsed a mass of black wings flickering in the shadows. I held my fire and sat quite still.

Having taken the air the geese remained silent for the space of a second or two and then, when they were swinging away for the high sands, they gave tongue all together in a fiendish babel of voices, and I heard the baying music die away upriver where for some moments they kept it up, the sound growing ever fainter.

Then an outburst of cackling came from behind me. I knew what had happened. D. M. had set another lot on wing and these birds were driving down the marshes. I saw a compact mass come low over the groyne and head straight for me. When I raised the gun I thought with a big charge of shot I should kill half a dozen, for they were not more than twenty feet up and coming slap at me. But I must have misjudged the elevation, either that or the charge of shot had had no time to spread. The recoil sent me back into the reeds but not a single goose fell, and that was the finish of operations for that night.

I have no excuse to offer; it was pure bad shooting, though I must say that my trigger finger was so devoid of feeling I never knew when I pressed the trigger.

I met D. M. at the groyne soon after 2 a.m. and found he had a single goose, a greylag, which had come over him as he was stalking his pack.

This brings to mind another occasion many years ago when I stalked a big lot of pinks on another estuary. This time we had located them at dawn, and I had a fairly easy stalk and got right among them. It was very dark, almost pitch dark in fact, and geese were feeding all round me, some within a few feet.

The professional fowler who was with me that morning told me afterwards that on one occasion, in similar circumstances, dark morning and good cover, he had crawled in amongst the pack, and had actually *caught one goose by the paddles as it walked past him!* I could well believe him.

But again, on that morning, I failed to get a goose, though they were all round me and sometimes dropping in over my head. The light was so bad I only had occasional glimpses of the birds and when at last I did fire at a bunch which came over me from behind I clean missed and put the whole lot up.

6. A Night under the Moon

THE tide is flowing and with the moon at the full it will be well over the 'plickplack'. It will be another couple of hours before it reaches me, ensconced in a shallow creek among the short reeds, two hours of magic for me this frosty January night!

I may get a shot or I may not, it matters little if you are a true coastwise gunner. There is a sense of release, a freedom from one's fellows, from the humdrum world of pavements and hurrying crowds. The imagination roves free, you think of others tucked up in their beds at this hour, the great cities with their lamplit streets, closing time in countless bars, the noise, the smoke, the smell in these warrens of human kind. And here am I, away on the wild marshes under the full moon, warm and snug as a fieldfare among the reeds despite the intense frost. There is no drowsiness of the senses. I am very much awake, eyes and ears are alert like those of a hunting wild animal's.

Now and again the shining muds, as yet uncovered by the tide, are dimmed as clouds drift over the moon's face. Then the pallid, dolorous light gleams forth again and the sands take on a metallic slabby gleam.

Out there on invisible sand-banks, far out in the flowing sea, much goose talk is going on. The ranks of birds are closely packed for the flow is constantly encroaching on their resting place, and as the minutes pass the clamour increases as goose answers goose. Birds do not, of course, converse in any set language, yet they communicate one to another their excited restlessness by sounds which are a manner of speech. Moreover, their bellies are empty, they have not been filled since afternoon.

Then they fed in peace in a low green field, full of sweet grass which the pinks love so much, seven miles away over the mountains. It is a long journey there, for they have to rise many hundreds of feet to clear the barrier. The journey undertaken in bright morning must be done again when the tide pushes them off to-night.

They have slept from 5 p.m., silently, in one vast mass on the high sands, safe from molestation. But now they know the time has almost come when they must set out again, set out in this moonlight to that same far silent field. It will be safer than at midday; the arch enemy, those puny two-legged things which frequent the daylight fields like busy ants, will have mysteriously disappeared, each and all will have crept into its shelter of brick or stone as a bee creeps into its cell.

From down river come faint clamouring cries as another big lot of pinks, flooded off, are on the move. They come, with all bands playing, but the time is not yet ripe to leave the sea for the land. They see their companions, ranged on the upper sand bars, and these they join. I hear them do so, the gabbling is continuous.

From the river mouth the dull boom of a gun rolls across the flats. Jim Jagoe is active there; even as the sound reaches me (and the geese) he must be busy with his cripple stopper. The much-feared sound stills the geese to complete, vigilant silence, and I hear now only the occasional mournful 'peep-peep' of a lone-voyaging golden plover, invisible against the stars.

Far across the saltings lights twinkle and shiver like stars, lights from the distant town whose glare is reflected on the sky.

On all the coastal estuaries I see these man-made stars, sometimes they seem so near, sometimes I imagine they are moving towards me. Their reflections shine across the muds; one can be easily deceived.

Then the goose talk begins again, *gabble, gabble, gabble.* A bird's memory is short, it lives in the passing second. And then party after party begin to rise from the banks and I can hear them passing away up-river, swinging round, dwindling, for the hills. A few parties pass high over me, but not until they cross the moon or pass before a film of cloud can I see them, orderly lines and Vs, all heading for the same compass point.

Can one wonder why these lovely creatures have such a hold on the imagination? Those stately processions across the moonlit skies, each bird calling to its neighbour, what other sight or sound can match this for sheer drama!

Many a time have I seen this massed flight-in under the moon, never does the spectacle lose its magic for me. For half an hour it goes on, this ordered movement of wildfowl to their distant feeding grounds. But at last the sounds die, the rearguards have gone in, and I have followed them by ear, and in imagination, for the first stage of their journey.

Though the geese have gone and I miss their clamour out there upon the unseen banks, other sounds tell other tales. The wigeon are moving and the curlews. The latter birds, restless too, now the tide is flooding, hungry also like the geese, are leaving the muds for the seaward fields.

Redshanks, also, can be heard, though these birds do not go inland like the geese and duck and curlew. They speed restlessly in piping bands along the edge of the tide, back and forth. The floodtide is ever a cause for anxiety and anticipation.

The creeks are flooding now and over the smooth firm sands the thin skin of advancing water slides at walking pace. It rustles as it comes, this advancing tide, a rustle which grows with every minute, dying away on the wind, increasing again. It is an uncanny sound, like the rustling of silken garments.

Now, too, the landward creeks are beginning to fill. A slight pressure on my waders tells me that even in my little creek the sweet, fresh thrust is making its way. Gurglings are heard at intervals, startlingly loud in the quiet of this frosty night.

The harsh purr of a wigeon duck comes across the flat and some other nameless fowl seems to laugh insanely.

If I look at the flats now I see a change. The muds seem to be moving, creeping, and with a start I see the rocking reflection of the moon just over the 'plickplack'. What a moment ago was firm sand is now moving water.

Peering down at my legs which are in the gutter I see small bubbles and clots of foam sliding by, pushing up the creek, and, yes, bits of reed and half an orange box come sliding past like waggons on a railway track. They move so surely, so steadily, it is quite uncanny: they seem pulled by invisible fairy tow-ropes.

And the next moment I feel an icy chill about my seat, where the secret advance of waters has overflowed my 'sit bag'. It is time to be up, it is time to move back into the reeds, to seek out the trodden path that leads back to the groyne.

The unwary, inexperienced gunner might think it best to make directly back for the sea wall by the shortest route. To do so would be folly.

Among the reeds the big dykes wind here, there, everywhere. Some are ten yards across and deep enough to drown a horse and cart. Up these big gutters the tide is thrusting with purposeful speed. Stand with me here at the fringe of the tall reeds and look down a moment at the bed of this big gutter. Flat cakes of foam are swimming up at a surprising pace, quicker than a man can walk, and up the glistening mud sides the flood is rising inch after inch. To-night the tide will reach the foot of the sea wall.

No, follow the path you know, back to the groyne, and there

you may stay until the tide pushes you right back to the land, you can walk along the stones (but take care this frosty night because they are filmed with ice).

Once on the groyne I can sit down once again, knowing I am secure.

It is very strange and sometimes very terrifying, this stealthy advance of the tide. On the Solway it comes, on some nights, with a perfect roar over the miles of flat sands and its fringe is a tossing ribbon of foam.

One shudders to think of being trapped far out from the shore. I have sometimes gone after a goose which has fallen a long distance out, and even when the tide is at the ebb one feels a horrid sense of insecurity.

Perhaps it is because distances are so deceptive, you can find nothing to gauge yardage by: even a redshank can look as big as a goose at times. That is why range is so deceptive over featureless sand or water.

Now I can hear the roar of the flood as it eats up the stones of the dyke, and in the moonlight crests of white foam rise and fall.

There will be no chance of a shot now, all the geese have gone in; the erstwhile muds, acres and acres of muds and sand, are now a seething mass of swilling, churning water.

But it is pleasant to stand awhile now upon the top of the dyke, and perhaps take a walk along the bank. One never knows, a few odd greys may have dropped in on the stubble by Curlew Bay; they were feeding there during the sunny afternoon to-day. I saw them through my glass, sitting at ease, and some were even asleep with intucked orange bills.

Against the greenish moonlit sky the dyke-top oaks and elms are etched, every little twig is visible. Behind, framing their delicate tracery of winter beauty, the broad bosom of the sea now glitters like molten silver. Away over the fields a dog is barking in some farmyard, persistently barking.

Sometimes, finding the beauty of the moonlit world too good to leave even for a snug bed, I have stayed out all night, and have heard the cocks crow one against the other. First, one begins and then from some far distant steading another answers.

The sleep of the cockerel, deep in the foetid blackness of the hen roost among his slumbering hens, is never so deep but he hears that distant challenge in the frosty night. Nor do these farmyard cocks crow only at the approach of dawn. I have heard those distant clarions at all hours of the night, it is as though they were the watchmen crying 'a fine moonlight night and all's well!'

Where are the geese now? Is it not hard to believe that an hour back the estuary was alive with their clamour? Yet now, every one has gone. They are stalking in the moonlight, away there over the snow-clad hills, cropping at ease on their chosen pasture, with an eye for prowling foxes who sometimes steal upon them over the glittering frosty grass.

And there they will feed until the sun climbs the sky once more to-morrow, and the labouring men come forth to work, and the cows get up in the pastures, and the lamps go out in croft and farmhouse.

Suddenly I feel a chill run up and down my spine. My shadow is black on the crisp sugary grass, from whose frozen blades secret blue winking lights glimmer and are lost, those strange fires which frosted grass blades seem to send back in the rays of the moon.

And I think at last of my warm bed away in the village, the glow of a dying fire on the ceiling as I snuggle down to sleep. The thought is good; now the geese have gone the magic has gone with them. And so I turn away and set my face for the silhouettes of the ricks in the distant farmyard.

Very soon this dreamlike, chill world of shadow and gleaming points of light will be merged into another dreamland as I sink to sleep (and the slumber of the longshore fowler is deep). What matter if I have had no shot? what matter indeed!

7. Curlew Bay

AFTER the pinks have left, flooded off by the tide, and the moon begins to set, the estuary is an empty place save for the waders. Hardly a duck is seen or heard. Then as the tide reaches the full sea mark and drops back, the little dunlin sprites, the curlews, and redshanks, descend like variegated butterflies upon the newly bared muds. Their breakfast table is spread and ready, though it is seven hours to dawn. As soon as the first wet band of mud is laid bare it will be thronged by these little gnomes, for at the full of the moon there is no regular nightly sleep for them, they can make it up later when the nights are long and dark, and how long those winter nights are when there is no moon!

As the tide drops back, this time silently and with no rustling, but with occasional gurgles, glugs, and gulps, the wader population follow the receding water on twinkling feet.

The curlews, who have been massed in their striped brown battalions on the arable fields, know exactly the state of the tide, as well as if they carried watches and tide-tables in waistcoat pockets. They come sailing over the sea wall, yodelling and whistling, usually in one compact mass, and with wavering gliding flight drop down to join the feast.

Curlews are curious birds. On the estuary I am describing they keep to one particular area, and rarely are met with lower down the marshes. A mile out in the muds is a low rock which is completely covered at high water. This is a favourite resting-place for them. After they have had their fill of sea worms and other marine creatures on which they feed, they repair to this rock, and will sit there during low water, the white gulls with them.

They will remain sleeping and preening until the tide again gives them notice to quit. But they do not fly directly inland but will keep a jump ahead of the incoming tide, running and flying in short stages. When they are within a hundred yards of the marshes they will either lift and go to the fields, or rest a little longer on a low stone causeway which lines one end of a small marsh.

One afternoon, wishing to get a close view of these lovely tawny striped waders, I concealed myself behind this causeway, covering myself with rush and grass. As the tide began to 'make', the curlews came and pitched just over the stones within a few feet of me. Trip after trip came in, until the broken ground in front of my hide was a mass of curlew, tightly packed, some four or five hundred birds. They kept up a continual low chattering which was almost goose-like in quality.

Then at last the tide began to creep about their feet and they were up and away. I longed for a camera to take a photograph of that intimate scene: I had never been so close to a large herd before.

As the sun rises, and soon after it has cleared the hills, parties of pinks begin to dribble back from their feeding grounds. The whole army will not come, but a few odd parties who feel the need of grit or sand or a rest, or it may be they have been disturbed off their pastures by labourers. They invariably return at a great altitude.

But some time, between noon and sunset, it is likely the big lot will come back; they cannot rest securely on the fields during the day and the sand bars are their beds; birds need sleep just as humans do. No inland pasture is really safe, but lochs afford sanctuary, and it often happens that they will rest on some island in a mountain loch or upon its still waters; any spot where no man comes near them.

The life of a wild goose is haunted by this dread of man. Unlike the rooks who can look after themselves and know when men are likely to be dangerous, these big birds must be for ever on the watch. Their very size is a disadvantage to them: their main objective when over land is to hoist themselves out of the range of guns, and when on the fields to keep strictly to the very centre of the pastures with always a wary eye on banks and dykes.

But what have the greylags been doing? Under the moon they may have been feeding on the saltings as I have shown, or they may have been feeding inland, though not far from the sea. They will most likely be back to the estuary at dawn, as soon as the moon has set, and will line the sand bars in their serried ranks.

As a matter of fact it is never very easy to say *what* the greys will do when the moon is at the full. I have noticed they are more fond of resting on the sea than are the pinks, and they will even 'ride out' quite a gale.

Should the weather turn blustery, enough to whip up the white horses on the sea, the greys have a curious habit of moving at high water, following the coast. The white shoulders of a moving mass of greylag geese are very impressive; they appear as white as gulls in some lights.

On the estuary I have in mind there is a small narrow marsh much favoured by them at high water and this marsh—Curlew Bay—which is near the mouth of the river, is regularly visited by the 'grand army' when the tide is at the full, and there is a certain amount of 'pobble' on the sea. They alight in a grey compact mass just off shore and will toss up and down, like a fishing fleet at anchor, for an hour or more, making a close scrutiny of the coast. If all is quiet and they see nobody about they will slowly swim in, wading ashore on top of the tide.

On this marsh there are many gorse bushes and I have often

hidden myself in these just before high water, and very occasionally I have had a shot. But the weather needs to be rough and the tide high.

Very exciting it is to lie concealed among the prickly gorse bushes and to see the 'grand army' or the 'grand fleet' cruising off-shore, scanning the marsh with hundreds of beady, penetrating eyes.

One foggy afternoon I remember particularly well. High water coincided with dusk, always a good time for an ambush, and since early afternoon a fog had come down. As on many of these northern waters, fog comes in on the tide. When I first got into my ambush the sun was shining brightly and visibility was three miles or more. But as the tide began to flow a wall of vapour came with it, and with surprising rapidity the whole scene was blanketed in a clammy mist.

The 'grand fleet' had appeared just before the fog came down, swimming far out on the sea, and of course, they were soon hidden. But their croakings came nearer and nearer as dusk approached. It was remarkable that the geese ever contemplated coming ashore in fog, but maybe they were hungry, for even during the day the greylags feed on the reed tubers if they can find some remote bay or section of coast when nobody is about.

It was quite impossible for me to tell which was mud and which was water, the whole area in front was a pearly blank, but before long I was startled to see a line of grey blobs, apparently floating, like wraiths, in mid-air.

They were the geese slowly swimming in on the tide.

I suppose it took them well over two hours to come in, and then they walked ashore about a hundred yards down-wind of me. First one bird slowly stalked ashore, and once he had dared to land, the others followed suit. Like all gregarious creatures they tend to follow a leader.

The procession of silvery grey shapes kept appearing out of the mist in one long line, they seemed never-ending, and at last all were well in to the 'plickplack' and hidden from me by a small, low, grass bank. They made no sound whatever, not a croak or a call, but I could hear them tearing at the reed tubers and sloshing about in the mud, though now and again every bird would remain quite still and silent, evidently watching and listening.

I bellied out from my gorse bush and managed to get to the low bank, giving them two barrels of 'BB' shot as they rose with a deafening roar. Two geese dropped out and another fell dead in the sea and slowly drifted in.

But this was an unusual occurrence; in most cases when they come ashore in daylight it is in clear, still, sunny weather.

From the amount of goose droppings on the turf of Curlew Bay, numbers of greylags made it a habit to come ashore during the night. On several occasions I have tried lying up for them under the waxing moon, but without success.

This particular little marsh was a treacherous place to walk, not so much from the point of view of creeks, but it was seamed in all directions, especially near the 'plickplack', with very deep narrow fissures in which one could easily break one's leg.

It was the best little snipe haunt anywhere on the estuary, and during the day when there was nothing doing with the geese we were always sure of some fun with these elusive little birds.

Redshanks, as well as curlews, frequented it in preference to the wider, more isolated marshes up river. When the tide was at the full and most of the marsh was covered with water, the redshanks used to mass in 'teetering' companies on the remaining exposed areas of turf.

Of late years, however, the redshanks have mysteriously disappeared from this marsh; indeed, they are not so common on the estuary as they were ten years ago.

There was a guardian of Curlew Bay which, on occasion, provided us with a little more excitement than we bargained for. This was Ferdinand the Bull. I have an idea that the farmer whose land adjoined Curlew Bay had placed Ferdinand there to keep off the local fowlers; at any rate, for the four seasons I shot there, this bull was certainly a nasty customer.

Curiously enough, when I made enquiries from the locals, it transpired that the farmer's father had been gored to death by a bull on this same marsh, many years ago, and the story is worth retelling, if only to show the treachery of these animals.

The farmer's father was an old man and very deaf. He loved his bull and every day would drive it out to the marsh and go for it in the evening. For a number of years this was the regular procedure, and so trusting was the old man that he never bothered to drive the animal before him but would precede it, the bull following behind like a faithful dog.

But one winter's afternoon, as the farmer was entering his own farm gate, with the bull close on his heels, he was knocked down by the brute, which then knelt on him and crushed his ribs.

My first encounter with Ferdinand happened in this way. I was shooting snipe one morning, working my way down the marshes towards the gorse bushes, when a friend, John Pattinson (who was my fowling companion that year), drew my attention to a brown object which was lurking behind a thorn bush at the foot of the sea wall, about fifty yards away. The bulk of the creature was hidden by the bushes. I saw at once it was a bull. He was standing with a wicked look in his eye, making himself as inconspicuous as possible, like a wounded buffalo lying in wait for a hunter.

I thought at first he might be harmless and began to make a détour out towards the muds so as to get round him. But Ferdinand came out in no uncertain manner when he saw what we intended to do. He was a small, thickset Angus bull, but whatever his size he was in an ugly temper.

Luckily the ground was boggy in places and this hampered his progress, but we only just reached the fence in time and John Pattinson removed the back of his breeches in getting over the wire.

We then crossed a deep burn which bisected the marsh, and

from the far bank exchanged pleasantries with 'Ferdi'. He was
a methodical beast. He wanted very much to get at us and made
those horrible, incredibly forcible, roaring grunts, which are as
awe-inspiring as the growl of a lion. And he tried the soft banks
with his forefeet, feeling for a firm foothold. Finding there was no
suitable place exactly opposite us, he trotted off down the burn and
tried again, as delicately as a girl feeling the bath with her toe.

We were angry at having been forced to give up our snipe shooting and John procured a half-brick which he hurled with great
force at 'Ferdi', hitting him a resounding thump in the centre of his
head. The rage of the beast was awe-inspiring. His little eyes
glowed red; he knelt down, roaring and foaming at the mouth, and
digging his woolly square head into the ground.

Then he rushed at a clump of gorse and tore and wrenched it,
sending the tough roots flying in all directions.

For three succeeding seasons 'Ferdi' guarded the marsh as
efficiently as a savage dog, and it was because of this, perhaps, that
the greylags liked the marsh so well; they were undisturbed by
gunners and were quite friendly with the bull.

What happened to him eventually, I do not know, but rumour
had it that Wullie Laing, a fowler from 'up river', and a fearless,
dare-devil sort of fellow, had shot 'Ferdi' one night when the bull
had cornered him by the furze bushes—and small blame to him.

These furze bushes were a very good spot for flighting curlew,
but the best stand of all was on the little narrow public road which
skirted the marsh. The burn came in there, and there was a steep
bank covered with broom bushes which made a wonderful hide
for a gunner.

But it was on the road one could enjoy the best sport, and on
some evenings the curlews, flooded off by the tide, invariably came
over one particular bend in the lane where there was a high Wych
elm growing on the bank. This tall tree seemed to be a guide
mark for them.

One night we had a great half-hour just at dusk with the water high. We had, I think, about five brace of birds. Of course, the cannonade was considerable, and I wondered at the time that it did not attract attention as we had no business shooting on the king's highway.

The following day we thought to repeat the performance (to the uninitiated I might say that curlew are excellent eating) but when we arrived there on our cycles I happened to catch sight of another cycle hidden behind a bush. I was suspicious and instead of dismounting I rode innocently by, and John and I saw two police-men hiding below the bank. After that we did not repeat our experiment, and no doubt the curlew still flight over the Wych elm and nobody has shot them since.

One January afternoon, while waiting for the curlew flight in the broom bushes at Curlew Bay, I saw two strange birds, about the size of starlings, feeding on some bright orange hip berries growing on the bank of the burn. I had my glasses with me and saw at once they were waxwings, the first I had ever seen.

A local fowler told me that he saw them every year at that place, and that years ago he had actually caught them with limed twigs set among the hip berries.

Perhaps one of the reasons why I had a great affection for this particular marsh was that one never knew what one might see there: it always seemed to be capable of springing some surprises. On occasion, when the weather was frosty, I put up a stray wood-cock on the steep bank above the burn, but we never succeeded in bagging it as it dodged away through the thick bushes of thorn which grew on the roadside. Strangely, too, we sometimes shot coot up the burn and there were plenty of moorhens.

It must not be thought that such lowly game was despised. Your true fowler relishes good meat, and coot are very good in an 'Oystercock Pie' which is the wildfowler's particular dish. Breasts of redshank and curlew, and plover too, where it was not protected, the odd pigeon, all were baked by our little landlady in one vast pudding and what a dish that was for two hungry men who had been out all day on the marshes!

Curlew Bay was essentially a daytime haunt of ours; for morning and evening flight it was useless, though sometimes geese came over the road and railway, a single track line which lay two fields off to the south of the Bay.

There was the chance at dusk of geese coming ashore, as I have described, and the gorse bushes were the best places in which to hide. I remember once an amusing happening on this marsh.

Up river was a horn of land which we named Bight Point, and we always took a spy from there before going on to the marsh. From this point you could see most of the marsh, and a careful scan with the glasses often revealed a goose or two well up on the grass and sometimes in a stalkable position.

One afternoon, just before high water, with a stiff wind blowing straight off the open sea, I reached Bight Point and settling against the sandy bank made my usual scrutiny. I could see the gorse bushes clearly and beyond them was a group of six or seven grey, lags standing with erect heads.

I immediately got down into dead ground and began a half-mile stalk, the latter part of it on my stomach, becoming very wet in the process. I was getting on well, and had heard no sound of the geese getting up when out of the gorse bushes in front, the very cover which I was striving to achieve before taking my shot, there arose a face crimson with rage and crowned by a woollen bonnet with a bobble on top.

The geese I had seen were decoys, and there had been a gunner lurking in the furze all the time. Why he had let me get so near, I do not know, unless he was so busy watching his decoys that he never thought of looking behind him, in which case he was a poor fowler.

One more incident will I relate of Curlew Bay, and then I will conduct the reader higher up the estuary to other haunts, each of which has its own stories and memories which must be rescued from oblivion.

One still, foggy night with a full moon I and my companion (Angus McCance I think it was that year) were walking up the marsh towards Bight Point.

There was a frost with the fog and though visibility was only a few yards the full moon shed a certain ghostly illumination over everything.

From time to time we stopped to listen to goose talk out in the estuary to our right and the frequent 'quar! quar! quar!' of an old mallard drake. On a normal night most of the geese and duck would have been inshore long ago, but to-night the fog had kept them prisoners.

As we neared Bight Point I thought I heard a hollow knock out on the water and we stopped in our tracks to listen. Then out of the fog stole a long, grey shape, a gunning punt with two men aboard. They glided by us like a ghost with not a sound, a dull gleam showing in their wake.

In a moment or so they had vanished up river. We had a wonderful impression of stealthy, deadly purpose in the watchful figures of the men and the forward-gliding punt, with its long barrel questing forwards into the murk.

A great number of geese were calling in mid-channel and about half an hour later the silent night echoed and re-echoed to the boom of the big gun.

Angus and I, sitting in the whins on Curlew Bay, optimistically hoping that the greys were swimming in to us, gave a groan, for it meant no sport for us that night. Listening carefully we heard, a minute later, the tiny pops of the cripple stoppers. So no doubt the punters had made a good bag. It was during the war years and wild geese were fetching fantastic prices.

8. Up River

UP river from Curlew Bay the character of the saltings altered; they were much more extensive, a quarter to half a mile wide, and with vast reed beds intersected by long stone groynes which went far out over the ooze—similar to those on the Tay in Perthshire. These groynes were very ancient and were built, it is supposed, by Dutch engineers in the eighteenth century in an effort to reclaim the soil. On the other hand it may well be that they were built to encourage the growth of reeds, which were valuable for thatching in the days when this method of roofing houses and barns was more prevalent. Up to a short time ago the reeds were still cut regularly and I used to see flat-bottomed scows ferrying away vast loads to the town at the mouth of the estuary. A high flood tide was chosen for their transportation, when the men could get their boats right up over the 'plickplack'.

For many miles along the sea wall was a line of trees, forming in some places quite a belt of timber. These were planted, no doubt, to act as a screen to protect the arable fields inland, or they may have been planted purely for ornament. Men had more of an eye for natural beauty in those days. One could walk for five or six miles along the bank-top, threading quite a woodland path. Hollies and other bushes clothed the steep bank of the river wall and under them, in hard weather, the woodcock used to hide. Local fowlers sometimes shot ten or a dozen down the bank in a single walk, especially before a spell of hard frost.

When I first saw these trees and walked along the winding leafy path, I was impressed by the fact that nowhere else had I seen such a curious combination of timber, marsh, reeds, and sea, unless it was on the estuary of the Beauly River in Hampshire, or the Tay. There was something incongruous to me to watch the skeins of geese coming in like high pheasants at a drive, over the tops of these trees.

Between Curlew Bay and the burn, which ran in by the fowler's house, there were no trees, but a straggling thorn hedge, with here and there thickets of thorn. It was opposite this stretch, which might have been a couple of miles long, possibly a little less, that some of the best places in the river were to be found for geese. The marshes at that point were very extensive, wider than at any point along the whole of the estuary, and the unwary wanderer could easily get lost in the tall waving thickets which stood well over his head, and were so dense in places as to form an almost impenetrable forest.

Through this wall of reed, at various points, I had my own private paths which took me out, after many doublings and twistings, to the short reeds and the 'plickplack'. It was no easy matter to locate the entrance to these paths in the darkness of a winter's dawn, even when I had taken the precaution of marking the exact spot of entry by scraps of white paper.

Somewhere in the centre of these vast reed beds was a fresh-water pool. I first heard of it from the local fowler, Jim Jagoe, and the story is worth retelling.

He had noticed that on occasion, especially on moonlight nights, the geese had a habit of dropping down into the centre of these reeds and he suspected that there must be a pool there. For some days he was unsuccessful in his search, but he eventually found it, a large circular pool of fresh water which was fed by a burn that flowed in from the shore.

At the next period of the full moon Jim hid up by this pool and killed a large number of greylags and pinkfoots which dropped in there to bathe and drink, and one frosty morning he stalked the pool, and killed no less than seven greylags with two shots from his twelve-bore. The geese very soon got wise to the fact their pet place had been discovered and thereafter he never had another goose from the pool.

Though Jim described minutely how I might reach it, I was for a long time unsuccessful and spent many weary, hot hours pushing about among the reeds in my search. But one September afternoon I came upon it unawares when I was taking a short cut through the tall reeds to the shore, and from it arose a cloud of teal, and I managed to drop two out of the bunch as it rose.

Then, strange to say, for a season or so I lost it again and only rediscovered it during a hard frost a few years later when it was covered with ice and I could walk from one side to the other!

It was not far above this pool that the 'Goose's Graveyard' began.

This particular locality was very nearly a fowler's graveyard on some occasions, for it was the most treacherous part of the whole marsh. It was bisected by very deep and wide channels, with smaller channels, also very deep, six feet and over, winding from it like the arms of an octopus. It was a perfect Hampton Court maze and the whole area was, of course, overgrown by the tall reedy thickets, so it was very difficult to keep one's sense of direc-tion. One could only negotiate the 'Goose's Graveyard' at low water when the creeks were empty, and even then it was no easy matter as the creeks themselves were full of deep adhesive mud in which one could very easily be stuck fast.

But when the tide began to flow these gutters and gullies filled rapidly, and in a very short space of time, unless one managed to get back to the sea wall, you were cut off and had to stand the tide out, or if it was a really high tide, swimming was the only method of saving your life.

Howard Seth Smith, another fowling companion who used to accompany me for several years (he now owns one of the Summer Isles in the far north of Scotland), was once cut off on the 'Goose's Graveyard'. In trying to extricate himself he went into one of the deep dykes. He was soaked to the skin and only saved himself by grabbing the overhanging herbage which fringed the creek. This accident happened in the early afternoon while I was below him near Bight Point, and when I met him about flight time he was still wet through, and had made no attempt to go back to our fowling H.Q. and change. How it was he escaped pneumonia, I cannot imagine, but he was a hardy fowler, as tough as nails, and as keen as mustard too. His shooting arm had been shot to pieces in World War I, and his hand and fingers badly mutilated. Never-theless, he had learnt to shoot again from the left shoulder, and was a good marksman too. He never used a three-inch case gun when he shot with me, nor did he believe in big shot. Four were his favourite shot, if I remember aright, and he had as many geese as I did.

We called that part of the marsh the 'Goose's Graveyard' because all the wounded geese in the river seemed to gravitate to it. After the punters had been out on the estuary, we frequently came across several wounded greylags and pinks hiding up the gullies.

One early morning, after a spell of arctic frost, when there were icebergs on the sea and great slabs of ice piled one upon the other on the 'plickplack', I came across a greylag with a shattered wing. This poor creature had evidently been haunting the 'Goose's Graveyard' for several days. As it moved up a deep narrow gutter it made a tinkling, rustling noise, and I soon saw that this was caused by large knobs of ice, like massive pearls, which had formed on the extremity of its breast and back feathers.

I managed to get between it and the sea, for I was determined to put an end to its misery, but when it saw that its retreat was cut off it came out of the gutter and ran at me with its beak open, hissing like a farmyard gander. A merciful shot put an end to its sufferings.

The behaviour of the main gaggle to a wounded companion is often inexplicable. I once saw a goose whose paddle had been shattered by a clumsy gunner land on the muds near a big gaggle. The others immediately surrounded it, cackling loudly, some hissing, and biting, and buffeting it with their wings, until the poor creature took itself off and sat moping some distance away.

This phenomenon has been noticed with other birds besides geese—crows and rooks, for instance. Gregarious creatures will not tolerate a sick or wounded member of the community, and the reason is, I think, *fear*, not that the ailing bird or animal can affect the safety of the flock, but that it's distress awakes in them the fear of pain and the knowledge that they are forever in jeopardy of their lives. So they either drive their companion away or actually 'finish the job' and kill it.

Wild geese when wounded sometimes show great courage. I once shot a goose, a very big greylag and the leader of the skein, on a marsh in Wigtownshire. He fell to the marsh about thirty yards away and came racing across to me. I was so startled I did not fire again (in any case he was close and I did not want to blow him to pieces) and the next instant he was savagely worrying the flap of my mackintosh.

Unfortunately, it is not always possible to make a clean kill. Geese are very tough birds and will carry a surprising amount of shot, and this is one of the reasons in favour of the eight-bore which can throw a dense pattern of big shot. There are far more clean kills with eight-bores than with twelves, but on the other hand one is tempted to take longer shots with the larger gun, until one has learnt wisdom.

The 'Goose's Graveyard' was teeming with water rails; short-eared owls roosted there also—no doubt they preyed on the wounded ducks and geese.

The cry of the water rail in the quiet of dawn is very startling. The old Norfolk fowlers call this 'Sharming', I believe. It is a very high, penetrating scream which slowly descends the scale, like a creature in its death agony. I believe it to be the challenge of the male water rail, and is the counterpart of the crowing of the farm-yard cock.

It was on the 'Goose's Graveyard', too, that I saw hen harriers, male and female: the male a lovely creature, dove-grey in colour. And what terror they spread among the numerous finches, tits and buntings which roosted in the reeds! I would see them tumbling down into the tall slender wands like pebbles.

It was curious to listen to the birds waking up in these reed beds just as dawn was breaking. Sometimes I have listened to the twanging musical notes of linnets singing all together like a choir of starlings, a very lovely concert, fairy-like and unreal.

There also the starlings roosted in winter, and as dusk fell over the river the waiting gunner would be startled by a sudden sibilant rushing sound which passed overhead and was gone in an instant. This was caused by the starling flocks at their evening exercises, each bird twisting and turning in unison like the little wader flocks on the shore, though without the charm of the latter, and that sudden gleam like silver smoke which shows when a dunlin pack turns on the wing.

Next, up river from the 'Goose's Graveyard', was Leaning Buoy, so called from the tide marker which lay on the edge of the 'plickplack'. This was a round metal buoy moored in the mud, to which was attached a long spear-like wand, on top of which hung a ragged flag. For many years it was anchored at that spot, but the last time I visited the estuary it had gone.

Leaning Buoy at one time was a very favourite haunt of mine. It was in reality a little bay, a bay of 'plickplack', bounded on all sides by tall reeds. It was possible to approach it by my own private hunting path through the reeds, which I had made myself.

I had concealed the entrance with skill, lest other vagrant gunners might discover my pet place, and it wound in and out, sometimes almost doubling on itself.

The greylags were very fond of coming in to Leaning Buoy to feed, and one afternoon I actually had a shot at low water, which was rather an unusual occurrence.

I was lying in wait in the reeds for the evening flight when I saw a party of about forty greys start walking in over the sands. It was very quiet and no other gunners were about. I suppose the geese were hungry and thought all was safe. At any rate, in they came at a steady pace, stopping now and again to take a good look round, and all the while I lay watching them like an old fox in the reeds.

Soon the leading goose walked into the 'plickplack' about ninety yards off, and as is their habit the rest of the gaggle followed suit. Soon they were hard at it, tearing up the reed tubers for all they were worth. It was a very fascinating sight to see these big grey birds all so busy, greedily chasing each other away from some particular titbit, stretching out their necks and hissing loudly. I had with me my single eight-bore, and taking a long shot I knocked over a couple. I felt well rewarded for a long and weary wait.

A quarter of a mile above Leaning Buoy was another favourite spot, Reed Island. This was not actually an island but a dense clump of tall reeds which grew apart from the main landward mass and was separated from it by a strip of short reeds about thirty yards wide.

This clump was on the very tip of a horn of land, and though the geese rarely passed over it, there was a deadly ambush in a creek fifty yards up river from the clump. I fancy that the geese, when flighting off in the dawn, steered by Reed Island, for it was quite a distinctive landmark from the sea.

Greylags were also fond of roosting in the short reeds behind Reed Island, between it and the main reed beds, and very occasionally I shot one by walking quietly out (on suitable mornings, that is to say, when there was no moon and a stiff breeze was off the sea).

By following a special path of my own, again one of my hunting paths, I was able to come out upon the 'plickplack' right on top of the roosting birds, and a snap shot could be taken as they rose with a vast beating of wings and hoarse croakings.

Close to Reed Island was the Short Breakwater, one of the stone groynes already described. It was half, or maybe a quarter, the length of the Long Breakwater lower down, but geese were always about it and were fond of sitting on a mud bank sparsely grown with reeds between Reed Island and Leaning Buoy.

John Pattinson lay out one moonlight night on this mud bank, and shot a very large greylag weighing about seven pounds, one of a bunch which came over his head. I shall always remember the triumph of that shot, for it was John's first goose. I had not gone out that night, as I had contrived to incubate a roaring cold and had deemed it wiser to stay at H.Q. Soon after midnight, when I was sitting by my fire wondering how John was getting on, and wishing I were with him, the door burst open and in he came, plastered with slime from head to foot, dripping liquid mud on the carpet, and holding up his prize by the neck. One's first goose is always an unforgettable moment in one's fowling career. No other trophy of the chase compares with it, unless it be one's first stag or woodcock. And John had deserved his goose because it was a bitter night, and he had to lie out some hours for it on his semi-liquid mud couch.

The groynes suggested that one might make a serviceable hide actually *among* the stones, especially far out on the muds. This was a snare and a delusion. We tried to build hides upon these groynes, but they were visible for miles away and the geese, when they saw a suspicious lump half-way along the length, sheered off and never passed within range.

They were, however, always *crossing* the groynes at all hours of the day (or night) but never at one particular point. Occasionally one might get a shot under the moon by lying on the stones, but only those who have shot from a cramped position will know how many an easy shot may be missed. To shoot well one's feet must be firmly planted; one must be standing up and have an easy swing. That is why a hide in a gutter or among the tall reeds was so much better in every way. Out in the gutters one could crouch down, and be quite invisible until the birds were overhead, or when they were just beating up nicely in range. Then, at the appropriate moment, one could stand up and take one's time. The geese saw you at once and towered, but if you had let them come well in, you had them at your mercy.

All the same, I must confess that a towering goose is no easy mark; somehow one always contrives to shoot below them, and it is quite extraordinary how so big a bird can spring upwards. They seem to stand on their tails and leap up, almost as if they had jumped off a spring board.

I do, however, remember one good stalk I witnessed on the Long Breakwater. My companion that year was Alan Rands, later destined to be a subaltern in the Argyll and Sutherland Highlanders. He was, I think, in his last term at school and had never been wildfowling before. Like most of the others, he was mad on the game and certainly deserved the goose he slew from the groyne.

In the darkness before dawn he had crept out right to the end; that in itself was a feat, for the stones were very slippery. In some way he had reached the end, or rather he had reached a gap in the groyne within thirty yards or so of the end, where a burn ran at right angles to the stones. Some greylags were bathing in this burn within range of the groyne and now and again he had seen an enquiring head, like the handle of an umbrella, rise up out of the bed of the stream, as he made his way along the stones.

When this occurred he lay low, and at last he found himself within eighty yards of the party. As they rose he gave them one shot with SSG. One lucky ball of lead pierced the neck of the leading bird and it pancaked, dead as mutton, on the muds. Alan put his gun down on the dyke and went after it. The mud was treacherous and he had almost reached it when he felt himself sinking. He managed to grab the goose, and then found he was stuck fast, and he had considerable difficulty in getting out, leaving his rubber boot in the quicksand. He paddled back to the groyne with one bootless leg, and in the process lost his stocking as well. But he went back for the boot and pulled it out, though his sock was never seen again.

A mile above Reed Island was Smith's Post. This was so called from the days when Seth Smith used to shoot with me. It was a good ambush, one of the best in the river, though it had one grave drawback. The geese, when flighting off at dawn, often passed over Smith's Post, which was simply a fringe of high reeds border-ing a burn. Maybe the geese followed the burn, it was a sort of landmark or 'flight mark' for them, and this is why it was such a good place. But a goose, shot coming up to the gun, invariably either fell in the burn (which was wide and deep and unless you had a good dog you lost your bird) or, what was almost as bad, fell way back in the tall reeds beyond you where it was a hopeless task to locate it. Many a goose have I lost in the tall reeds. No matter how carefully you marked their fall it was impossible to keep a straight line, once one was well into the thick tall wands, and hours of search were fruitless.

Nevertheless, Seth Smith shot several geese from there, and so did Major Oakey in later years; indeed it was the latter's favourite stand.

I always remember one curious happening when Seth Smith was shooting there one year. He fired at a couple of greylags which came in very late one frosty January morning, and I saw the shot. He hit one bird very hard and it set its wings and fell out in the vast stubble field over the sea wall. We both immediately went to fetch it, but we searched for most of the morning and never found it. Going again across this stubble for evening flight I found the bird. It had fallen farther away than we thought, into a small hollow of the field, and unfortunately the carrion crows had been at it, and of course the carcass was spoilt. Both of us must have passed close to the hollow in the morning, but had somehow missed our quarry, and that year we had no dog with us.

The burn which ran past Smith's Post was, as I have said, wide and very deep. It was on the banks of this burn, close to the land, where the old fowler's house used to stand. Many a morning Jim Jagoe must have got in his punt and glided away down this gutter, for it wound away across the sands well below the level plain and was a deadly approach to fowl.

One very arctic winter when I was shooting with Seth Smith, we lay out near this gutter, building ourselves a hide of ice cakes. Seth Smith dropped one greylag into the short reeds. He went across to get it, but it came to life just when he was stooping to pick it up and flew across the gutter. Another shot crumpled it up and it fell on the frozen burn, exactly in the centre.

The sloping banks of mud were sheets of ice but Seth Smith somehow tobogganed down this slope. Unfortunately the gutter was not strong enough to bear his weight. Had he gone through he would have been lost, for the water was eight feet deep or more and flowing strongly under the roof of ice.

When I came up he was lying on his back 'scissoring' with his legs, trying to reach the body of the greylag. I dissuaded him from these rash experiments and fetched my black labrador, Bride, who quickly fetched it in, much to our satisfaction.

I shall never forget the estuary that winter. Out on the sands the ice was piled up in glittering bergs and castles; one could walk over the most treacherous places, and when the tide began to flow, the noise out in the river was awe-inspiring. Bangs and cracks echoed over the saltings as the rising water burst its bonds. And again when the tide dropped and the 'ice roof' fell in along all the gutters, the noise was deafening, the same sounds that the polar explorer hears.

We got few geese that winter as they were all driven away, and what birds we did get were very thin. Their feeding grounds inland were frozen up and, as is their habit, the big skeins had all departed for warmer climes.

That winter I saw a snow-white goose with the small parties of greylags which haunted the frozen estuary: it was, I think, an albino grey.

It was amusing to watch the geese riding on the ice cakes as the latter were pushed up or down the river on the tides. The birds seemed to enjoy their novel rafts, and the ducks also.

Nor did they seem alarmed at the hideous clatter and bangs of the floes grinding one upon another: no doubt this was a very familiar sound which they had heard many times in their arctic breeding grounds.

Once over the burn by Jim Jagoe's cottage the character of the marsh underwent a complete change: here the 'woodland walks' began, the holly shrubberies, and the lines of oaks and elms. In my early days on this part of the coast I had many interesting experiences, for at that time no aerodrome had been built and the pinks had not been scared away. But descriptions of this section of the coast, and the little adventures I met with there, must be left to a later chapter.

9. The Island Loch

AS a change from shooting on the shore, I think it might be
of interest if the reader accompanies me on a wildfowling
expedition which I undertook with Charles Oakey in the
early December of 1948.

As I keep a 'journal' of all my wildfowling trips I can very easily
describe in detail the day-to-day happenings. So, for a space, we
will leave the broad estuary with its marshes and reed beds, Smith's
Post, Curlew Bay, Leaning Buoy, and all the other beloved haunts
and sample a very different method of fowling, inland, on a Highland Loch.

I am not going to give the exact locality, though maybe many
will recognize it from my description.

It might be well to say first how it was that, on the 11th of
December, 1948, Charles and I found ourselves discussing a very
good lunch in the north-bound train from Rugby, both of us feeling
that schoolboyish glow of satisfaction in knowing that we were
heading back on the old trail, the trail of the grey geese.

In the preceding summer I had, one day, a letter from 'Mac',
the heavy artillery merchant, asking me if I would care to join
him with a friend in shooting the Island Loch in the following
December.

Now I was already acquainted with this loch from the writings of Millais, who describes in one of his books how he once built a hide upon one of its islands, and had lain in ambush with the gaggles feeding all around him. He also describes the dramatic arrival of the geese in the autumn, how he saw the huge skeins dropping down from a vast height, weary after their long journey from the arctic.

The Island Loch has been a meeting place of the pinks and greylags for centuries; it is one of their main airports. There they arrive in October; there they mass before their return journey in the spring.

It was too good an opportunity to let slip and, as I expected, Charles needed no persuasion. Always an asset to any shooting party, he is a first-rate shot. Good marksmanship, which ensures there will be something in the bag, acts as a wonderful spur to lesser marksmen such as myself. Mac's brother was also joining us, thus making a party of four guns.

An amusing happening occurred on the journey up, which I cannot omit.

The train, strange to say, was on time; indeed, it arrived a few minutes early, and came roaring in while we were having a hasty sandwich in the refreshment room.

There was a scramble for a porter to take our hand luggage (the bulk of our gear had gone on before) and we only just managed to pack into our carriage before the train drew out. I noticed on the rack above Charles's head a large, battered green box tied with cord, without label or lock upon it. On top was piled our gun cases and the rest of our hand luggage.

We had several changes *en route* and the battered, heavy case was carefully transferred, together with the rest of our gear. On arrival at the hotel this same cumbersome luggage was carried to my room and dumped on the floor. I yelled at Charles and told him it was not mine. The following dialogue ensued:

"Not yours! What do you mean?"

"Isn't it yours, Charles?"

"Mine! Certainly not! I thought it was *yours*!"

Who was the rightful owner of this box we never did know. Next morning we contacted the local stationmaster—who arrived with a suspicious look in his eye, took all details, and departed with the mysterious trunk.

This little story, which certainly has its humorous side, reminds me of another *contretemps* which occurred the year before, when I went with Angus on a fowling trip, and is again too good a story to omit.

We had arrived at our destination, a little wayside station in the highlands, close on midnight. I got out of the carriage first and Angus followed with his gun slung across his back. I noticed Angus stumble just as he was getting out, and apparently the muzzle of his gun caught on something near the top of the door.

We retrieved our cycles from the guard's van, and as we pushed off into the darkness, we were puzzled to see the train still stationary in the station with porters running to and fro and much shouting from the guard. We thought no more about the incident until next morning a policeman arrived at our digs and enquired why we had pulled the communication cord! Apparently Angus' gun had somehow caught the cord as he descended from the carriage and so had automatically applied the brakes.

But to return to my story. As the following day was the 'Sawbath', there was, of course, no shooting, so we made a tour of the district in Mac's shooting brake, and I was able to form some idea of the geography of the place.

What a bright, clear morning that was! Cold and glittering, but few clouds in the sky. The rain of the night before had given a sparkle to this colourful country, and had made the dead bracken and the newly bare birch woods unusually rich and glowing. Against the madders and buffs of dead grass and old heather, the stems of the birches were silvery white threads, spotted and banded with black, and the crests of the mountains which surround the loch were clear and sharp in the morning sunshine, with no snow upon them.

Out on the loch white horses gleamed here and there, and in the lee of the islands we made out the black flotillas of duck. There were three islands on the loch, two of them so wooded the trees overhung the water. At the eastern end was the main island, the Laird's Island, so beloved of the geese. It had no trees of any size, and in this it differed from the others. It was low and flat and through the glasses it appeared to be of fine, soft turf. At one end was a small square ruin, all that remains of an ancient monastery which dates from the sixth century.

The northern shore appeared swampy. All down that side was a thicket of willow and alder. The southern shore was practically bare, as bare as the banks of the artificial islands in the Serpentine. Mac, with his telescope glued to his eye, exclaimed, "There they are!"

I knew what he meant by 'they'. He handed me the glass. Looking through it I saw a small party of greylags sitting comfortably on the short grass in the lee of the monastery. It was a domestic scene. The birds appeared very comfortable enjoying the sun; some had their bills tucked into their backs, not one had its head up. They had the air of having complete confidence in their impregnable position, it was *their* island, and nobody could approach it without their knowing it. It would take twenty minutes for a motor-boat to cross that tumbling, blue-grey strip of water, and long before any danger threatened they would be up and away.

The geese had another reason for confidence. The Laird only shot the loch four or five times in a season; ours was to be the fourth.

As we watched the resting greylags a biggish skein came beating up over the mountains, and for a quarter of an hour we watched them circling a dark maddery moss on the opposite shore, as though they were looking for a place to feed. Later we were to know this moss well, with its boggy acres, its fringe of dark Scotch firs, its winding ditches. Then they swung in towards the island and alighted alongside the resting greylags.

We had another interesting view of geese on the way round the loch. There was a ploughed field near the road and Mac stamped on his brakes with a suddenness which nearly dislocated our necks. I knew he had sighted geese and automatically unslung the glasses.

There, within two hundred yards of us on the dark slabby plough, was a small party of pink-footed geese, ten or a dozen, and among them a semi-albino 'pink'. Its colour was a pale dove grey, very beautiful, the same colour as a hen harrier. Only its primaries were dark; the rest of it was a uniform, pale, ashy grey. We saw this same bird again in the afternoon when we revisited the field. It flew in with the same bunch right over the road and pitched on the spot where we had seen it in the morning.

That night, after dinner, the head keeper waited on us, and advised us where the guns had better be placed for morning flight —on the moss on the northern shore. Plenty of geese were in, he said, more than in the preceding winter when the loch had been very low. Now it was full: this suited the geese.

It was with great confidence we retired that night to bed. But, as usual, I found it hard to sleep with the prospect of shooting new ground at dawn. It must have been well after 2 a.m. before I could drop off, and then my dreams were full of shadowy skeins. . . .

It was a windy dawn and cold. As soon as I was dressed I went to the stable for my dog. Judy, my labrador, was a new acquisition (my other bitch, Bride, had been run over and killed in the autumn) and she had not been entered to geese. Ducks, I knew, she retrieved well, but this was to be her first experience of wildfowling.

We found the keepers waiting for us in the yard, and Mac

backed out his shooting van. We piled in, Mac, his brother Tony, Charles and myself, the two keepers, and my dog.

Twenty minutes' drive, and we drew up at the side of a farm. There was still no sign of dawn, though the waxing moon gave a fitful light, gleaming on the distant waters of the loch, which I could see beyond the madder-black tones of a wild-looking moss.

We tramped off over the fields, the wind in our faces. I heard mallard getting up from some flood flashes on a potato field, their quackings died away towards the loch.

Tony and Charles went left with the head keeper, and Mac and I accompanied the under keeper towards some hides built right on the edge of the shore. I found my hide was very snug, of thatched straw, with a comfortable place on which to sit down, so that my head was well out of the wind. Not true fowling, you will say, and I would be the first to agree with you. Nevertheless, I felt moderately excited as I watched Mac and the keeper disappear into the darkness on my right, where gorse bushes loomed black and sinister.

Judy curled up at my feet; I slipped two cases of BB shot into my Magnum, heard the well-oiled breech snap to with a sweet click, and settled down to enjoy the drama of the dawn.

The wind piped plaintively in the thatched reeds of my hide, and the waves, tumbling on the stony shore a few feet away, drowned all other sounds. Slowly the light grew, and I could make out afar the dim shape of the Laird's Island, a mile out in the loch, and the hills beyond.

One thing I was quick to notice, and that was how different is dawn on an inland loch, compared to dawn on the coast. There is not the same sense of restless energy in the fowl, no trips of teetering waders flying up and down the tide, no decided movement of birds in or out. I knew that the churning white surf just beyond my hide was stationary, that no encroaching tide would flood me out, nor would it recede to lay bare the muds. There was a certain lifelessness in the scene and I was to notice this more markedly during our stay.

Nevertheless, the distant half-heard croaks and callings of geese gave hope of things to come, and very soon I heard geese moving behind me over the dark moss. This was unexpected. I had imagined the geese would come in from the direction of the island.

I swung round. A ragged black mob was coming low over the heather and rushes. They flew about rather aimlessly, calling to each other, and then swung in towards me. I thought at first they would come directly over me, but when within eighty yards they veered a little to the left and passed low over the stony fore-shore forty yards off.

I had my first shot. I missed with the first barrel but scored with the second. The goose I fired at threw up its chin and crashed in the water about ninety yards out, and immediately began to drift parallel to the bank.

Other geese were on wing over the loch, so I did not send Judy right away which, as it turned out, was unfortunate. There was a pack now coming in on my left, and as they passed over Tony I saw one fall like a stone. The rest broke formation and came raggedly over Charles, another shot, another goose fell, sending up a plume of spray. It landed in a little bay close inshore. This was good shooting, a good beginning.

I then sent Judy for my goose which had now drifted farther out in the loch, and was hidden now and again by the heavy waves. She could not see it, and after swimming round for a minute or so came back and shook herself, looking at me with 'I don't believe you' expression. A moment or so later the floating body of my victim was lost to view in the tumbling waste of grey waters.

However, I did not give up hope. The wind which was blowing parallel to my hide would drift it in higher up, and no doubt the keepers would collect it later in the boat.

Another bunch of geese now came over Charles and again he

scored, the goose falling with a thump among the rushes within a few yards of his hide, though I did not see him go out and retrieve it.

That was all the sport we had that dawn and when day had fully come I saw Charles and Tony walking about among the rushes looking for their birds. I took the dog over to help, but not a single goose did we pick up on that first morning's flight!

It was unbelievable: two geese, at least, I could have sworn had been dead birds, but we searched the rushes for some hours and failed to find them.

It was, I think, the most disappointing flight I ever remember: five geese down (Tony had had another shot after his first, which I had not seen, and had dropped a second bird) and not one gathered!

This only demonstrates a maxim I have always held—that if you get a goose down *retrieve it at once*, even if other geese are on the wing. Time and again I have been robbed of my game by not observing this rule.

Wild geese are very tough and if wounded will creep away and hide in the most cunning fashion, not even a hunted moorhen can conceal itself so well.

So ended our first morning's flight, and we returned home to breakfast feeling that we had somehow made a mess of things. Though the keepers later retrieved the bulk of the geese, we resolved in future to collect our birds at once.

10. The Laird's Island

IT was the 16th of December. Mac, Tony, Charles, myself, and Judy were walking through the birch scrub of the northern shore. The great moment had come, we were going to cross to the Laird's Island: that is, if we could make the passage. For some days it had been unapproachable because of high winds which had whipped up the loch into a miniature Atlantic. No small boat could live in it. This afternoon it was little better, the same westerly wind prevailed; even well back in the birch woods we could hear the continuous roar of breakers.

The keeper thought we might 'make it', but certainly not from the boat house at the far end of the loch. He would not risk the long pull in a heavily laden boat. His plan was to run up on the leeward shore and then join us on the fringe of the birch wood and make the crossing (about a quarter of a mile) where the loch narrowed.

At that point the island broke the force of the wind, the waves were not so turbulent. Yet, as we emerged through the silvery stems of the wood, the water seemed to me to be in hideous, churning turmoil. White shutters of foam tossed up and sank, and impressive waves were running in among the willow scrub in front of us to break in a welter of dirty foam. Would the keeper decide to cross? I got out my glasses and scanned the upper part of

the loch but could see nothing but the white bars of foam appearing
and disappearing.

The wind was piercingly cold, but I had on my American
'hunting' coat, which is the best garment devised for shooting, with
capacious pockets and a belt. No cold can get through it.

Across the loch black clouds hid the mountain tops (there had
been snow at dawn), scud came flying overhead in tattered ribbons.
But at times the sun gleamed forth, and then the heaving waves
before us were turned to molten silver. There was little visible
movement on the Laird's Island. Now and again a bundle of duck
would rise up (I could see them through the glasses) to drop down
in the lee of the willow swamp which fringed the northern bank.

During the last few days, when we had been storm-bound on
the shore, I had many times looked longingly at this promised land.
Sometimes I had seen masses of geese descend upon the flat green
turf by the monastery walls. They had fed and slept there undisturbed for most of the day.

We had shot one or two more greylags on the moss at dawn, but
they had never come again as they did on that first morning's
flight.

"Wouldn't like to go in to-day," said Tony, gloomily eyeing the
grey waves, "not in this get-up, anyway." He looked down at his
thigh boots and leather coat.

I 'couldn't agree more', as the saying is, and I must confess
I began to hope the keeper would not come.

We sat down on a fallen Scotch fir and watched the rolls of
yellow foam being whipped up like meringues and whisked into
the heather, where they feathered and burst. The waves made so
much noise we had to shout to make ourselves heard. Then
Charles grabbed my arm and pointed out over the loch. On the
roaring wind came snatches of goose talk and turning I saw a great
mob beating in low for the Laird's Island, possibly seven or eight
hundred birds. Hardly had they dropped out of sight behind the

monastery walls when another straggling skein came over the fir woods on our left. They too joined those on the island.

The sight put a new heart into us.

"My goodness!" exclaimed Charles, "if we can get there we shall be in for some fun to-day!"

I switched the glasses round, and immediately saw little white plumes of spray rising and falling far down the loch. These plumes, which appeared like shell splashes, were higher than the waves. I knew it was the keepers on their way down. Soon we could see the black prow of the motor-boat rise and fall, sometimes there would only be a pillar of flying spray which blotted them out.

We stood up, watching. We could see bunches of duck disturbed by the boat's approach rise up and toss away down wind. From the Laird's Island—no movement, no sign that down there on the green behind the ruin close on a thousand geese must be massed!

At last the boat drew near and then slewed round in the shallows, wallowing, rocking.

"What about it?" yelled Mac.

"Och aye, we'll have a try," shouted the keeper. "It'll be a bit rough, nae doot, but we'll chance it." He was hardly audible above the racket of the surf.

This didn't sound reassuring to me. I have a horror of deep water, due no doubt to once being half-drowned in Rugby School swimming bath.

We waded out. The waves came running in over the sandy ledge, banging and slamming the boat. Judy came grunting after, swimming strongly, and we lifted her aboard. Then we all piled in, the keeper walking alongside until the water became too deep, pushing us off-shore. The engine spluttered to life, we swung round into the teeth of wind and wave.

It was not a pleasant journey, though there was no real danger— not then. Spray broke aboard us. Tony up in the prow at times took it green over his back. But all eyes were now on the island which was steadily drawing nearer. Still no sign of life, not a goose lifted yet; all were hidden behind the ruin and the low swelling hill of turf on which it stood.

There was a lively chance of a shot, so the keeper said, if we could run ashore among the willows, place two guns in the butts (barrels sunk in the turf) which lay a hundred yards from the swamp, and then the keeper, Tony, and Mac would go round the shoulder of Monastery Hill to put the geese up. With the wind where it was it was quite likely they would come over us.

The landing was made: at last we were on the island which had so long remained impregnable.

The keeper, Tony, and Mac set off over the turf, and Charles and I got down into our barrels. These were fine big butts with plenty of room for Judy and an old oil drum for a seat. Sitting down, my head was well below the level of the ground; standing up, it was possible to peep comfortably over the rim, through the low rampart of straw which was placed all round the mouth, and how snug it was to be out of the wind! I will describe the view from my hide, as it will give the reader some idea of the geography of the place.

Behind me (to the north) I could see the willow swamp, a bit of foreshore, and the boat tied up behind some willows, rocking gently. The stems of the willow trees were a rich madder colour, which made a fine contrast to the bleached tussocks of rush and coarse grass of the swamp. Over the top of the willows I glimpsed the strip of loch we had traversed, beyond it the birch wood, and beyond again, the high shoulder of the mountain. The sun was out at that moment and the whole of the upper slope was bathed in light, the crest powdered with snow.

Looking south there was not so much to see, just the ground rising up into a little hill, and the top of the grey stone monastery showing over it, backed by more mountains, dark blue-grey against the afternoon light.

It was from over this crest the geese might come.

About ninety yards to my right, a little way up the slope, I could see Charles in his hide. Charles's headgear amused me as much as mine amused him. I favour a deerstalker, he an Edwardian cycling cap, one of those small perfectly round caps, made in sections, with a skimpy peak and a diminutive button on top. We both must have looked like an illustration of sportsmen of over half a century ago.

All at once there came the sudden clamour of uprising pinks. I slid my safety catch forwards.

The next moment the near horizon fairly spouted geese, all flying in a ragged formless body directly for our butts. They were well up and the wind was in their tails. I saw Charles's gun swing up and bang! bang! went both his barrels. No goose fell. A lot swerved and came over me and I hit one very hard with BB shot. He carried on for a few wing beats, faltered, and then turned over in the air, falling in the fringe of the rushes which bordered the swamp.

Remembering former experiences, I wasn't going to chance my first goose of the trip getting away, so I jumped out of the barrel with Judy and raced across. After a search I saw it lying in the rushes. But Judy did not recognize it as game. She galloped over to it, sniffed it, and turned away, bringing me instead a small greyish, very frightened, rabbit which she found under a tussock and pounced upon! I took it from her and let it go and it ran off none the worse. It was annoying about Judy, but the next moment the best possible thing happened.

Mac, and the head keeper, who had seen me run across, joined me. We were talking about the result of the drive when a single goose came over our heads, and Mac brought it down with one shot from his single eight. It fell stone dead about fifty yards away and Judy saw it fall. I sent her for it and she retrieved it to hand at once.

We then went back to our butts.

It was not long before more geese were on the move, and a nice pack came over Charles and me. Charles dropped one in the willow swamp. I missed (both barrels). I sent Judy for Charles's goose, and after a chase in and out among the willows she grabbed it and brought it back to me.

Shots now began to sound from the far side of the island, and now and again as a skein came straggling across I would see a bird drop out. The bag was mounting. Charles had been right—it was a day of days to be here, when the distant sea was too rough for the birds and they were continually on the move. Sometimes I would see the skeins coming in over the mountains at the head of the valley, poised for minutes at a time as though they were hovering, for they were meeting the full force of the gale.

I saw two very large skeins beat in and for a long while they strove to pass along westwards of the loch; for some reason they did not wish to come down on the water. They had in mind some set goal, but the wind was against them and for twenty minutes I witnessed a gallant struggle.

In the infrequent lulls they would creep forward a yard or two, and then a fresh gust would push them back. Time and again I saw them resolutely return to the attack, undulating, ever creeping forward.

Finding that they could make no headway they then tried another tack. Down they went until they hugged the mountain; they seemed to be only a few feet above the heather. Inch by inch they crept along the mountain side and I thought the battle was won. But as soon as they came out from the shelter of the hill the old enemy met them and forced them back, and at last, with what seemed a gesture of despair, they scattered and let the wind whip them away towards the sea.

It demonstrated to me how these big birds are very much at the mercy of the winds and how, on their journey from their arctic breeding grounds, they must be careful to choose propitious weather.

Towards sunset the wind increased in fury. We stayed on, hoping more geese would come with the rising moon, and when at last we foregathered under the monastery walls we found we had twelve geese to show for our trouble.

Under the moon the island was a ghostly place; black shadows from the monastery, goose calls to left and right, and all the while the continual fret and roar of the waves beating on the shingle. As we chugged out of the lee of the island, and felt the push and thrust of the swinging waves under us, the clanging cries of geese sounded loud overhead and everyone stared upwards to the stars, fingering guns, but we saw nothing.

It was a heavy load for the journey to shore and a grisly passage it proved to be. We had at times, so the keeper told me after, only two inches of freeboard. We were tossed and shaken and shipped some water, and when at last we reached the bank the moon had gone behind dark storm clouds and we misjudged the landing place.

For some perilous moments we wallowed helplessly just off shore, broadside on to the waves. Our screw was powerless and now and again a great roller would heave us round, canting us up until I thought we should turn over.

But all unpleasant things come to an end. We ran ashore at last among the willows where we had embarked in the early afternoon, and how good it was to feel the firm earth under our feet and smell wet winter woods about us!

It had been a successful day. Perhaps the high spot had been a shot of Charles's. A skein came over him and he had fired at what he thought was the white goose. Actually it turned out to be a barnacle, a very rare visitor to this inland loch. It was a beautiful bird, an adult male, in perfect plumage and was, incidentally, the first barnacle Charles had ever shot.

We returned to the island a few days later. It was an afternoon of tranquil calm, and though a few parties of geese came over we only had one bird. But the long spells of inactivity enabled me to explore the old building and find, among the rabbit burrows below its crumbling walls, the complete top of a human skull, as yellow as parchment. No doubt it was the skull of one of the old monks who long ago prayed and chanted within the walls of the ancient building.

It was queer to think that these men of God, over a thousand years ago, had also seen and heard wild geese passing, that they had looked out on those same mountains and harkened to the roar of the surf on winter nights. Certainly they could have chosen no better haven from the world than this green island set in a grey loch, with no sounds but those of wind, wave, and wildfowl.

11. The Moss

A FAINT glimmer shows to the east as we make our way across the potato field. There has been rain in the night, and it is sticky walking; the mud balls up on our waders until they weigh as heavy as slave irons.

In front of me I see the silhouette of Donald, the head keeper, carrying in one hand a spade, and in the other Mac's Pandora's Box which contains the decoys. In front of him again sways the large figure of Charles in his Edwardian cycling cap. His wader tops are rolled down, they flap outwards as he walks, like wings. Behind comes Tony. Mac has gone to the shore butts with the under keeper; long since he vanished into the darkness. We plod on across the field.

There is, oh! such a sweet keenness in the wind which blows from the loch. It is spiced with rich mossy smells, the damp earthy flavour of heath and dyke. A great happiness pervades me as I am sure it does Charles, that sense of expectation, the knowledge that there are yet many days of sport like this, dawn ambushes, evening flights, good company, yarns around the fire at night!

It is, I am sure, the smell of the wind which engenders this feeling of happiness, which is very akin to boyhood's holiday glow of exultation.

For some mornings past, as we have come off the moss, we have noticed a party of greylags on a small stubble adjacent to this potato field. Tony has the idea that a hide by the potato clamp will yield a good dividend, for we have noticed that the geese fly over this, especially when disturbed. I favour a hide on the far side of the stubble field where there is a low wall. Charles good-naturedly says he doesn't mind where he goes, but I suspect he has a good spot in the back of his mind, he usually has.

We see Tony well ensconced behind his potato clamp and the decoys are put out on the muddy field. Then Charles goes plodding off towards the dim glimmer of the loch. He has a notion, I believe, that he can intercept the geese as they come out.

The head keeper and I go off to the stubble. We find that the wall is not too good but at the far corner of the stubble field, where it joins the moss, there is a little rushy corner. The rushes are tall and thick, the ground boggy.

Donald goes on ahead with the spade and the next moment is floundering in a bog close to the fence. No good there for digging. But here, close by, the ground is soft but not oozy. This is the place.

Donald is a powerful, braw laddie, and he puts his back into his work. In a few minutes he has excavated a respectable hide. He is working against time, for the light is growing over the fir woods.

"Try that, Sirr," he says, climbing out of the hole.

I sit down on my goose bag and find that I need a little more leg room. Donald puts this right in a moment, and arranging the rushes round me (I feel very pampered) he goes off to join Charles and the under keeper in the whin bushes on the west shore.

Judy presses close; I feel her warm body shuddering with excite-ment. These shudders come in waves. For a second or two she is quite immobile, then she is seized as with an ague. But it is not cold, simply sheer excitement.

Close behind me, along the banks of a deepish dyke, are some tall naked trees. Soon after it gets light some fieldfares come to these and for a long time they sit upright on the topmost twigs 'chack chack, chacking', turning their bold lean heads from side to side.

A few gulls pass overhead, and then a bunch of a dozen or more, on their way to the pasture. They remind me of country labourers setting forth for the day's work. They will not return until night-fall. All day they will be following the ploughs, perhaps, or winning their sustenance on green flood-washed meadows.

I like to watch the gulls pass, it is one of the sights which the flight shooter never fails to enjoy. Their wings, those narrow angular wings, move rythmically in unison, gracefully and unhurried. The birds hold a dead straight course.

The keen wind hisses in the rushes and among the bare branches of the trees. The fieldfares have gone, it is now quite light. My foreign surroundings grow plain in the new light of day and the stubble field, which seemed so vast in the darkness, is now, I see, quite small.

Then there is a single shot from Charles's direction and I wonder what that wily old bird has slain. It sets me on the *qui vive* and I cautiously raise myself, and peer about me towards the madder-brown moss. I see nothing but the dark Scotch firs, over there by the water's edge.

Then looking right I see, quite close and sailing in over the wall, a small party of greylags! Down I go into my hole and slide forward the safety catch, my heart knocking at the base of my skull.

Will they come over me?

I hear a single croak and then—silence. Are they down? I am just about to take another look when there is a swish of wings. Five greylags loom up over the tips of the rushes. I raise the gun. They see me at once, check with a startled croak and wheel away. I fire both barrels, but they go flapping on towards the potato clamp.

I hold my breath, Tony is there waiting for them. He will have heard my shot.

I see the geese flapping onwards, rising a little over the potato clamp. One goose slumps to earth and a second later I hear the shot. The others go on out of sight.

Half an hour passes. It is quite light now. The sun has risen, it shines quite warmly on my corner. Gulls in hundreds are now coming off the loch. Then I hear a great outburst of cackling and see a skein of forty or more greys coming along from the fir woods. They are, I know, looking for a place to feed; no doubt they have in mind this stubble field.

But the geese are wary, they circle about, cackling all together at intervals. No doubt they have heard the shots and are suspicious. Then they begin to lower and set their wings. They pass wide of Tony and come smoothly in towards my field. I know they will circle once before alighting and it looks as if they will come slap over my corner.

Down I get, doubling myself over the shuddering body of Judy. But there is no swish of wings. The minutes pass, I am sure they are down on the stubble, and raise myself cautiously to take a spy. No! they are not on the field. Then where, in Heaven's name, are they? I peer about on all sides and then give up the mystery.

The geese must have sensed danger and passed on over the moss. Half an hour passes. The sun shines on the mountains, tawny red, gold, and buff. I see the labourers going out to the fields, carts on the move, and on a distant hill a shepherd and his dog are walking towards the fir wood.

Taking out my glass I scan the moss and the far whin bushes where Mac must be, and at once see the gunners are 'coming off', in other words they consider the flight is over. Charles sees them too and, as I watch, his figure rises up like magic from the heather away there by the firs.

It is time I 'packed in' too. I rise from my rushy couch, and on the instant there breaks forth a tremendous 'whooshing' noise, followed by an outburst of hoarse cackling. From over the low wall in the next field lifts the big lot of geese. They had been there all the time! When I had bobbed down they had just dropped in over the far side of the wall. Had I known it I could have had a perfect stalk.

I cite this instance of what occurred one morning on our trip as a typical example of goose hunting. One must be for ever watchful and alert, and if geese, once seen close at hand, seem to vanish into thin air, then a very cautious 'recce' is indicated. This I had omitted to do.

Afterwards, when I joined Tony, I found him very disgruntled, and still hunting for his fallen goose. It had fallen like a dead bird (I was a witness of that) but he had been unable to find it. I put Judy on the line of the fall, and she followed it a little way among the rushes. But the moss was so thick and intersected by so many gullies and drains that it was a hopeless quest. Actually we found Tony's goose next day right on the shore and half-eaten by crows and stoats.

A few moments later the other guns came up, Charles carrying a snow-white ermine on a thong of rush which he proudly displayed to us, thereby earning the soubriquet of *Ermine Hunter in Chief*.

In actual fact these pretty little white stoats were common on the moss. A morning or two before, while waiting for morning flight, I had seen a flash of white snaking in and out along the tide edge. I had shot it, another perfect ermine. These little creatures seemed to make it their business to hunt up the shore soon after dawn, no doubt on the chance of finding carrion. The keeper told us that every year he saw them there. Certainly the winter of 1948 was very mild and open, so it was not snow or frost which made them change their coats.

There is one other locality which I will describe before saying good-bye to this magic haunt of geese.

At the eastern end of the loch was a long low embankment of

green turf, thickly grown with willows. Beyond it was a beautiful pool of some three acres, hedged all round by woods and with an island in the centre. It was a queer place, a sort of ornamental pond, and seemed quite apart from the loch, though it was connected with it by a deep narrow channel at one end of the raised rib of turf. I was surprised to learn that when the loch was low a good crop of hay was carried from the bed of this 'pool' which was, in reality, only flooded land.

One evening very late, when waiting for duck near the pool (they often came down on the quiet water beyond the willows), we heard some greylags go in. It soon became clear that they were using the pool as a sleeping place.

This was very curious. As will have been shown, wild geese are very wary birds and dislike the proximity of cover. In the pool they were hedged round with trees with no exit save over the low willow-girt bank.

An examination next day, however, showed that they were not only using it at night but had landed on the embankment. Their droppings were scattered about and quantities of grey feathers showed that they frequently came ashore and perhaps slept on the bank.

Accordingly, an early morning raid was planned.

Tony, Mac, and the keepers rowed up the loch in the darkness before dawn and managed to reach the willows before the geese took alarm. Then the whole mob lifted from the pool and came out over their heads, and Tony managed to drop one in the loch.

Needless to say the manœuvre was not repeated, and the birds gave up using the place, at least for the time being. Only on a private shoot could this have occurred and no doubt after our shooting lease had expired, the greylags would return again to this quiet sanctuary among the trees. It certainly was an ideal dormitory as, however rough it was out on the loch, the pool was always calm and sheltered.

All good times come to an end, and at last there came the frosty morning when Charles and I stood on the platform waiting for the train to bear us south.

It was a frosty, sunny dawn. The platform was white with rime and as we waited we saw the gulls coming out over the village from the loch. We saw, too, one small skein of greylags, high up over the chimney-pots, and their clanging cries on the frosty morning air were in the nature of a salute and a farewell, for we were not to hear that gladsome sound again until the following season.

12. *Sea Lavender Land*

NO two localities haunted by wildfowl are similar. What could be more different than the vast grey-green saltings of the Wash (where, in my early days, I did the bulk of my wild-fowling) and the estuary, say, of the Severn, or the tidal basins and wilder bays and indentations of the north of Scotland or Ireland?

Even the extensive Solway marshes differ in a marked degree from those of the Wash. On the east coast you do not get those fine 'lawns', so beloved of the barnacle, with areas of grass so delicate and cropped they might be bowling greens.

There the marsh vegetation is coarse; sea blite, sea lavender, and all manner of wild bog-loving plants make the Wash marshes a rough ground to tramp over, and the numerous dykes and gullies, winding hither-thither in a perfect maze, necessitate constant jump-ing. One has only to fly over the Wash to get a good idea of the intricate pattern of the drains; some are yards across, others so narrow you can step over them, but all wind like snakes in every direction.

At one time I knew the Wash marshes as well as I knew my native fields and woods at home, those happy hunting grounds where I served my apprenticeship to the sport of wild shooting. Of these meadows and spinneys, woods and lanes, I will speak in another chapter, as the inland gunner has his own form of wild-fowling.

A description of the Wash saltings may, therefore, be of interest to those who have never seen them.

In passing, I might say that I am writing of the saltings as I remember them a quarter of a century ago. Of recent years great schemes have been set afoot for draining much of these tide-washed areas, sea walls have been built, and in a very short space of time, probably in the next decade, there will no longer be any marshes worthy of the name, all will have been 'tidied' up; the acres and acres of sea lavender and gullies, haunt of duck and waders, will have gone and in their place will be the black rich fields which are such a feature of this flat and inhospitable land. A pity, a great pity, from the sportsman-naturalist's point of view. The farmer wants to make more money (just as if he hadn't enough already!), so away with all the waste wild places, plough them up! grow corn, and sugar beet, more money! more money! It is the same avaricious longing which lays the axe to the green woods I love. To most men trees are of no more account than cabbages, the only difference being they are taller and make a good deal more cash in the market place.

Again and again I realize that for a man of my tastes and feelings I have been born half a century too late, that all the things I hold most dear are regarded by others as of naught. Most of the fine places where once the wildfowl used to frequent in their thousands have been either drained or built over, or turned into bombing ranges or aerodromes: indeed, aerodromes seem to have picked on all the good 'goose' country. Even our lovely forests (such as remain to us) suffer, and at the time of writing (1948) that splendid forest of Savernake, where once Hudson used to roam, is still occupied by the military and access is forbidden.

Mankind seems such a quarrelsome, greedy animal that he who would enjoy nature and wild life must take himself off to a desert isle and be content to live a solitary existence, cut off from his fellow men. If all this despoiling of the wild places means civiliza' tion, then I don't like being civilized. Attempts will be made in the not so distant future to stop all shooting and fishing by Act of Parliament. It is these urban'minded people, these money grab' bers with the minds of pen'pushing clerks, who would bring all this about.

But I am getting a long way from the subject of this chapter, which is the marshes of the Wash.

From Boston in the north to Hunstanton in the south there are (or were) thousands of acres of wild salt marsh which in winter are thronged with all manner of wildfowl from grey geese to jack snipe. In some places these marshes are a couple of miles wide when the tide is out, and beyond the fringe of sea blite are thousands of acres of firm sand where the geese and ducks may rest undisturbed, unless the aeroplanes worry them.

Out on those vast golden levels they are as unapproachable as bustards on a Spanish plain, and certainly I have seen more geese on the wing at one time along this coast than anywhere else in Britain.

On a good old 'coarse' morning when the geese are 'in', the sky is striped like a zebra's back with the skeins flighting to feed. Their chief food is on the potato fields inland and as long as the ground remains unfrozen they will resort to them, flying out at night to the sand'banks in the Wash. Like the geese of the north they will feed by moonlight, and the biggest bag on record was made on a potato field owned by a friend of mine, a Lincolnshire farmer, who incidentally is a great authority on geese and ducks, and a keen sportsman into the bargain.

Some of the gullies on the Wash are ideal for hiding in, narrow but deep, and fringed with sea blite. When the geese are beating up, one can get right down in these creeks and be completely hidden, the only drawback being the glutinous mud they contain, which tends to anchor your feet, thereby making an easy swing and follow through a difficult business.

My plan used to be to go when there was no moon, and get as far out on the marshes as I could.

The narrow creeks are deepest and best near the shore; as one gets farther out they become wider and afford less cover until, where they debouch on to the sand, they are simply wide shallow runnels which are useless for hiding in.

Pits may, of course, be dug far out on the sands and excellent sport may be had from them, though I have never tried this method, the reason being that if one ventures away 'in front' one should employ a local fowler as a guide and I am always averse to this; I prefer to hunt on my wild lone and find my own way around. In any case, your local fowler is sometimes amazingly stupid, and will go to a vast amount of needless walking, crawling, and manœuvre when the chances of a shot are nil.

Your very good wildfowler (such as Charles Oakey) may appear rather a lazy man, he 'packs up' too soon at darkling, or will not go out on such and such a morning because he says it will be sheer waste of effort. He knows, you see, just when conditions are favourable, just when to pluck the flower of fortune with the minimum of effort and discomfort. And quite right too! There are some fowlers I have met who never bother about dressing in suitable clothes; they say they do not bother about wet feet or frozen toes, any old jacket is good enough and one can always change when you get home. Though these fellows are hardy enough and can stand a vast amount of exposure, they pay for it in later life when the hot fires of youth are sinking and the blood begins to chill. Then rheumatics take their toll. Many an old long-shore fowler of my acquaintance has been crippled with rheumatism long before he need have been if only he had taken care of himself. It isn't molly-coddling oneself to see that feet are always dry, and that you have a comfortable air-cushion-cum-goose-bag to sit on in a dyke. It's just common sense, and there's no reason at all to be cold and uncomfortable when wildfowling if you take the precaution to dress properly.

Newspaper sheets cut to the size of the foot, and as thick as you can comfortably wear them will keep the feet beautifully warm. It is well to remember that there's nothing like paper for retaining heat.

I remember many years ago, when shooting on an estuary in Scotland with Charles, how we lay out on the frozen muds during an intense frost. It was a moonlight night and there was no cover to speak of, just a few sparse stalks of short reed, as we were outside the 'plickplack'. Under normal conditions one could never have waded this far through the treacherous mud. There we lay, stretched out like two corpses under the moon, hopefully waiting for an incautious greylag to fly over us. Underneath our waist-coats we had several layers of newspaper, so that we crackled alarmingly when we moved. But we were warm enough despite the fearful frost.

The only time one gets really wet and cold is during a stalk and then, I must confess, there is no clothing yet devised which will keep out the water or warm the hands. Yet there are occasions when a stalk is your only chance to get a goose and it must be undertaken. I have always looked upon stalking geese as rather in the nature of a last desperate measure. It is safe to say that ninety per cent of geese which are shot in Britain every year come to the gun of their own accord, and the gun does not go to them.

But to return to the Wash. It was there I shot my first goose. It amuses me to think of my very early efforts. I was quite unacquainted with the habits and ways of wildfowl and, for the first day or two of my stay, I went out during the day. Not only did I never get a shot at a goose but, strange to say, I never *saw one*, for the simple reason I arrived at the marshes long after they had gone in and departed ere they returned! I might have been in a country where no geese were ever known, for I was too unobservant to see them on the fields.

Of course, I soon got wise and I was lucky enough to get a goose on my first dawn flight, a pink-footed goose, and I shall never forget the wave of exultation which went through me when I saw it fall.

On one or two occasions I have known geese come over a gun where there was no cover whatsoever. Once on the Wash I was out with an old fowler I had chanced to meet at flight, and we were making our way back to the shore over a flat area of mud.

The flight was over, and it had been a good one that morning, thousands of birds having gone inland, but all had passed in about two miles up the marshes and we had not had a shot. Suddenly my companion laid his hand on mine and told me to get down. We both lay on the mud, or rather crouched in a kneeling position, and a bunch of pink-footed geese came right over us. We both stood up and fired, my companion bringing one down, which fell at our feet.

On another occasion I was walking across a grass field in Northumberland. It was a bright sunny morning in January, and I was not thinking of geese. All at once I heard the well-known cry, and looking up, I saw a party coming towards me, rather high over the next field. I knelt down and kept quite still, and when they were overhead I stood up and brought the leader down, the biggest pinkfoot I have ever shot; it weighed over seven pounds.

The charm of the Wash, as of the Solway, is the variety of fowl which one sees: all manner of ducks, mallard, wigeon, teal, pintail, waders by the thousand, plovers by the countless thousands, and the two kinds of geese, pinks, and an occasional whitefront. Greylags, for some reason, are uncommon on the Wash, though they are sometimes shot. The reason is, I think, that the grey is more fond of grazing on fresh grass than the pink, it is essentially a pasture-loving goose, and it certainly does not resort to potato fields in the way the pink does.

One of the most wonderful sights that the longshore gunner can see on the Wash, and indeed on any large estuary, is the flight of the dunlin and sanderling flocks. Their silver breasts curl and gleam like pale smoke along the tide line and can be seen from an immense distance. Always, at high water, the little waders indulge in this spectacular display, and it is very wonderful how each bird twists and turns as at a given command; it is a sight I never tire of watching.

High water is a sort of play hour, a relaxation, when they mark time until the water begins to drop. But in very wild weather, when the great winds boom over the flats, they will not fly but sit hunched head to wind in one dense carpet, shoulder to shoulder.

This reminds me of a very pretty and unusual sight I saw many years ago on the outskirts of Dundee, close to the Tay bridge.

I happened to be passing that way one day, along the lower road. It was a very wild winter's afternoon, with a ferocious wind and flying snow, and the tide was running very high, well up on the sea wall which runs alongside the pavement.

Upon the top of this wall the dunlin were massed in one vast company. I cannot estimate the number I saw, but I would say that nearly a thousand birds were perched along the top of that wall. Now and again a panic would seize them and away they would go across the tossing waves. But in a few moments back they came to settle once more on the heavy coping stones. They were doing this continually, flickering and alighting like a flock of grey and white butterflies, and though I was within a few yards of them they showed no alarm.

All their favourite sand-banks were, of course, covered and even the low-lying green marsh higher up the coast was flooded by the tide that day, so there was no place for them to rest, no firm hard surface but the top of the wall.

Some gunners will shoot these fairylike little creatures, but it is a crime to do so, nor are they good to eat.

Knot are just as attractive, even more so, being comfortable, dumpy, little grey and white birds who show little fear of man. They are, however (unfortunately for them), excellent eating, as good as plover, and puntsmen, as well as shoulder gunners, will sometimes send a charge of shot into their close-packed trusting ranks.

I remember once when wildfowling up at Lindisfarne seeing a punt gunner fire at a stand of knot on the slob. How many he gathered I do not know, but for two days afterwards I was picking up dead and dying knot along the tide line; I must have found at least two score of bodies.

The handsome sea-pie or oystercatcher is also shot by gunners, which again is a pity as they are no good on the table. Moreover, they are stupidly trusting birds, though pretty to look at in their black and white pied plumage and their sealing-wax red legs and bills. They are so vividly and clearly marked with the charming patterns and harmonies of intense black, snow-white, and pillar-box red that they sometimes appear to me to be carved and painted birds, with a curiously wooden appearance—Noah's Ark birds, in fact.

Of all the wader tribe they are the most hysterical when the tide is at full flood. They fly about the saltings in peeping bands, and show no fear of the figure of a man with a gun under his arm.

Another bird which has this rather artificial appearance is the shelduck. For some reason I have never been an admirer of the shelduck, though with some naturalists it is their favourite duck. They are fond and courageous parents, and when they are leading their brood to sea over the dunes, they will not desert their charges.

It seems queer to me, too, that they breed in rabbit burrows, as at first this would seem to be a most unducklike procedure. Yet the reason is not far to seek. They are vividly marked; you can see a shelduck for a mile away if it is sitting on the marsh, and this distinctive colour would betray a sitting bird, even if it was hiding in a dense bed of reeds. Carrion crows and other birds of prey would see that striking white, dark-green plumage, and the orange-red bill. So the shelduck has been forced to breed in burrows, where they are hidden from the eyes of their enemies.

W. H. Hudson in *Adventures Among Birds* has a charming chapter on the shelduck. He was very fond of this species and he has some interesting things to say about their courtship and breeding habits.

But from the longshore gunner's point of view they are inedible. I have never tasted anything so obnoxious as shelduck; the true gunner will never shoot them.

With the redshank it is rather different. Though they also mass together at the high sea mark, and though they also will fly in teetering companies along the tidal ways, they are more wary than either the dunlin or the knot, and are almost as difficult to shoot on the wing as snipe. Moreover, they are almost the snipe's equal on the table.

Curlew, as I have said, are fair game and on the Wash I have had some excellent fun with them. And this reminds me of an incident some years ago on the Wash which caused me at the time some embarrassment and certainly a good deal of amusement. But the telling of it must be left to a later chapter.

When the tide is out on the Wash the sea is invisible, the grey-green plain stretches away and away to the horizon and even the main gutters, twenty feet deep and many yards wide, are empty save for a tiny trickle which winds its way down the centre of the mud cushions.

But at the flood tides in spring and autumn this grey-green expanse is one vast churning mass of waves which flood higher and higher until they almost lick the top of the sea wall.

Woe betide the incautious gunner who happens to be far out in the maze of winding creeks if he neglects to watch the rise of water. It will be too deep for him to stand it out and nothing but a long swim will save him and that, on a day in mid-winter, will probably be the end of him.

The water runs away very quickly as soon as the tide begins to ebb. First appear the inshore clumps of sea blite, then the higher areas of marsh, and upon these the homeless wader flocks descend in their millions like flies on meat.

Soon every gully and creek is a roaring torrent as the tide races and scrambles back towards the sea, as though it had suddenly realized it had overstepped its bounds, and felt itself in danger of being cut off by the land.

Old baskets, planks, trunks of trees, all the flotsam and jetsam of the marsh which a moment ago were bobbing along the sea wall, go aground. (Once, during the war, I found a stranded mine.) Soon that same grey-green expanse, albeit very draggled and sodden, reappears, and the water in the creeks sinks below the rim of the marsh.

These high tides, especially when backed by a wind, drown a lot of hares. On the Wash marshes in the days when I shot there, hares were common. We never walked the saltings without having one in the bag at the end of the day, and sometimes a brace of pheasants as well.

Pitiful it is to see the poor hares cut off by the tide, retreating first from one piece of high ground, then another, until weary of swimming they are drowned by the rising flood. They do not seem to have the sense to make their way back to shore when the waters begin to rise, but will swim from island to island in an aimless fashion until their strength is spent.

I remember once on the Solway seeing a score of hares drowned in this way. Through the glasses I could see the marshes dotted with little woebegone black figures hunched up miserably on their tussocks, ears flat, noses raised heavenwards.

And after the tide had dropped, I could have collected a sackful.

13. Early Days

ABOUT two years after I had shot my first goose on the Wash, I went again with my cousin, Tony Wilson, and pitched a tent below the sea wall. The time was September, and the curlews and plover were then assembling on the saltings in very large flocks. Duck, also, were plentiful and we lived very well, mostly off what we shot, which is a fine experience for young boys.

We had chosen a snug place for our encampment among some trees on the landward side of the sea wall. Actually, I suppose, we had no business there, but in those happy carefree days, when restrictions were not as they are to-day, nobody said anything to us and we were left undisturbed. In any case, we were some way from a farm and the nearest house was Shep White's cottage on the bank.

From there we got our milk and bread and also, I remember, some extremely good pickled samphire which the shepherd's wife gave us in a stoppered jar. She had picked the samphire herself out on the marshes and, of course, prepared it also.

Pickled samphire should form part of every true fowler's diet, for it tastes of the saltings over which the grey geese fly. I am not aware one can purchase pickled samphire in the shops; perhaps some of the big London stores supply it—I do not know. But I have never tasted it since that day, and next time I am down Shep White's way

I must ask him (if indeed he still dwells in his windy little cottage on the sea wall) whether I can have another jar of it.

When I think of those early days, when one never saw another car, or met a fellow fowler, and then remember the last time I visited that spot, I feel very sad. There was a procession of cars at flight time which disgorged amateur shore poppers, gull shooters, or Milford Snobs, as Colonel Hawker would have termed them, and I realized that never again would I shoot a goose from the sea wall or lie out in one of the seaward dykes to await the dawn. Just when the geese were lifting from the bars some gawking idiot would come mooning over the sea wall and stand gaping at the oncoming skeins. How sorely have I been tempted, time and again, to pepper these idiots at long range. I am sure I was never so stupid when I was learning the game! Indeed, I know I was not!

I knew, at least, that I must take cover when geese were on the move, and when I got the hang of the thing I was careful not to spoil the sport for other people.

Some professional fowlers, who have a jealous disposition, will sometimes purposefully spoil your sport. I remember once waiting on a marsh in the north for some geese to swim in to me. I was well under cover and the birds were coming in well, when suddenly they all turned their heads and went swimming out again.

I looked round and saw a villainous specimen of a fowler, with a rusty gun and an enormous game bag, tramping down the shore. He saw me in my hide but did not alter course. On the contrary, he came and posted himself in the reeds, like a ragged old heron, not twenty yards in front of me. There he stood without a vestige of cover, and eventually I moved away. I am a man of peace and cannot bear rows with locals. And when at last I looked back he was still standing there, like some old weathered post, staring out to sea.

But to return once more to my camp on the Wash. We shot plover, mallard, curlew, and redshank, and every night we enjoyed a savoury Oystercock pie. We had our fishing too, for in the deep muddy dyke below us we caught fat writhing eels which made delicious breakfasts. We captured these on night lines tied to our tent pegs, and every morning we would find an eel or two wriggling on the end.

One evening, when we were just finishing supper, Tony and I became aware of a tantalizing feminine perfume wafting in our direction. Looking up I beheld two attractive girls coming along the bank. Both wore fur coats; one was slim and pretty, the other big and handsome.

They stopped on the bank above us, and asked us how we were getting on, and what we had had for supper.

I omitted to say that we had just finished a very good dinner of partridge which I had poached with my ·22 off the ploughed field opposite. It was lucky I was circumspect, because it soon transpired that the handsome girl's father owned the land. However, we persuaded them to inspect our tent, and finished up by inviting them to supper the following night, an invitation which was accepted.

Promptly to time the girls turned up; Jill, the big girl, and her friend, whose name I forget. I cannot remember what we gave them for supper (probably another of her father's partridges) but we all had a very merry time, and afterwards we were frequent visitors at Jill's home, where I met her father, a dear old bearded man who kept up the tradition of family prayers morning and night, when all the staff attended. Thus began a friendship which has been a lasting one, and every autumn for some years now a brace of pheasants arrive from Jill, now married and with a large family, and still living in the Fens.

The morning after this supper party, Tony and I were shooting curlew along the bank past Shep White's cottage. The tide was flooding and the birds were coming off the saltings in little trips of a dozen or so. For over an hour we had some magnificent shooting.

At last I had one down, a runner, and it fell on the plough behind us.

We had no dog, so after it I went, running hard across the furrows. Anyone who has ever been to Lincolnshire, and is familiar with those vast fields, will know what a chase I had, and by the time I had caught it (I had deemed it wise to leave my gun behind) I was a long way from the sea wall.

I had barely regained it when I heard the familiar cry of the enraged *homo sapiens* whose territory has been invaded. Turning round I saw a squat, red-faced fellow coming along the bank.

He was inarticulate with rage, as these people always are on such occasions, and demanded to see my gun licence. He accused me of shooting pheasants and swore that he would report me to his master, a neighbouring big farmer, whose land adjoined that of Jill's father.

"All right," I said, "go ahead and report me! I was only retrieving a curlew," and I held up the bird to show him I was telling the truth. I also emptied my game bag to prove my innocence: in short, I was as obliging as I could possibly be.

Still he ranted and raved and again asked to see my gun licence. I showed him one which was out of date (I had a current one in my wallet) and, with smug satisfaction, he took down my name and address and handed it back.

That evening Tony and I thought we would go and see the bailiff's master and explain what had happened, that we were not poaching his pheasants, and that it was only a curlew I had shot.

We made various enquiries, and at last found this farmer's house. It was a pretentious place with a lodge, and we went up the long drive and rang the bell.

Its clanging had barely died away when I heard a fearful racket of dogs, and as a rather scared maid opened the door, I saw four or five great mastiffs advancing across the polished floor. Behind them was a big man, not unlike the Aga Khan, but with a far less genial expression. He reminded me of Giant Despair in *Pilgrim's Progress*.

I explained what had occurred and, after humming and hawing, he said it did not matter. Only our youth and innocence made us so honest as to go and 'own up', but in all fairness to the farmer it must be said that occasionally vagrant gunners, even in those days, would poach pheasants and partridges from the sea wall, even from the roads, and after all, we ourselves had also erred in that respect!

Some weeks after I had returned to my home in the midlands, our local sergeant called on me and asked to see my gun licence. I showed it him and then he grinned.

"Seems as though somebody down in Lincolnshire wanted to get you into trouble, sir, one o' them amateur policemen, I suppose."

The bank from which I shot my curlew and duck is now no more, waving corn grows where I used to ambush the geese, and where flickering redshanks followed the creeks seawards, yelping as they flew, the plough turns a dark furrow.

That particular part of the coast, especially the bank by Shep White's house, will ever be associated in my mind with one particular morning.

That year my companion was Desmond Phayre, now a Major in the Royal Artillery. We were friends at Rugby School, and have kept up our friendship ever since.

In the school holidays we paid several visits to the Wash, staying at the Talbot Inn, a small hostelry near the centre of the town. They fed us like fighting cocks at the Talbot, and our landlord's pretty daughter waited on us.

Unfortunately, what was not so pleasant, it was next door to a granary. Every night, as soon as the light was doused, the rats and mice came out to play—to use an Americanism—and how! They scampered about under our beds and even ran over them. One mouse scurried over Desmond's face as he lay in bed. He swore it was a rat—it may well have been, he should know.

We purchased many tins of Rodine, and after putting down the poisoned bait we retired to bed and heard our guests enjoying themselves. By midnight every scrap of bread had gone. Next night and henceforth a beautiful silence reigned, no squeak or scratch was heard. I often wonder how many we slew that night.

One morning, when Desmond and I reached the sea wall, we found half a gale blowing off the land, and we knew that if only the geese would come they would have to battle their way in. I had with me my single eight-bore loaded with BB shot, Desmond an ordinary game gun.

He elected to go out on the marsh, I stayed on the bank, and soon after dawn the geese began to move in on a long front of a mile or more. I have never seen so many geese as I saw that morning, and nearly every skein was in range from the top of the wall.

The trouble was that on such an extended area it was difficult to judge the exact spot where the geese would pass. Sometimes they would go in behind me and at others just out of range above.

Then I found that if I watched the geese leave the sand I could more or less judge the crossing place of those skeins which came over my section of marsh. I had to allow for the push of the wind, which was gusty, and several exhausting runs I had, burdened with the heavy gun, in my attempts to get under them. At last one big skein passed in over me and I had a shot with Belching Bess. The bird I fired at landed on the slope of the sea wall ten yards away. As I ran down the bank to pick it up there was a heavy thump on my left and I saw I had shot another goose. A single pellet of BB shot had penetrated its neck. This is the nearest I have ever got to a right and left at geese. This is rather strange, as one would think that a tolerable shot would have no difficulty in bringing off a right and left out of a big skein. Yet this rarely occurs even with the best shots. I do not think that Charles, who is a much better shot than

I am, and has been at it longer, has ever had a right and left at geese.

That morning on the Wash when I had two at a shot will always remain in my mind. I had the bigger of the two geese set up, and I still have it in my gun room, a pleasing reminder of that stormy and eventful morning.

Desmond, out on the marsh, had never dirtied his gun, which only shows the element of luck in wildfowling. All the geese had passed in just out of range of his hide.

14. *The Unquiet Spirit*

THE marshes are seldom visited by the inland gunner in summertime, but I have on occasions been to the Wash at the full flowering time when thoughts of wildfowling are far away. And indeed it is an odd experience, the marshes are so totally different as to be almost unrecognizable. In the dykes the rushes are green and thick, not dead yellow as in winter, the fields inland are sprouting rich crops, lucerne, sugar beet, and potato. No longer does the wind pipe a melancholy tune in the wayside telegraph wires, and the black surface of the rich fenland earth is masked by growing corn.

Sea lavender is in flower and the air is full of odd, pungent perfumes, scents of flowers which love the salt marsh but are foreign to an inland nose.

Redshanks soar above the creeks, trilling their mating song, snipe drum, and mallard, bold with the days of truce, rise quacking from the drains as you walk out to the sea. Even Shep White's cottage on the bank seems less exposed and the oaks along the sea wall, which you last remembered as bare and wind-tossed, are as heavy in leaf as any midland forest tree.

Much of the romance is gone for me then, yet, if you come again three months later, in autumn—mid-September time or early October—you will begin to feel the old magic stirring. By then the stubbles have been cleared, and the potato haulms will have rusted and flattened themselves along the furrows. And at flight, in the evening, the creeks will be alive with duck.

Curlews, their breeding season over, will be flying in musical bands about the tide and everywhere you feel the restlessness of migration time. Yet you listen in vain for the clamour of geese, though any day now you will hear it. And with that first far-up crying you will know that *they* have come back to their winter quarters, and will be stationed there for the next six months. At this season, late September and October, the geese seem to resort to the Norfolk coast more than the Wash, and at Wells, that Mecca of all wildfowlers, the whitefronts will have arrived, and will be passing back and forth to the high upland stubbles, saluted by ineffectual popping of guns.

At Wells the inhabitants talk and think of geese as those at St. Andrews talk and think of golf. Stuffed geese adorn the tap-room walls and thigh boots stand in hotel vestibules. One passes men in the street dressed for the shore, some are glassy-eyed with goose-fever, occasionally one will have a superior jaunty air, which means he has shot a goose.

Everywhere there is a restlessness, uneasiness, among the feathered population, which in some mysterious way communicates itself to the longshore gunner as he waits in his creek at evening and hears the deepening violet sky throbbing with wings.

I suppose the mysteries of migration have always intrigued earth-bound man. Without artificial aids we are very immobile, our two legs carry us at a snail's pace over the ground, and if we would go faster we must hoist ourselves on wheels or into our ingenious flying machines, and thereby lose the blessed silence of natural motion.

The hum and vibration of a car, train, or flying machine blots out all natural sounds, the very motion itself feels artificial and unnatural. The bicycle is the least objectionable mode of mechanical transport, as it has the merit of silence, and as one goes along the familiar sounds of the outdoor world are yet audible. In any other mode of transport the body is enclosed as in a box, a sort of second house where you are shut away from the air, wind and sun.

No wonder, then, we have this envy of the birds who can wander where they please so effortlessly and in silence!

The uneasiness shown by the migratory birds in autumn and spring certainly finds an echo in mankind. Mists at morning, cleared stubbles, the smell of weed fires in the evening, and the robin's song in the woods, all these signs and tokens tell of the dying year. At these times I feel very strongly the urge for change, not to fly away over the ocean to foreign lands, but a strong desire to be in my old haunts by river and estuary so that I may watch the arrival of the ducks, geese and waders.

Even in the midlands, where for the moment circumstance forces me to live, I sometimes hear on starlit October nights the curlew passing over, the sad pipe of golden plover and, on rare occasions, geese. I notice, also, the passage migrants which every August and September haunt the reservoirs and field ponds in my neighbourhood.

There is a little horse pond I know of away in some lonely field which every autumn is visited by greenshanks. They stay there for about three weeks, from the second week of August to September. Wheatears, also, I see on passage and occasional flocks of golden plover.

All migratory birds, not only ducks and geese, plover and waders, suffer from this 'pain', as I like to call it, that sense of 'uncomfortableness', to use a clumsy word, but which Hudson frankly terms as *fear* at the migration times.

This fear can be observed in the martin and swallow flocks which congregate on the telegraph wires at the end of August.

They will sit in long lines for hours at a stretch, preening and talking one with another, when suddenly every bird will be seized with an uncontrollable excitement or frenzy. They will dart away in an agitated throng, uttering the alarm notes with which they salute a hawk or other threatened danger. They seem actually *terrified*, hurrying about the sky in every direction, wildly, as if pursued by a bird of prey.

Wild geese, though heavy and cumbersome by comparison with the airy swallows, must also feel this age-old 'fear' at the time of departure from their arctic breeding grounds. Certainly we can observe this uneasiness in early spring when they are preparing to leave these shores for the arctic wilderness.

They congregate in vast companies at their chosen points of departure, gathering like passengers at a vast railway terminus. For a day or so the numbers grow and the cackling and hubbub is redoubled. Like the swallows, they are seized with sudden panics and alarms, flying hither and thither in gabbling companies.

The longshore gunner, armed now with binoculars and not with a gun, can observe his beloved sea game thronging the sand-banks in a grey carpet; countless hundreds, one might say thousands, of geese, all filled with a restlessness, like hiving bees. And then one morning when he goes forth with his glasses he finds the sand-banks bare, not a goose calls anywhere, the whole vast company has left in the night and will not be seen again until the following September.

All that remain are those other lesser travellers who seem to be waiting for 'local' trains, the redshank and the curlew, whimbrel and duck. Yet even these scattered parties dwindle as the weeks deepen into summer; the redshanks are off to their breeding grounds, the plovers to the uplands, and the only feathered passengers he will see will be those that are breaking their journey on their way to other lands.

To give an instance of the intense 'pain' the geese suffer at migration times, a friend of mine, an old 'coyman, whose family has worked a 'Decoy Pipe' for three hundred years, told me recently that he keeps wild geese on some ponds near the decoy. They are, of course, pinioned and sometimes, at migration time in the spring, the pink-footed geese get out of their enclosure and walk away in a direct line for the north—sometimes wandering three or four miles distant before he can find and overtake them.

It almost seems as if there is some mysterious polar attraction which draws them like a magnet.

W. H. Hudson gives an interesting and touching account of a pair of upland geese at migration time. One had been wounded and was unable to fly, and when the urge came to migrate it began to walk and its mate would not leave it. It flew on ahead and returned again and again, but at last could stay no longer and flew on, leaving its mate still following—on foot.

About the only naturalist who has ever made a detailed study of our passage migrants on the coast in summer is Abel Chapman who did most of his bird watching on Fenham Slakes at Holy Island. In his chapter, 'The Globe Spanners', he reveals some astonishing facts and describes the immense journeys undertaken by some of the wader family such as knot.

The mallards, like the geese, become very restless and soon after the turn of the year they move about the country and cross the seas; they are great wanderers.

I once reared a wild mallard from the egg. I found the deserted nest of a wild mallard in a marsh and I put the three eggs under a broody hen. She hatched out two; the third was addled. One duckling was accidently trodden upon by the hen, the other survived and for a number of years was a very interesting and lovable little creature. It was a drake and when in full winter plumage was a never-ending source of delight to me.

I made him a small pond in which he could swim and bathe, and in his pen there was a sloping board up to his sleeping hut.

His great delight was to toboggan down this. He put both his paddles together and descended like a fireman on a greasy pole.

Absolutely fearless, he would take tit-bits from my fingers, and he showed also great intelligence and affection. But in spring and summer a terrible restlessness possessed him. He would rise up in his pen and beat his wings against the wires, even food had no interest for him. I dare not let him free as he would have been shot by the first lout with a gun, or even picked up and carried off to make a roast, for he let himself be taken up and even stroked, and had no objection to being handled. I thought to placate him by offering him a mate. I could not procure a wild duck so put a runner duck in with him, a foolish, portly creature which had not a tithe of the sense that my little wild drake possessed.

One winter, just before Christmas, some village thief raided the pen which was in my garden and took away the runner duck. The wild drake was very muddy and scared next morning, and I judged that he had been too nimble for the rustic fox, or had been deemed too insignificant to steal.

Thereafter he was less trustful and seemed to be fearful of some unknown enemy. Three years went by and again and again I was tempted to set him free, for I was sad to see his pain at migration times. During the moonlight nights at these spring and autumn periods, he was especially uneasy and I would hear him quacking loudly at all hours.

In the winter of 1948, when I was away with Charles Oakey shooting the Laird's Island, the same thief struck again. When I returned I was met with the news that my little mallard drake had been stolen on the night of the 15th of December.

It had been a bright moonlight night but no one in my household had heard a sound. Next morning my wife missed the usual quack with which the little drake always greeted the 'switch on' of the kitchen light. She went out and found that the thief had coolly rolled up the wire of the pen and taken the drake out. It would not have run away, it would have sat and allowed itself to be picked up, as it always did.

The motive of this theft must have been spite, as a wild duck is too small to make a labouring man a meal. In every rural community you find these despicable sneak-thieves. They are like human foxes. They do not strike often, but only now and again when they are least expected.

Then they will raid a hen house or steal a turkey and in nearly every case they get away with it; the village policeman is powerless. Even if the thief is caught there is a nominal fine, less than the brute invests on his precious football pools each week.

The graceful alert carriage of a wild duck compared to his domestic relation is very marked, as is the difference between the wild goose and the tame. The pink-footed goose, which is smaller than the greylag, has a very upright carriage and springy step, and in all the wild geese the waddling roll of the domestic goose is absent, nor do they have the hanging pouch of flesh between the legs.

Though the departure of the geese has never actually been witnessed, as the main skeins depart in darkness, the arrival in autumn has been seen on many occasions. A friend of mine saw the pinks arrive one year on Rockcliffe Marsh on the Solway, and a very impressive sight it was. He was duck-shooting one evening in September when he heard for the first time that year the cry of the geese. For a while he could see nothing until at last he spied at an immense height above the earth a single goose, wheeling vulture-like in wide descending circles.

As he watched, other specks appeared, slowly climbing down, round and round in graceful sweeping spirals until the whole sky was full of gliding specks as goose after goose came into view.

In the space of about two hours no less than three thousand geese had descended and the marshes, which in the morning had been silent and devoid of life, were now ringing with the wild clamouring chorus of the newly arrived birds.

Millais, as I have said, witnessed the same wonderful spectacle over the Laird's Island and it is one which I have yet to see. Only those who happen to be on the spot can hope to witness it.

I have seen a few geese on the Solway in August but these may have been pricked birds. On most large estuaries there are geese to be found all summer, pricked birds which were unable to follow the skeins when they left in the spring. Many of these birds recover, especially if they have access to grass feed, and perhaps the following spring they, too, can go away with their brethren and follow the age-old trail.

What of the goose population in Britain to-day? There are others far more learned than I on the subject and Peter Scott with his Severn Wildfowl Trust may be able to give a definite answer. But I should say from my own observations that the peak of the 'goose years' was between 1925 and 1939; at least, I am speaking of the numbers of geese which frequented the Wash.

Since that time, due no doubt to the building of aerodromes and bombing ranges and the reclamation of marshy lands, the numbers have fallen off. Certainly the barnacle geese on the Solway are decreasing yearly, and it will not be long before they are comparatively rare on that part of the west coast. This is entirely due to the persecution by visiting gunners and, even though the marshes are extensive, extending for many miles, the geese get little peace and are harried by day and by night.

My own expeditions to the Solway took place many years ago before it had become overrun and when it was rare to meet with a fellow fowler in a day's shooting. In those years the barnacles were resident in considerable numbers, and I enjoyed many a moonlight hunt on my wild lone.

15. *The Hounds of Heaven*

ON reading through what I have so far written concerning
wild geese, it occurs to me that I have not done justice to
their peculiar haunting and far-carrying voices, nor have
I stressed the very deep impression made on me by the music of the
skeins.

I do not think that any man who has a spark of imagination
within him can fail to be moved by the almost unearthly music of
a large skein of wild geese upon the wing.

In remote country districts of England, especially those inland
and far from any river or estuary where these noble birds congregate,
the clamour of the geese passing over, often at dead of night during
the migrating seasons, causes much disquiet and concern in the
rustic mind and is the source of many legends. The inland villagers
still regard those heavenly voices as the clamour of ghost hounds, or
of evil spirits in full demoniac cry through the upper darkness.
Shepherds on lonely hilltops are especially prone to these superstitious tales, and they will never believe that the sounds they hear
with so much dread are but the signal cries and squadron orders
of migrating birds.

The reader may think that this statement is far-fetched, that I am romancing, but I can assure him that what I say is true; I have met many old villagers who believe that to hear the ghost hounds bodes ill to them and all mankind.

On the coast, as might be guessed, the sound of wild geese passing in the night causes no comment. The villagers of the Wash or Humber districts would make much fun of such silly old wives' tales.

Yet the fact remains that there is no other sound in nature so unearthly and, to my mind, more lovely, than that of the passing skeins, especially if you hear them, as they should be heard, in the quiet of a starlit winter's night, perhaps from some lonely hilltop or upland pasture. It is a most unbirdlike sound, and is rightly likened to the cry of hounds, yet no hound on earth possesses that celestial *chiming* voice which is so characteristic of the clamour made by a large skein of pink-footed geese. No bird in the vast company has an identical call, some are high-pitched, others are deep and resonant, some cry out all together, others call singly. Mostly the birds are invisible, and are perhaps at a great height above the earth. You hear that melodious baying draw nearer and ever nearer, and then gradually die away into the distance, and even I, a hardened longshore gunner, cannot listen to that magic music unmoved.

I shall always remember one night on the Solway when I was far out on the marshes, and on ground which was unfamiliar to me, hearing the geese pass over, and how they brought me deliverance from peril.

I had been out all day and had seen many interesting birds, merlins, barnacle geese, pintail and grey plover, but sport had been nil and my game bag was empty. In the late afternoon, when I was far from shore, a fog suddenly came down, and in a remarkably short space of time I was completely enveloped in a dense opaque wall, the only visible thing being the setting sun, as yet well above the horizon, and partially veiled by the thinner upper mists, immensely swollen and red, suspended like a huge coloured balloon in the wall of white vapour.

I had no compass with me and very soon I had the uneasy feeling that I was lost. For some time I walked in the direction of the setting sun, as I knew that land lay that way, but soon even that massive rose-red globe was swallowed up and I did not know which way to turn. To make matters worse I knew the tide was making, and before long I heard in front of me the low hissing murmur which told me it was advancing across the leagues of sand.

I have never known the tide to advance so rapidly as on the Solway, and as it comes the murmuring roar, like that of a tidal bore, has a most menacing quality.

Between me and the land I knew there were dykes and gullies, some of great depth, and how to get out of the mess I was in, I did not know.

After walking a great distance, as I thought, towards the land, I still found my feet upon the sands and the roar of the tide drawing ever nearer.

That dreadful sense of isolation at being cut off from all life is most unpleasant, and one has to keep a firm hand on oneself to avoid complete blind panic. I have been lost in woods and upon moors, but I have never had the sense of hopelessness and dread that I experienced that night.

As I stood debating what to do, surrounded on every hand by that impenetrable wall of fog, which reduced visibility to less than four feet, I heard in the far distance the cry of wild geese. Very faint at first it came, from my right, and growing ever louder, it passed directly over my head, though I could not, of course, see any sign of the birds. I listened to them go right out behind me until the clammy silence closed around me once more.

This silence of the fog, even on marshes populated by many wildfowl, is very strange. It is as if every creature that has wings becomes dumb and apprehensive, and that their safety depends on keeping absolutely quiet, as indeed it does.

Certainly geese do so when resting on the sands in a thick mist. Those I had heard were, of course, far above the fog, and it would appear to them as a dense white coverlet masking the whole estuary.

But I knew now which way the land lay, and I set off as best as I could judge in the direction from which the birds had come. In a very little while I was brought up by a deep and formidable drain, or, as it seemed to me, a river—for I could not see the farther shore —and from the flow of foam-spotted water which was pushing up I formed a rough idea of the direction I must take. I knew, however, that I must cross this river, for I thought I recognized it as one I had seen earlier that afternoon. So I followed the bank along until I spied a crazy wooden bridge which spanned it from bank to bank—at least, I judged its farther end rested on the bank, but all was shrouded in mist. It seemed like a fantastic, enchanted bridge resting on thin air, inviting me to step into nothingness. It appeared, also, as though it had not been used for years. The wooden slats which formed the floor were rotten and here and there large gaps showed. The whole contraption was suspended by rickety posts and rusty wire. However, I knew I must try to get over or the tide would overtake me, and at best I should have to stand it out all night.

Very gingerly I started on my way across, feeling with my toe and hanging on to a strand of wire. I got over successfully, and I was thankful, as nothing could have saved me had the bridge given way. In my heavy fowling clothes I would have stood no chance, as the banks were steep and slippery cushions of mud.

Once over I felt a good deal better but my troubles were far from over. For hours I wandered about in that dreadful mist, several times finding myself once more on the banks of the deep, wide river.

In the early hours of the morning I felt I could go no farther, and sank down among some furze and dropped off to sleep; under the circumstances a most foolish thing to do as I was wringing wet with perspiration and the night was frosty. When I awoke I felt my clothes frozen on me, I was shivering and coughing, my head ached and I felt horribly ill.

I had committed the worst folly of the inexperienced wildfowler. On a frosty night I had gone to sleep in an overheated bodily condition. But one mercy—the fog was lifting, and as quickly as it had come down it drew away, and I saw the gleaming lights of the farmhouse where, sixteen hours before, I had left my cycle.

I reached the farm after a terrible walk, my feet like lead, almost on the point of collapse from thirst and ague. There was a pump in the yard, and from it I drank copious draughts of ice-cold water, another foolish thing to do. Somehow or other I reached my fowl-ing quarters, after a grisly ride of several miles. As I endeavoured to keep my feet on the pedals I was shaken from head to foot with palsied fits.

The next morning I was down with pneumonia, and I was gravely ill for some weeks.

This, I may say, is the only occasion when I have got into difficulties, but I might have been in a worse case had I not heard the geese pass over, for they gave me the direction of the land.

The voice of the greylag differs from the pink. It is much deeper; it does not make such a musical hound-like clamour when in full cry. Also an old greylag, sitting by himself out on the muds in mid-estuary, can make his voice carry an immense distance. It is a sort of resonant 'Ank Kank, Ank Kank', while the pink-foot calls 'Quink! Wink!'

It is amusing to the waiting gunner to listen to a large company of pink-footed geese deep in conversation after they have reached the sand-banks. They surely must be exchanging views and opinions and are discussing, maybe, the excellence of the day's fare, or the evil habits of longshore gunners.

But let a distant shot echo over the water, then every voice is stilled, and for a minute or more they will remain silent. Then one hears very low and subdued conversation beginning again until soon all are at full gabble once more.

The alarm note of the greylag, when he is feeding on the fields and sees something which arouses his suspicion, is a rather low duck-like quack. It is the sound uttered by the sentry as warning to the feeding gaggle, and instantly every bird is on the alert, heads are up and each goose is ready to spring. A greylag when he is suspicious, and on the point of rising, usually walks away a few steps from the source of suspected danger, each bird uttering that same low 'quick wick'. Then they will all stand motionless for a second, necks extended, feathers depressed, and finally with a simultaneous leap, they are up.

For a second or two, being heavy birds, they have to fly almost level with the ground to become truly airborne. Sometimes they will give a touch or two with their paddles in a running motion, like a swan rising from water.

I have known a fast retriever dog catch a greylag as it was taking off. It happened at night when I was walking with a friend across a Solway marsh on the way back from flight. It was very dark and unbeknown to us a party of greys were sleeping on the grass just in front of us. The dog winded them and dashed forwards; we heard an agonized squawk in the blackness and the sound of a beating wing. A moment later back came my friend's dog with the grey-lag in its mouth, while the others went cackling away for the sea.

I have also seen a dog pull down a rising goose in broad day-light. A flock of pinks were feeding near a hedge, and a fowler and his dog were lying in a ditch not far away. Suddenly the dog, disobeying the frantic shouts of his master, dashed out and caught one of the hindmost rising birds by its hanging paddle.

The whitefronted goose has perhaps the most musical and unearthly cry of all the wild geese, and it is to my ears a very beautiful sound indeed.

That of the Canada goose is impressive, possessing a bell-like quality similar to that of the whooper swan. It always reminds me of an Alpine cow-bell, a sort of 'Honk Tonk, Honk Tonk', the only goose which really 'honks'.

The brent, the small dark sea goose, which rarely visits the salt marshes, has a cry unlike any other wild goose, unless we can compare it to that of the barnacle. Actually the sound is, I think, a cross between the honking of the Canada and the yapping of the barnacle.

A big barnacle skein in full cry always reminds me of a pack of excited peke puppies as compared with the true hound-like baying of the grey geese.

On moonlight nights on the Solway I have heard the barnacles moving over the merse and a very bewitching sound it is, but without the rather supernatural quality of the pinks or greys—possibly because they never fly high.

On still frosty nights when there is no wind the barnacles frequently indulge in long flights up and down the marshes, presumably for exercise. At such times they show little caution, speeding along in one vast yelping pack not twenty feet above the merse, and if they happen to come your way two barrels sometimes take deadly toll.

The most fairylike 'Hans Andersen' sound made by birds is undoubtedly the song (I will not say call) of wild whooper swans. It is not very loud and cannot be compared with that of any known creature, no dog or other bird: it is a trumpeting as on silvery trumpets, possessing perhaps the same timbre as that of the 'post horns' discovered in Tutankhamen's tomb.

It is easy to associate with it the desolate tundras and mosses of the whooper's native land, the dark endless forests of pine, the red-stemmed willows that grow in far northern bogs.

Some people consider that our own domestic farmyard goose makes but an ugly discordant sound. Yet I disagree. Heard from a distance the old farmyard gander is exceedingly musical, and his robust voice has much in it to attract me: I consider it vastly superior to the thin crowing of the rooster. It has almost the same noble quality as the brazen bassoon—like the call of a cow.

It has always been something of a puzzle to me why the voices of birds carry so far. That these comparatively small creatures can emit a sound which will carry a much greater distance than the loudest shout ever made by man is puzzling.

This brings to mind the call, or rather song, of a bird which impressed me as much as the call of the wild geese, and, strange to say, the author of this song was not a goose at all, or yet any of the swan or duck tribe.

I was staying some years ago in a little Devon village near the River Dart, a delightful spot and a favourite springtime haunt of mine. There I sometimes go to greet the first spring migrants for they arrive in the lanes and hanging woods a full fortnight before I hear them in the drear midland plain where I now live.

Every morning before breakfast I was in the habit of rising and going for a long walk and my way invariably took me to a wild little gorse-clad common on the top of a bare hill.

And very soon I began to hear a strange fluting cry, or song, which was quite strange to me. I knew it was some bird, but of a species I had never heard before, certainly not in my midland fields.

Morning after morning I went up to this common with my glasses and whenever the sun shone and the air was tranquil I heard this same elfin call mocking me. It came from across a meadow where there was a raised earth bank such as is common in that part of the world. Along the top of the bank grew trees, oaks, ashes, and elms, and there was a hedge of hazel along the rim of the red rabbit-drilled earth.

I searched the trees with my glasses but saw no bird, and when I climbed the gate, and tried to get closer to the edge of the field my mysterious songster fell silent and not a note would he favour me with.

And then one specially bright warm morning, towards the end of April, as I was leaning over the gate on the edge of the common, looking out over the hedgerow—now yellow with primroses—I heard *two* voices answering each other, and after a little while up rose a pair of dumpy birds high into the blue sky, the early bright sun shining upon their breasts, and they were singing all the time.

After a moment or so I managed to focus these mysterious feathered magicians in my glasses and saw at once they were wood-larks. And from that day to this I have thought the song of the woodlark almost my favourite wild bird's song! It has almost a ventriloquistic quality and possesses immense carrying power; it is a musical resonant trill 'ueueueueueueueueue', with a tremor and shake in it which affects the ear most strangely.

And with the song of my Devonshire woodlarks I will bring this chapter to a close, with perhaps an apology for including one small bird in the distinguished company of the wild grey geese.

16. The Upper Reaches

ABOVE Jim Jagoe's house on the bank of the burn, the estuary altered a good deal in character. It was not so wide, being, I suppose, not more than a mile and a half across, and the reed beds on the opposite shore were clearly visible. Nor did the geese frequent these upper reaches in such numbers, though their main feeding grounds, on the vast green lowland fields, lay in this direction.

Nevertheless, I have memories of some very successful days there, and cover was more plentiful than down river; the reed beds were thick and tall, the stone groynes in better repair. There was one immensely long groyne, the longest in the river, and in a sense this was an historic spot because years before an old fowler nearly lost his life in a quicksand off the end of it.

The story is well known in the district, it has been written about by several authors, Millais included, but it will bear repeating.

Towards the end of the last century there was an old fowler named McInnes. He lived, I believe, in Jim Jagoe's cottage, but of this I cannot be sure. At any rate, he was a great character, and was well known along that stretch of coast, one of the real old 'bank' men. He made a precarious living from the sale of the fowl he shot, and by doing odd jobs for the farmers at threshing and harvest time. There was not a reed bed or dyke, quicksand or mud bank, he was not familiar with on the whole length of that six-mile stretch. He was, I understand, something of a poacher too, and was often in trouble with the keepers on the estate which adjoined the marsh.

One year, when the geese came back in the autumn, McInnes noticed a white goose among the skeins, a beautiful bird as white as driven snow, and the old fowler determined to bag this rarity. He would no doubt be able to get a good price for it, for albino geese are very uncommon. Not only that: this lovely creature seemed to be a challenge to his skill and he made up his mind to have its skin.

All that season he strove to shoot the bird. Morning after morning he would see it go out with the skeins, and again at evening, when the geese came back to the sands, the white goose would be there, very conspicuous in its spotless plumage which made such a vivid contrast to the sober greys and browns of its companions.

Once or twice that season he came near to success, but something always happened to spoil his chance or aim; winter passed to spring and still the white goose flew free.

When at last they went away McInnes thought that he had lost his opportunity, that he would never again see that lovely creature. But when next autumn came, and once more the glad cry of the geese sounded high in the grey skies—there, sure enough, was the white goose!

McInnes would not be a man with imagination, he would not wonder where the goose had been, what adventures it had met with away there in its arctic home, nor would he wonder at the power of those broad white pinions which had borne the bird so many thousands of miles, across wide oceans to a strange ice-bound land and back again.

All he bothered about was how to slay it and surely, if it stayed throughout the season, he would have another chance!

But the weeks went by and that chance never came. Sometimes the white goose would go away for a week or so when the weather was frosty and the fields frozen, but as soon as the mild weather returned and the skeins came back, there would be the Goose Queen, as he called it. And still the days went by.

Every year, for four seasons, this happened, and with each autumn McInnes looked eagerly for the bird and, sure enough, there it was, seeming to mock all his efforts.

It will never be known how many times he had an opportunity to slay the Goose Queen. It is certain that he nearly succeeded on several occasions, but the bird seemed to bear a charmed life. And then, one January evening, as he was walking along the tree-lined bank above the cottage he heard the well-known cry of the geese coming in from the fields. He ran to a gap in the trees and looking up he saw a big skein of pinks, and among them was—*the Goose Queen!* This time he had his chance, but whether he was nervous or his aim was bad, he failed to make a clean kill.

The bird, mortally stricken, came down upon the muds where it 'herpled' along towards the open water.

In an instant McInnes raced down the bank and out over the muds in hot pursuit. Had he had a dog, all would have been well. A wounded goose can walk very quickly yet, even so, he gained on his victim, and when it was almost in his grasp he found his way barred by an impassable ditch, and had the agony of seeing his prize stagger away until it reached the water. But the effort was too much for it. Hardly had it gained the river when it fell lifeless in the tide, and began to drift down river for the open sea.

Even now, McInnes would not give in. For four years he had striven to shoot this goose and he was not going to be beaten. He remembered the Long Breakwater which stretched far out into the ooze. Past this the goose would be sure to drift and so, with all haste, he hurried down river, panting and groaning in his eagerness to reach the groyne in time.

He did so; somehow he scrambled along the slippery stones to the very end, just as the white goose, lifeless now, came drifting down upon the tide!

He saw it was going to pass wide of the groyne, but not so far he might not reach it. Casting his clothes and gun upon the dyke he set off, floundering like a demented creature through the mud until the tide was deep enough to float him.

McInnes was an indifferent swimmer but he could keep himself afloat, and despite the frightful cold he gained on the drifting body. He had almost reached it—indeed his hand was stretched out to grab it—when he went aground on a submerged sandbank. He could neither swim over it, nor yet walk upon it, and when he dropped his legs he was immediately held fast in the quicksand.

McInnes must have been in such places before, he knew all about 'rolling out', but somehow, in his frantic endeavours to keep an eye on the goose, which was now some eighty yards away still going out to sea, he lost his head, and it was soon apparent to the hapless man that it was now a case of saving his own miserable skin. The harder he struggled, the deeper he sank until he was up to his armpits.

Luckily for him the tide was ebbing or it would have gone hard with him. As it was, he struggled for over an hour, held like a fly to a flypaper, but at last, when his strength was almost spent, he managed to roll out, and somehow gain the dyke and his clothes.

This awful night so affected McInnes that for weeks he would not go near the river, the sight of it was actually abhorrent to him, but after a while he came back to his old way of life, though he never again ventured on to the muds without a spaniel, which he purchased as soon as he regained his health and strength.

All along the bank from Jim Jagoe's cottage to a point some four miles above, there was a thick belt of trees, oaks, elms and other hard woods, with here and there a fir. The sloping side of the sea wall was also heavily bushed in places with hollies and thorn. Among the trees, on top of the bank, wandered a footpath—it was almost like a path through a private plantation. When the chances of geese were nil I have passed many an entertaining hour shooting the wood pigeons. In some years thousands of the little foreign pigeons frequented these trees and every morning, at about flighting time, vast flocks came up this wooded belt and offered really first-rate shots. They roosted in some big fir woods on a private estate higher up the estuary.

It struck me sometimes as very strange to be sitting in a brush-wood hide (one of Jim Jagoe's, be it said, for the old man had built these hides all along the bank, and I believe that he made the bulk of his cash from shooting pigeons), hearing and seeing the geese coming off the fields.

It was queer to see these birds in such a setting, framed, as it were, in delicate tracery of bare twigs, and to hear also the loud clear call of woodland birds, tits and finches up in the trees, and to smell the rich leafy scents all around me. And there, not forty yards away, were the vast reed beds and the estuary.

One misty evening I was sitting thus, looking out over the land and waiting for the skeins to return, when I saw a single goose flying over some haystacks on the far side of a field. Over the hedge were some electric pylons supporting their heavy cables, and to my amazement the goose struck two of the upper cables; it flew directly into them.

It turned over in the air, and seemed to batter its way down through the centre of the wires and dropped almost to the ground.

I thought it had been killed, but it lifted again and flew off strongly for the sea. This made me wonder that there were not more accidents, especially to the skeins which were always flying back and forth over these cables.

I have many times seen partridges killed against telephone wires, especially during partridge drives, but I never thought to see a goose meet with such an accident.

On very frosty moonlight nights the Long Breakwater was a good place for duck, and many a time have I followed that winding forest path and seen the shadows of the bare oaks banding the track before me, and sometimes the form of a roosting pheasant up in the firs. Pheasants were numerous in the reed beds, and Jim Jagoe bagged a goodly number, especially when the birds had been 'shot up' on the estate.

I myself have sometimes put them up when walking out to the Long Breakwater, but I did not shoot them as they were, of course, the rightful property of the owner of the Castle near by.

I remember one rather curious incident which happened during the day close to the Long Breakwater. It was a sunny, mild afternoon, almost like spring, with the thrushes singing loudly; the sort of day which would have made old Colonel Hawker exclaim, "Bluebottles buzzin', flowers buddin', doctors gallopin' in every direction and a regular Philharmonic of blackbirds and thrushes", etc.

I was certainly not thinking of geese when I heard a party of pinks gabbling over the edge of the tall reeds. They were sitting well out from the 'plickplack', and were so engrossed in conversation I was able to stalk out through the tall reeds until I was within a hundred yards of them.

For about half an hour they chattered and gabbled, now and again trooping down to a little freshet which came in over the muds just there, for a bathe and a preen.

I wisely refrained from disturbing them as they were out of range for even my single eight, and it was, moreover, a very pleasing sight.

Before very long I heard the cackling of geese from behind me beyond the oak trees and the geese on the mud immediately set up a great calling, those in the burn hurrying back to join their companions, and all stretching up their necks and crying to their comrades who came sailing over the trees.

As soon as the geese in the air saw those on the mud they corkscrewed downwards like curlew, passing right over my head and making a strange whirring sound with their broad pinions. I fired and brought down the leading goose.

Just at dusk on calm frosty nights when there was no moon the greylags had a habit of swimming in to the 'plickplack' hard by the Long Breakwater. Many a night I have lain out on the end among the stones hoping for a shot. Sometimes a single bird would fly straight in, and land among the short reeds with a terrific 'slosh', but is was by then usually too dark to see it.

Once as I was lying there listening to the croaking of a big gaggle which was swimming in to me, another party came over the groyne behind me, not ten feet up; the sky was black with outspread wings. I fired my eight-bore, but, like the time when they came over me by Reed Island, I failed to hit a bird, probably because they were too close.

Once, too, when I was returning home and walking back through the short reeds armed with the single eight, I put up a woodcock. I shot it with BB shot at long range and my dog, after a long search, found it.

Jim Jagoe told me that sometimes he had shot capercailzie in these reeds, and he told me also of the other rare birds he had seen and heard, spotted crakes, little and common bitterns, and hen harriers.

I once had a lovely view of a magnificent cock hen harrier by the Long Breakwater. I was watching the little birds going to bed in the reeds, scores of tits and finches hopping restlessly about among the slender wands, when all of a sudden every bird closed its wings and dropped like a stone down into the thicker undergrowth. For a moment I wondered what had scared them, and then over my head floated a lovely hen-harrier cock, as grey as a wood pigeon, his fierce eyes turning this way and that in search of a victim.

But the little birds remained absolutely still for a long time, long after the round-winged freebooter had passed on up the coast.

The terror of all the small bird tribe at the approach of a hawk is very impressive: they fear a bird of prey much more than a human being because their fear is so much older; it is inherent in them. They regard man, perhaps, as a treacherous animal, but one which on occasion, can be strangely gentle and harmless. But a hawk is their greatest dread and, so overcome are they by terror, they seem to lose all power of motion, like a rabbit pursued by a stoat.

Many an evening, walking back along the foot of the bank, I have heard the geese coming in from the fields, and sometimes I have been lucky, the skein has come over the tops of the oaks on the bank directly above me and I have had an easy shot. I remember one bird, a big greylag and leader of the skein, falling from a great height and splitting himself half open on the frozen ice at my feet.

Now all those lovely trees have gone, felled in the last German war, and the geese have gone too, along with their feeding grounds. Ugly army huts now dot the flat levels where the grey legions fed undisturbed, grey tarmac stripes the green grass where once the ploughs forged up and down. Worst of all, the roar of planes is ever predominating, from dawn to dark and all through the night as well. Blazing lights glare around the vast hangars, flare paths illuminate the sky. No wonder the geese have gone elsewhere.

I am glad I knew it in the old days.

There was one other locality on this stretch of the coast for which I had a great affection.

There was a farm right on the sea wall, a large house with a lodge entrance, called, if I remember rightly, by the romantic name of 'Seaside'. It was surrounded by trees, and a large orchard, full of old fruit trees, flanked the house. There was a duck pond, too, and a rutty elm-girt lane leading from the by-road to the sea wall.

Many a frosty morning I have tramped up this rutty lane and seen the tame ducks asleep on the pond, white blobs on the ice. I have crossed the orchard, and come out upon the bank, and followed a sloping track down into the reeds, my feet rustling in the drifts of oak leaves.

Exactly opposite the farm was a short dilapidated breakwater, and on either side of it two big islands of reeds. This was, at one time, a very favourite spot of mine as the geese seemed to prefer it to any other in the estuary. I had made my own reed paths, cunningly winding with 'bomb bays' and angles, well trodden so that I could steal upon the geese without making a rustle in the quiet of dawn.

I have had more geese from 'Seaside' than from any other point on the shore. But now they come no more.

I visited this place two years ago, and on several mornings I went out, crossing the orchard, and threading the same reed paths, but I found the 'plickplack' deserted; the only birds I saw were redshanks running on the muds.

And now, I think it is time to say good-bye to this estuary, and to all those good times I had there in days long past.

17. *Solway Side*

IN the years between the wars, I made several expeditions to the Solway: indeed, after the Wash had become overshot and spoilt by the bombing ranges at Holbeach I went there several seasons in succession, staying, as I have said, at Glencaple, that charming little fishing village on the Nith.

The countryside around Glencaple possesses great charm. The hotel stands almost on the quay where there is (or was) an old warehouse, for at one time a considerable amount of shipping of small tonnage came up as far as the village, though what merchandise they loaded or delivered, I do not know, unless it was wool or hides.

Exactly opposite the hotel, over the river, are saltings, and beyond them the imposing bulk of Criffel dominates that part of the coast.

A narrow country road lined with trees leads from the village southwards to Calaverock Castle, a romantic ruin set in woods standing almost on the marshes.

All the way from the village to Castle Corner are extensive saltings which are flooded in the spring and autumn tides, a great place for waders of all kinds and many species of duck, though the latter keep to the open sands of the estuary.

There was a local fowler living in the village who took me out

on several occasions, a broad-shouldered, big man with a remarkably fine head. His name was Jimmy M'Noe.

It was Jimmy who first instructed me in the geography of the
place, and he was a great goose hunter and a fine shot, unselfish
and in no way grasping; indeed, when I used to offer him payment
for his services, I had some difficulty in getting him to accept
a penny, very different from the professional fowlers on the East
Coast. In all fairness to them, however, I must hasten to say that
Jimmy was not a professional fowler. I seem to remember he had
some job connected with the quay and warehouse, and in the
fishing season caught salmon in nets.

This reminds me that they fish for salmon in the Solway in a very
primitive fashion. When the tide is flowing you will see the fishermen, in their long wading trousers, far out in the sea, each with
a long pole from which drags a net which is a sort of stationary
trawl.

They stand in the channels waiting, as patiently as herons, for
hours on end until a fish swims into the bag of the net which floats
out behind them. They feel at once if anything enters the trawl,
and they then come ashore with the salmon floundering wildly in
the meshes. I have never seen them capture a salmon, but one never
does see a fisherman catch anything as long as you stand and watch
him.

Sometimes in the winter evenings, Jimmy and I would tramp
out across the grey-green saltings below the village and stand in a
muddy channel off-shore.

The greylags sometimes came in that way, and when it was
almost dark they frequently (so Jimmy said) passed low over the
waiting guns if the latter stood quite still. At intervals along
that part of the shore are long poles stuck into the sand which
support fishing nets, and the geese no doubt mistake the figures
of men for these poles. (They are frequently taken in the nets, by
the way.)

I must admit that, knowing the grey geese as I do, I should have thought their sharp eyes would be able to distinguish the figure of a man below them, and I never did see them come in anywhere near us, but we shot a few duck coming down this channel.

Even though I was with Jimmy I hated going out on to the muds, and this 'channel standing' was far from pleasant as one slowly sank down into the mud; after about half an hour it would be up to your knees; nor could you obtain an easy swing with your feet anchored in this way.

Many a dawn I went with Jimmy to Eastpark, a famous greylag marsh beyond Calaverock Castle and about eight miles distant from the village. (It was on Eastpark, by the way, that I was lost in the fog on that dreadful night which I have described in an earlier chapter.)

It entailed a vast amount of walking over rough ground, and it was very rarely that we ever got a shot, though there have been occasions when Eastpark and the marsh in the neighbourhood of the Pow have yielded several geese. The pink-footed geese, strange to say, I never saw there; they kept to the Cumberland side of the Solway on the private marsh of Rockcliffe. Why Rockcliffe should be private I have never been able to ascertain, unless it is that the Cumberland men had not the spirit to stick up for their rights. I am inclined to think that the braw Scotties would never allow their own fowling grounds to be interfered with on the Scotch side of the Solway. Not very long ago the Rockcliffe marsh was anybody's shooting ground.

Nevertheless, as at Holt in Norfolk, the preservation of the marshes on the Cumberland side has meant that the geese have long periods when they are undisturbed, and occasionally the fowlers on the Scotch side benefit when the pinks come across to feed on the fields.

There are, I believe, one or two 'free' marshes on the English side, but I have never explored them. Even so, I once managed to get myself into trouble on the Castle Corner marsh by Calaverock Castle.

There is no fence or visible boundary between the free marsh and the private ground by the castle, and one afternoon I was having some fun with the rabbits in the furze bushes by the wood.

Before long, I was accosted by a bellowing keeper who ordered me off. I understood I had been poaching.

"And whom does the ground belong to?" I asked.

The man looked at me with a shocked expression. "Dinna ye ken? It belongs to His Grace!"

"Who?"

"His Grace the Duke of Norfolk."

The keeper thereupon took my name and address, but I heard no more about it. If His Grace should ever read these lines I ask his forgiveness. I did think, however, that there might have been some fence erected between the open marsh and the preserved ground, or at least some notice to say it was private land.

The character of these Solway marshes on the Scotch side interested me. I have said that no two goose grounds are similar, and here I found quite a different terrain compared, let us say, with the Wash or Holy Island. The saltings are very extensive, and not grown all over with coarse crab grass or sea lavender, nor are there numerous winding creeks and gullies seaming the surface in every direction. One finds, instead, level green lawns beloved of the wigeon and the barnacle, and when at last the sea is reached there is no mud or 'plickplack' but a definite 'brew' or miniature cliff where the clean sands join the soil of the marsh. This little cliff or 'brew' is about three feet in height, and all along its length lie tumbled turves of all sizes behind and between which the waiting gunner can find cover.

Another feature is the shallow bath-like flashes in the surface of the saltings, full to the brim with crystal-clear ruffling water, and usually surrounded by the fine lawn-like grass.

These flashes are not always shallow, some are four, or even five feet deep, and one has to beware of them when coming off the marshes in the darkness. They are favourite places for wigeon and the droppings are scattered around, mixed sometimes with those of the barnacles.

Somehow, these prettily marked little geese never seem to me to be true geese, and I shall always remember my astonishment the first time I ever saw a big pack.

One bright windy morning, when I was walking out from Castle Corner, I saw what I took to be a big flock of green plover flying in the distance. They wheeled about and settled on the grey-green marsh, and when I focused them in my glasses I saw to my astonishment that they were barnacles. I had always imagined them to be much bigger birds; in reality they are not very much larger than a big mallard duck, though some weigh up to five pounds. The average weight is four pounds, compared to six pounds in the greylag. Incidentally, while mentioning the weight of geese, the record greylag is sixteen and a half pounds, but I once saw a greylag on the Moray Firth which must have beaten this record. I saw it on several occasions, both on the wing, and feeding with its companions on the fields, and it dwarfed its fellows. It appeared to me to be about as big as a small turkey.

Due west of Castle Corner there was an island which was much beloved by the barnacles. I called it an island, but it was in reality a small area of marsh separated from the main marsh by a tidal creek.

When lying in wait for the barnacles at night, one had the uneasy feeling that the tide would come in and cut one off, and sometimes this happened, and there was nothing then but to stand it out, a cold job on a winter's night.

Once Jimmy M'Noe and I, when crossing this creek at low water, got into difficulties, or rather Jimmy did so: I, being a light weight, a mere ten stone to Jimmy's seventeen, got over without much trouble.

As we entered the shallow water, Jimmy called out: "Keep going, keep going! It's a wee bit soft." As I got in mid-channel I felt the suck of the quicksands trying to drag me down, and I 'kept going' with a vengeance and only just got through.

But Jimmy, with his seventeen stone, was not so lucky. I saw him leaning forward, the sweat standing out on his forehead with his exertions, but he was slowed up, finally stopped in mid-channel with the water coming up to his thighs as steadily as a rising tide.

An inexperienced gunner might have lost his head and struggled, which only causes one to be sucked down with greater expedition. There is a horrid story one hears in the taprooms of the district of an inexperienced wildfowler who got 'stuck' in a quick-sand somewhere near this spot. He sank to his armpits, and was only rescued in the nick of time by some fishermen who happened to hear his crazed screams of fear. They fetched straw from the nearest farm, and trod it in round him, but when they at last hauled him free from the clutches of the semi-liquid sand, the man was a lunatic and, the story goes, he never regained his sanity.

Whether or not this is true, I do not know, but to be trapped in mud or sand far from help is an experience that will test the strongest nerves.

If ever the reader gets trapped in this way and even 'rolling out' won't avail him, let him blow down his empty gun barrels. The noise produced is like a ship's fog horn and carries for a great way. This has saved many a fowler in fog or other unforeseen circum-stances.

But, to return to my story. Jimmy cast his gun with all his might to the opposite shore where it landed on the turf, and getting down in the sand and water he rolled himself out, though, I must admit, not without great difficulty.

Apparently this was all in the day's work to Jimmy, and when the moon got up he went off down the coast towards Eastpark, wet as he was, and left me to find myself a hide. This I did under the brew, where I stayed for a couple of hours until the moon rose. It was a very frosty, silent night, and I could hear the wildfowl far out on the sands, the quacking of duck and the 'wheeos' of wigeon.

Soon there was a rushing sound and a pack of wigeon came over my head, taking me so completely by surprise that I never fired a shot.

My next excitement was a party of greylags which came croaking by, following up the sands, but they were too far out.

The broad estuary, silvered by the moon, spread out on either hand, was a lovely sight. Now and again the silvery expanse would be dimmed by a cloud passing over the moon. Far in the distance danced the lights of Silloth, while to the south-east a glow in the sky showed the position of Carlisle.

Soon after two in the morning I heard two very distant shots up towards Eastpark, and not long after, the faint clamour of a barnacle pack on the wing. The sound drew nearer, and the next moment they came flying up the centre of the marsh between me and the land. In the moonlight I could see their white breasts gleaming. They wheeled round and came back past me, offering me a quick shot, and I brought one down ten yards away.

Then followed a long wait of an hour or more when again I heard the yelping chorus drawing towards me. This time they all pitched about two hundred yards away near the creek, and for a minute or so remained perfectly still and silent.

I could not see them, but knew they were there, and very soon they began to feed, and I heard the guzzling clamour and the familiar 'buzz' of contentment. Domestic geese when greedily at feed make very much the same kind of sound.

I got out of my hide under the brew and bellied across the salt-ings, a horribly cold and wet business. The buzz became quite

deafening, but I could see no sign of the birds until I saw the reflection of first one barnacle, and then another in the waters of the
creek. They came trooping over the edge of a brew, and seemed to
be going down into the bed of the creek.

As I was peering and squirming, trying to see something to
shoot at, one of them must have spied me, for in a moment they
were up with a roar of wings, and I never touched a bird with my
two barrels. It is absolute folly to 'fire into the grey' and this I had
done.

So ended my sport for that night, and about an hour later I heard
the approach of Jimmy and saw him coming towards me over the
merse, the glow of a cigarette fitfully lighting up his face. He was
covered in mud and soaked to the skin through having had to roll
out of another quicksand, but he carried two beautiful barnacles
by their necks. He said he had stalked them down a creek and had
fired both barrels as they rose.

Sometimes big bags are made by local gunners out of a pack
which comes over them in the moonlight, but since that night I shot
my barnacle I have never had another, nor have I a great desire to
slay any more of these lovely little geese, which seem to me to be more
at home in a private ornamental water than flying wild over the
saltings.

Wigeon, however, are a different matter, and I have had some
wonderful nights on the Solway after these beautiful and most
edible of all our wild ducks. A cock wigeon in full winter kit is
the most exquisite creature, with his sulphur caste mark on his
forehead, his rosy-pinky-brown head and breast, and the delicate
wavy pencillings of his flanks. It is my favourite duck. I like, too,
the vivid snow-white and black on his shoulders and wings, his
neat head and slender legs. There is nothing cumbersome about
him, all his curves are streamlined and perhaps the only other wild
duck which approaches him in delicacy of plumage and trimness
of build and line is the pintail.

Pintails are fairly common on the Solway but are not easy to shoot, and only at a high tide and in rough weather will you bring one to bag.

But of all my Solway memories one remains, that broad silvery moonlit expanse on a frosty night in midwinter, with the moon riding high and masked at times by clouds, and away in the distance the dancing lights of Silloth and the bulk of Criffel rearing up a blue-grey silhouette against the stars.

And then, growing in volume each moment, the whisper of the tide, the excited cheepings of the wader flocks as they race to and fro in smoke-like clouds along the edge of the advancing water. Minute by minute that whisper grows to a troubled murmur and the murmur to a roar as the tide comes swilling across the miles of sand.

And in a moment, the erstwhile bare sands are transformed into a crinkling moving film of water, oystercatchers fly in piping bands overhead, and sometimes, as a climax to the excitement of the coming of the flood, one hears the baying of the barnacle pack as it sweeps along over the merse.

And a second memory remains, the tramp home along the shadow-banded road from Castle Corner in the silent night, the furze bushes standing sentinel, like cowled monks by the wayside, and finally the cosy, lighted bar of the Glencaple Hotel, presided over by mine host, Mr. Leyland; surely the most comfortable fowler's pub in Britain.

But do not think that you will shoot geese or duck to your heart's content at Glencaple. I have been there for days at a stretch, and have never shot anything but a curlew. Favourable weather is necessary to have any sport at all, and there are one or two days each winter when the tides are high and the weather wild, when all the blank days are forgotten. It was from the tree-lined road near the Glencaple Hotel that that fine shot and first-rate wildfowler, Colin McClean, had a right and left at geese, a pink and grey with two shots. That occasion is still quoted in the taproom o'nights when the wind knocks in the chimney and fowlers drink a last round before setting out for their lonely moonlit vigils on Eastpark.

There are better places in which one may hunt geese, but I know no other where the surroundings, company, and the good fare make up for all the fruitless days and the cold glittering vigils on the midnight shore.

18. The Inland Fowler

AS a change from shooting on the shore—that magical world of saltings and sea lavender, creeks and estuary, where wind and tide never sleep—let us look for a moment at the shoot-ing grounds of the inland fowler, let us see what recompense he can find when he dwells, albeit uneasily, far from the lands he loves.

Let me say at once that organized drives and shooting parties are distasteful to me. True fowler that I am, I prefer to hunt wild game on my wild lone, and though on occasion I walk the stubbles, and take my stand beside the woods, I find my greatest happiness in waiting for duck by some willow-girt pool or, at worst, ambush-ing pigeons in their winter roosting woods.

Abel Chapman rightly says that the wood pigeon is the wild-fowl of the inland shooter. The bulk of them are winter visitors from the far north lands; they are most difficult to stalk, savoury in the pot, and are worthy game for any exile.

For some years I had a shoot adjoining a large reservoir in the midlands whereon in winter great numbers of duck, wigeon, pochard, mallard and teal congregated. In autumn and spring I even heard the curlews crying.

It was interesting for me to see how the habits of these inland fowl were very similar to their brethren on the coast. On moonless nights the ducks came out in a main big flight at dusk, but when the moon was full they seemed to come off at all hours. The wigeon always sat on the water long after the mallards had gone in and came off when it was practically dark, certainly when it was too dark to shoot.

A large inland reservoir attracts rare birds on passage. I have seen black terns hawking on sooty wings just above the surface of the water in June, and many rare ducks, such as garganey and pintail, were often seen.

The flight lines off this reservoir were just as erratic as those on the coast. It all depended on the direction of wind and where the birds happened to be feeding. Only on one occasion did I ever have a good flight, and that was when snow was on the ground, and a strong wind blew from the east.

My most curious experience happened in March of 1946.

There was a thick small wood near the reservoir which was on my shoot, and this was much frequented by pigeon and carrion crows. It was a good little spot where I always had something, a pigeon, a rabbit or two, and the occasional pheasant.

One March evening when I was ambushing pigeon, there came on a violent snow blizzard which lasted until dusk. The pigeon came well that night and I speedily filled the bag, shooting over a dozen birds before it got too dark to see. Then the carrions began to caw at the far end of the wood, and I stole through the trees to get a shot. The night was so wild and rough that I noticed the moorhens were coming in off the reservoir and roosting in the thick blackthorn underwood. Soon I saw what I took to be two carrion crows near the top of an oak tree. The light was very bad and I could not see clearly, but they appeared to be two carrions sitting side by side.

I fired and a single large bird fell. I thought it was an owl and felt sorry I had shot. A moment or two later I was more than sorry, for mark what happened. I sent my labrador to retrieve the bird, and she came back with her tail between her legs. I ordered her off again and she bustled away, but again she returned looking very crestfallen.

I thought then that I *must* have shot an owl and that it was wounded. I walked over. At the foot of the oak the underwood was very thick and, parting the branches, I peered in. At first I could see nothing. Then I made out the form of a pale striped bird lying under the brambles. Still I thought it was an owl, and pushing my way in I picked it up. I found to my horror that I had shot a bittern!

I see in Witherby's handbook that bitterns do occasionally roost in trees, so my mistake was excusable. It must have been the wild snowy night that drove it in to shelter. It had possibly been on passage and had noticed the sheet of water and the thick wood, and decided to rest there for the night. It was an accident which might have happened to anybody, but it made me feel very bad for some time afterwards.

When the reservoir froze over, the number of birds dwindled rapidly. The wigeon departed for the coast, and only a few mallard remained, spending the day far out in the centre of the ice in one compact throng.

The best shooting was, of course, in August when the young ducks were flying to stubble, but as I had not the shooting rights round the reservoir I only had the odd birds which came in my side.

It was sometimes easy to imagine that I was by the coast, especially on those still misty autumn evenings when the mallard were lifting in little bunches, and flying off against the last glow of the western sky. And better still, when I heard the 'wheeos' of the wigeon packs, and I could close my eyes and imagine I was in my old haunts up north.

One hard and snowy winter the old crossing-keeper told me that he had seen a skein of fifteen grey geese that morning, flying in at dawn.

The news was exciting as wild geese were only occasional wanderers. I had seen an odd greylag and a pink-footed goose on rare occasions, and there was always a party of Canada geese on the water every winter.

Incidentally, I heard an amusing story from the old crossing-keeper about these Canada geese.

They had a habit of flying past his cottage on some evenings, and one night a party of guns ambushed them in his hedge. Dead on time the Canada geese came clonking over in a long line and one of the guns fired at the leader and killed it. It fell from a fair height, right on to the top of a car which happened to be passing. It went clean through the sunshine roof, injuring a woman inside.

But to return to the report of wild geese. The news, I must confess, was treated with some reserve, for I had never seen more than an odd bird on this water. But, nevertheless, I took with me my Magnum and a couple of three-inch cases of BB in case I found that the old man was correct.

It was towards sunset when I reached the shoot, and after scanning the water with my glasses, I went cautiously along by the side of the wood.

It was one of those leaden-grey late afternoons with no sign of any sun or open sky. Heavy clouds were slowly coming over from the north, and as I reached the wood, the first wavering flakes began to fall, wandering about, some lighting on my coat and lodging on my moustache.

Beyond the wood there was a narrow field bordered by a fence, rather a 'goosey' looking field, and the fence even reminded me of 'goose country' fencing, post and wire. This field was separated from the reservoir by another field, and between it and my goose field was a thorn hedge and a ditch.

Snow, of course, was everywhere, but it lay thinly; it crunched underfoot and was powdery like sugar, a sign of frost.

As I reached the thorn hedge I thought I heard a goose call the low alarm note. I got down in the ditch, and peeping through the laid thorns in the bottom of the hedge, I immediately saw a party of fourteen white-fronted geese at the far end of the field. They were not feeding but all stood with erect heads looking in my direction. One, I noticed, was a magnificent old gander with a heavily barred breast.

I lay for a moment or two hardly believing my eyes. Geese on my own shoot nearly a hundred miles from the nearest sea!

After a little while they began to walk about slowly, all save the old barred beauty who stood very still, turning his head.

I got down into the ditch, trembling with excitement, and crawled along in the snow for fifty yards. When next I looked, I saw that they were in range of the bank if I could win another twenty yards. They were now all feeding, even the old gander, and seemed quite oblivious of danger. The wind was blowing from them to me, though I do not believe that wind direction matters a very great deal when stalking geese.

Luckily that afternoon I had left my dog at home, as the one I had at that time was not good at waiting, very different from my present bitch, which can be put down and will not stir until I wave my hand.

I crawled another twenty yards when the most miserable thing happened. A cock pheasant 'exploded' in front of my nose. It had been crouching behind a pile of hedge clippings on the shore of the ditch! It rocketed up over the hedge in a cloud of snow, 'cocking' for all it was worth, and I immediately heard the geese rise with a thresh of wings. Away they went with sundry croaks, far out over the water. I hoped they would settle, but no, round they flapped, and climbed away over the fir wood on the opposite shore, and though I waited on to dusk I never saw them again.

The only other time I surprised geese by my shoot (again off the same field) was a couple of years later in the severe winter of '47.

Snow had covered the land for weeks and one evening, walking along with my dog and not expecting geese, a party of greylags rose croaking from the centre of the meadow, far out of shot. These, too, went away and I did not see them again.

I have said that pigeon are the great standby of the inland fowler and most winters I shoot a great many, both in the small wood on my shoot and in another lovely wild spinney called the Colonel's Cover.

Of all the woods and spinneys I know, the Colonel's Cover is my prime favourite. This wilderness, which was planted primarily as a fox cover, is about five miles from my house. It lies away from a narrow country road, and, being so quiet and remote, is the home of many uncommon birds and animals, and holds a quantity of 'wild' game.

To reach it I turn off the road at the crest of a hill, cross two spacious pastures, and there below, in a large hollow, is the Colonel's Cover.

It is of considerable size—about four acres in extent, a kind of vast bowl set in a fold of the fields, planted for the most part with dense blackthorn. Ridings and paths have been cut through it to allow access to the Hunt, and at one end, on the southern side, are tall trees, oaks, elms, and ashes, ideal perching trees for pigeons. In winter thousands of starlings roost in the thorns and all manner of migrant birds, redwings, fieldfares and the like.

Badgers are common, and, of course, foxes also; the Colonel's Cover is a certain find, whenever the Hunt comes our way.

It is there I go, every spring, to greet the first of the migrants, and what happy hours they are, lying quietly under the thickets with the warm sun shining down upon me, listening to the tender falling scales of the willow warblers, and the lilting 'chiff-chaffer-ings' of the chiff-chaffs. What a joy it gives me to watch the delicately tinted leaf warblers hopping happily among the 'pussy' willows and snow-white blackthorn sprays! One day you will not hear one of these travellers, but the next, the whole cover is melodious with their songs. They seem to arrive in the night, usually about the eleventh or twelfth of April, though the chiff-chaff is sometimes a fortnight earlier—sometimes I hear the latter bird at the end of March.

Lying quite still among the old dead bracken fronds, with the cloudless sky above, I see the exquisite beauty of the white blossom printed on the flat blue background, with here and there a glimpse of an intense black twig showing between the snowy bloom which seems to give an added value to its pattern. Now and again comes the sweet scent of violets which cover all the sunny banks of the ridings and perhaps, mingled with it, the elfin perfume of flowering wild cherry bloom.

If I lie there long enough the rabbits will come out and sit in the pathways sunning themselves. A wild rabbit, when it is sunning, sits in a peculiar way with its head up and its ears drooped flat and downwards. At such times you can stalk them without cover, for their eyes are shut, they are dreaming in the vernal warmth, oblivious of all danger. Sometimes, too, I see them sprawl luxuriously on the close-cropped grass, lying as a man does in a warm bath, in curious unrabbit-like attitudes. Old ones and young ones, and small bouncing babies, how they delight me!

At this time (late April and early May) I do not shoot them, though I always carry my little gun with me in case I have the chance of a pigeon.

In the spring wood pigeons flock to remote covers and woods. It is just before the winter flocks break up, and in the sunny hours vast numbers come to the tall trees of the Colonel's Cover where they remain most of the day, if undisturbed, basking, like rabbits, in the soft sunlight.

At this time of year there are no teasing flies to bother one, the 'summer hum' has not yet come. Queen wasps and bees are about, the latter eagerly at work among the white bloom.

On topping the rise above the cover at this delectable flowering time, the whole area bursts into view as a sheet of white, as if every bush was covered in snow. As soon as I appear on the sky, line the pigeons, roosting in the trees, take wing. For a moment or so the blue-grey mass of wings covers the hollow with a moving carpet. If I wait under the trees odd pigeons will soon come wheeling back, and it is not often I come home without at least half a dozen fat birds in the bag.

My labrador has sometimes a difficult job to retrieve them. Many fall right back in the dense blackthorn jungles; occasionally a bird becomes lodged in the intricate branches above the reach of the dog's nose. This necessitates a painful crawl on my part before my victim is located.

All kinds of little adventures are sure to be met with in the Colonel's Cover. Very often I come upon a bunch of grass snakes, all tangled together in a Gordian knot, upon some warm and grassy bank, their beautiful glistening coils stirring and moving among the violets. Some would have viewed this sinister spectacle with ignorant horror. Some keepers always club them to death, or shoot them as they slide away into the herbage, but I recognize them as beautiful, shy creatures, absolutely harmless, fashioned most wonderfully in their plated green and primrose armour.

The glory of the blackthorn is of short duration, it only lasts ten days or so, and then the dense green leaves arrive to make all close and secret. But other glories come, the wonderful and even more entrancing hawthorn snow, which flowers at the very peak of the year. Then this wilderness in the hollow of the fields is a bowl of perfume.

The blackthorn has no noticeable scent, but that of the haw, thorn or 'May' is strong. Some dislike it, but to me it has always been wonderful. It is not sweet, but has a herby *leafy* bouquet. I prefer it to the scent of roses.

The Colonel's Cover is so impenetrable that few poachers venture there. I like to think it is my very own private kingdom where I can be sure of wandering all day long, week after week, month after month, and meeting with nobody but rabbits, foxes, and badgers.

This thorny wilderness forms a veritable sanctuary for vermin. Jays and magpies abound. The latter build their vast domed structures of woven thorns in the tops of the squat may trees, choosing those which grow right in the centre of the thickets.

To reach these nests is a formidable task and, once located, the actual ascent of the tree is a very painful operation. The long skewer-like thorns pierce the thickest jacket with ease and when at last I struggle to the base of the nest, my hands and face very often streaming with blood, it is by no means an easy matter to find the opening and sometimes, despairing of doing so, I break a way in, to feel the five or six greenish speckled eggs nestling in the fibrous cup. These eggs, like those of jackdaws, seem to me to be much more than mere 'shells', I value them as much as if they were precious stones, gems pilfered from Nature's treasure house.

Magpies are so wary and their hearing is so keen that I never surprise the mother bird upon the nest, and on only few occasions do I see her leave it. No doubt I advertise my coming by my struggling with the dense and thorny barricades. When I do see the black mass of the nest in the top of the hawthorn crown, there is no way of telling whether it is old or new, the climb has to be undertaken in a hopeful spirit. Perhaps the finding of eggs, under these circumstances, gives an added enjoyment.

I spoke just now of the almost spiritual delight I find in a bird's egg, whether it is the heavenly blue and black spotted thrush's eggs (as blue as the April skies) or the greenish streaked eggs of the crow family which seem to me to have taken their colour, their ashy greys and sombre greens, from the thick oak trees on which the lichen grows.

But I have this same deep sense of pleasure when I look at birds.

The wonderful blue and white watermark on the shoulder of the jay seems to me to be a masterly touch, and the painted appearance of a cock chaffinch is something which gives me a delicious sensa-tion of pleasure. The pinks, greens, and blues, chestnuts, blacks, and whites; what a trim and gem-like bird he is! I have an affec-tion also for the more sombre-hued greenfinch, whose soft greens are so obviously copied from the dense leafy arbours where he lives his life.

At one spot in the Colonel's Cover there is a thicket of gorse. The underwood is more open there, and later in the season the rose bay grows in profusion at that place, it is a sort of clearing in the waste of thorn.

There the linnets nest; and the cock bird, twanging his wild sweet windblown notes, is another favourite. In captivity the cock linnet does not show the wonderful wild rose blush on his upper breast. But in its free, wild life it is a gallant, colourful little bird, chubby of cheek, and with an upright carriage.

It is a delight to seek among the prickly armoured bushes for the nest, to spy a whisp of straw or bent, and peering in to see the cosy white woolly cup so snug, so neat, in which the delicate spotted eggs securely nestle.

After the time of the May bloom the tender greens darken, and soon the neat leaves of the blackthorn are no longer fresh. Multi-tudes of verminous caterpillars spin their ugly webs from spine to spine until, in some summers, the bushes appear quite mildewed and grey. The ridings become narrower with the high tide of mid-summer growth, the dog-roses flower, and then the berries form; the oaks on the southern fringe assume a dark burnished hue until at summer's end, the new brilliant growth at the tips of the branches dresses the oaks in a false spring attire.

Lying under the tired foliage I hear the clatter of the reapers busy in the hot fields round about and all the underwood is brittle and baked by the heats of summer. No longer do the powder puff rabbits gambol on the close shaven grass of the ridings, and here and there among the thorns a single rose or amber leaf tells of the coming of autumn.

Then come the frosts and day by day each bush and tree in my lovely wilderness turns colour with the blended dyes of autumn. Mists and winds, the sadness of the fall—my paradise is changed beyond all recognition!

The commonest bird in the cover is perhaps the bullfinch and in these late autumn days I see scores feeding on the heads of the dead meadow-sweet which grows thickly along the ridings.

As I am writing I recollect that the Colonel's Cover is the only locality near my home where nightingales sing.

With the changing moods of this lonely wilderness so does my spirit change. In those sunny days of spring, when the willow warblers sang, the lust for hunting slept. But when the first frosts tinge the thorns this hunting lust grows within me, and many a happy hour I spend there, and I have some happy memories. That day in gold October when I shot a brace of pheasants in the open space where the gorse bushes grew—that is a moment I remember.

The labrador, feathering eagerly on and knocking against the dead willow herb stalks, stopped as if stricken with paralysis, and from under his nose the beautiful cock bird burst forth with a frantic bustle and loud cock! cock! Up went the little gun and the bird fell forty yards away. I ran forward, sniffing as I did so the keen reek of powder; another cock got up on my right, just beyond the gorse. I downed that too.

And again that misty November afternoon when I flushed a woodcock from the marshy hollow near the oak (where the frogs made such a 'hoax coax' in spring). I had him as well.

Though the Colonel's Cover is not a particularly good locality for uncommon butterflies I am sure of seeing commas there in spring. These tattered gipsy butterflies always seem odd to me.

They have the same colouring as the gipsy, the same red-brown sun-stained tint upon their wings. They frequent the same gipsy haunts—forgotten roads and brambly wastes.

One other wood is productive, and this is the 'Jubilee J', a spinney planted in the shape of the letter 'J' on top of a small conical hill. This little wood must have been planted about the time of Queen Victoria's Jubilee—hence the name.

It is a very small place, and contains not more than a hundred trees, perhaps, but they are all well grown, oaks and ashes and one or two elms. At the foot of one of the trees I have made a thick hide of fir branches, and from this ambush I take deadly toll of the pigeon flocks through the winter months.

Pigeons love a spinney on a hill, especially if it is isolated and stands fairly high like the coppices and hangars on the downs. I have never returned empty-handed from shooting the Jubilee J, my best bag being fifteen birds one afternoon of gales in March.

The birds do not roost there, it is simply a port of call for all the pigeons in the neighbourhood. They prefer a solitary sheltered cover for roosting, and are shy of consorting with other birds such as rooks or daws. They need quiet, and once they have used a wood for several seasons, they will never leave it; every year they will resort to it in increasing numbers. I like to see the winter pigeon flocks coming in from the east. Invariably they fly very high.

Both pigeons and stock doves fight savagely in the spring, striking each other with their wings until the feathers fly. They sit side by side on a branch and flap their wings, striking each other with their shoulders until, like boxers, they are exhausted.

It will be seen, therefore, that one can have enjoyable days rough shooting inland, and though true wildfowl are hard to come by, save on the big reservoirs and sewage farms (the latter places are magnificent duck preserves), even the odd pheasant and rabbit provide delightful sport.

When I was a youth I had some red-letter days, and the following is an account of one of them.

It was one golden and hazy afternoon in the first week of November that I set out with my spaniel to shoot over Barrett's Farm. I had never shot there before, but had always cherished a desire to do so, and a lucky encounter with the old farmer himself, over the matter of a load of manure for our garden, led to a hearty invitation. "You'm welcome to have a walk a-round," he said. "You won't get much, but you may pick up a pheasant or two in the Ma'sh Spinney, and they're plenty o' rabbits; you can shoot as many as you like o' they."

There is an added interest in shooting over unknown ground, and I looked forward to my 'walk a-round' with keen anticipation. I could not have been more fortunate in the choice of a day. It was one of those peerless afternoons we sometimes get in the English autumn, still, and tranquil, the sun shining from a cloudless sky, but with a gentle warmth. There were wasps and big flies busy round the ivy bush on the farmhouse cart-shed wall and, late as it was, some red admirals were sidling on the Michaelmas daisies that peeped over the garden fence. They seemed to me perfect specimens, lately hatched, without tear or blemish. Yet these insects, bees, wasps, and flies, seemed to me a little lethargic, they moved from flower to flower with a certain hesitation; the red admirals did not quit their feast when my shadow fell upon them. Despite the sun they sensed the coming of winter; they were not deceived.

I thought it strange, though, to hear no twitter of swallows over the barn roof. I searched the sky but saw none, only countless starlings, which glided about over my head, clumsily fly-catching. They do this in the first warm days of spring; it is a sign, as sure as the opening of flower and leaf, of coming summer, as it was now a token of approaching winter.

Leaving my cycle by the farm I went down the muddy lane which led to the fields and spinneys. Major, the liver-and-white spaniel, was beside himself with joy, frisking about before me, grinning up into my face, scampering before and behind, throwing himself full length on the wayside grass, panting with out-flopped tongue.

But as soon as we reached the head of the lane, and passed through the gate, he came to heel. He sensed my will by looking at my face; he knew his place.

I stopped a moment, when through the gate, to take a look at the boundaries which had been pointed out to me a day or two before by old Mr. Barrett himself.

The pastures sloped away from the farm quite steeply, and the field I was in was rough with tussocky grass. Below was a fine old double hedge, some ten or twelve feet high, ablaze with the clear yellow of the dying maples and pink and rose with the hawthorn leaves. There were, I remember, many crab-apple trees in this hedge, and that year they bore a heavy harvest. The yellow apples shone from a distance on the bare branches (they had mostly dropped their leaves) and many lay below on the hard-caked earth, for it had been a dry autumn. You could have gathered many bushels of the bitter fruit. Some appeared as red and rosy as orchard apples, some showed a faint maiden's blush on their mellow-yellow cheeks.

This double hedge (always a good place to 'hunt out' with a gun) led over two fields to melt into a maze of other hedges, well timbered with oak and elm, with here and there a scattered spinney of oak and ash poles. A faint pearly mist hung over the distances, and in the hollows in the hills. Many of the stubbles had not yet been ploughed in, and over them I could clearly see flocks of rooks and grey wood-pigeons, all busy at their gleaning.

We first of all tried the double hedge. I sent the spaniel in the middle while I walked on the sunlit side, wishing I had a second gun to guard my flank. Major was a good dog at hedge-hunting; he never worked out of gunshot and, if at times, when for instance he got on the trail of a rabbit, and excitement and keenness made him forget my rule, he would poke his head out at the limit of gun-shot range, waiting for me to come up with him. There are not many spaniels who will do this and only months of hedgerow hunting had made him wise. He had found that if he put up the game too far away all his efforts (and mine too) were useless. It had taken him two years to learn this.

For some time nothing happened. I heard Major scuffling along among the crab-apples and the dying nettles, and occasionally caught a glimpse of his busy stern wagging in a gap in the bushes.

With a loud clatter a few wood-pigeons left the oak-trees which grew between the hedges but, pigeon-like, every bird left the far side of the tree where I could not see them, and offered no chance of a shot.

All at once something moved in the nettles in the ditch about twenty yards in front of me. At first I thought it was a rabbit; the next moment I saw it was a hen pheasant. She was running for all she was worth down the ditch. I only caught quick glimpses of her, head down, back hunched, and long tail stuck out behind her. An instant later Major darted through, standing for a moment in an opening under a rail, looking with a puzzled and very excited expression up and down the ditch in each direction. It was laughable to see his tense face, the ears cocked forward almost hiding his white muzzle, and he gave two little jumps so as to see over the dead 'gix' in the hedge bottom.

I ran, with my gun at the ready, and Major, turning round and at last using his nose, ran too, down the ditch, and getting a little too far in front, I had to call him back with a whistle. He stopped at once and waited for me to come level with him.

The pheasant had evidently darted back through the hedge again. At any rate there was no sign of it. I told Major to 'follow on', and he vanished again. I was afraid that the bird would break cover the far side, so I shouted to the dog to go right through, at the same time hurrying on down my side. I had now come to another hedge which joined the tall one at right angles and the only place where I could get through was at a gap and two rails. I was on the top of the rails, with the sun almost in my eyes, when I heard the sound of the bird rising with a great bustle of wings.

She rose out of the ditch, rocketing right up, evidently making for a small spinney which lay across the stubble field in front of me.

Somehow or other the gun came to shoulder and at the report I saw a cloud of feathers burst outwards and glimpsed the pheasant falling to the stubble thirty-five yards away. Major was out in a moment, and racing away, and by the time I had climbed down from the top rail of the fence he was trotting back, head held high, the bird in his mouth.

This was a good beginning, so good that I sat down under the hedge and, giving the dog a biscuit which I always carry with me as a reward for good work, I filled and lit a pipe.

On every twig the spiders' webs glistened in the sun, the filmy threads shone in the pale sunlight very clearly, and I saw that they were laced, even from the tips of the stubbles, so that, looking into the sun, it appeared as if there was a pathway of shining webs stretching right across the meadow. Redwings were clucking in the oaks.

Some rooks, disturbed by my shot, wheeled and cawed over a far field. Some alighted in the trees of the little spinney. After smoking for a little while (the dog lying panting beside me and trying to bite some burrs out of his long ears by pulling them downwards with his paws over his nose) I got to my feet and continued along the hedge. Where there is one pheasant there is often another, perhaps the whole brood, and the bird I had shot had evidently been hunting for the acorns which lay about in the stubble under the oak-trees. These trees were still in full leaf, indeed they showed little sign of decay, only an upper branch, here and there, had turned to that soft buff yellow which is the tint of undressed leather.

Major went in again and we had nearly got to the end when I heard him give a muffled excited bark (a thing he very seldom did). I thought he had another pheasant. But the next moment a rabbit rushed out within fifteen yards of me.

It ran out into the stubble and stopped, its eyes wide with fear, not knowing what to do. Perhaps I was between it and its hole. Just as I was raising my gun it bolted off down the hedge, offering an easy going-away shot which any schoolboy could have made a showing of. But for some inexplicable reason both my shots went wide, the rabbit rushed on with bobbing white scut, and dived into the hedge again some ninety yards away.

Major then emerged, looking at me with the most laughable expression on his face, and then gazed pathetically in the direction the rabbit had run. I shook my head at him and he came to heel. This little failure had sobered me down.

We next went across to the little spinney. I felt sure I should find another pheasant or two there; it looked just the place for them, quiet, lonely, and with several large oaks growing among the ash poles. We cut across the stubble and entered it. The hawthorns which formed its underwood were lovely, every tint of yellow and rose; some leaves were almost scarlet. But the field maples were the loveliest, their black, slender twigs showing through the veils of incandescent yellow.

As I pushed through them these leaves fell in showers. Major had only to knock gently against one of the bushes to send a flurry of them on to his back.

We went slowly and with caution. The spinney smelt deliciously of damp, wet leaves and rich earth, a wintry smell. There was a little boggy ditch in the middle and long coarse grass

and a holly or two. I had just passed the bole of an oak when a bird
flew up. (I thought it was a partridge by the way it rose, though
I should have known no partridge, save a wounded one, would be
found in the middle of a spinney.) It went straight up with great
swiftness, Major standing beside me, rooted to the spot.

And then I saw what it was. A woodcock! Never before, in all
my wanderings about these midland pastures, had I ever seen
a woodcock, yet there was no mistaking it, the long bill carried
downwards, the large but rather snipe-like wings.

It soared over the yellow maples and the rose-red thorns and
turned left. I glimpsed it in a gap, straightening out, and at that
instant I 'followed through' and fired. By that time the bird was
out of sight, for a spray of maple came across my gun, but I thought
I heard him drop, and Major darted off.

I stood among the trees, waiting for him to return, hardly daring
to look in his direction. It would be awful to have missed, yet it
was a difficult shot. Imagine my joy when he reappeared with the
woodcock in his mouth. He trotted up to me, but instead of giving
it into my hand, as he did the pheasant, he put it down at my feet
and licked it. He was not used to woodcock; it was the first one
he had ever retrieved.

I was beside myself with bliss. I could have danced. When we
get older we lose this surge of inner joy at the successful accomplish-
ment of a shot. What a pity that is!

I took the warm bird up and held it in my hand, looking at it
intently. It was the first woodcock I had ever shot, it was the first
I had ever held in my hand. The stout and stumpy body, the fine
full eye as full of expression as a gazelle's, the exquisite tints of its
barred plumage, what a miraculous treasure it was! I could not
bring myself to put him with my pheasant in the game-bag for fear
his delicate plumage might be soiled. I wrapped a handkerchief
round him and put him in my pocket. I would never forget this
moment. I would have him stuffed, I would have him mounted

in a case with dead oak leaves about his feet, I would look at him for years after and remember this golden autumn afternoon!

And now, as I write, I seem to be standing once more in that little tinted spinney with the weak sunlight filtering through the half-bare branches; I smell again the rare aroma of the leaves, the earth, and hear, as I stand in a trance, the sweet trickle of a robin's song somewhere in the thickets and the faint 'caw caw' of rooks.

I cannot remember anything more of that afternoon; it is strange that I should recollect so clearly the events which led up to that moment.

Major is now no longer by my fireside; Barrett's Farm is far away, many, many leagues; old Mr. Barrett, like Major, is dead (God rest their souls), and I am almost middle-aged. Is it not strange I can still live again that experience so vividly when other far more weighty and important occasions have been forgotten and passed out of mind?

19. Shooting Party

MOST boys begin shooting at an early age and I have described in other books some of my youthful experiences, of how I saved up my pennies week after week to purchase my first weapon, a twelve-bore (hitherto I had possessed a crazy ·22 rifle and an equally crazy four-ten. The ·22 had blown up and injured my eye when I was firing at a tit, a well-deserved punishment, it seems to me now).

But one's first shooting party, surely, is a great occasion. (In my case it was unusually memorable.) I do not think that this account is out of place in the present book, and it will also serve, perhaps, as a horrible warning to other boys who are referred to by sporting relatives as the 'young entry'.

When I was about fifteen years of age I went to stay with my godfather who was by way of being a sportsman-naturalist and to whom I owe, perhaps, my own love of shooting and wild life generally.

A neighbour of his, whom I will call 'Major Heathcote', was a peppery old gentleman who lived about three miles from my godfather's house. He was as keen and punctilious over shooting matters as are some men over foxhunting. He reared a large number of pheasants (he was a very rich man, and employed three keepers on his large estate) and an invitation to one of his shoots was considered an attractive fixture by the sporting gentry of the neighbourhood, especially as the hospitality provided was renowned.

I cannot think what induced my godfather to take me with him on that fateful day unless it was the fact that I had by that time become (though I say it myself) an unusually excellent shot for a youngster. I seem to remember the Major had been let down by a gun at the last minute, and had in a rash moment asked my godfather to find someone to fill his place.

I was quite terrified when I was summoned to the latter's study and told that I was to 'stand in'. The idea of shooting in company did not appeal to me; my idea of the true joy of a gun was to potter about the spinneys at home with Rollo, our spaniel. One saw more of the wild life of field and wood, and one had to work for one's game. Mechanical slaughter was (and is) distasteful to me.

It was with some trepidation, therefore, that I found myself sitting beside my godfather that frosty December morning en route for 'Blaydon Manor', with the guns in the back, and Hughie Bell, my godfather's groom, in his best tweed coat and breeches and mirror-like leggings, looking very neat and spruce. He was to act as my godfather's loader, a rôle in which he was well versed. Between his knees was Bruce, a black labrador which my godfather had recently bought on Bell's recommendation, a 'second season' dog whose parents had been Field Champions and which Bell had pronounced to be a 'grrand worrker'. (Bell was a keeper's son and knew a lot about shooting matters.)

Steam from the pony's nostrils puffed on the keen air as we drove along and I was glad of my thick tweed overcoat and scarf which the housekeeper had insisted on, much to my disgust.

I noticed the puddles in the road were white with cat's ice, the wayside grass crisp and furred with rime. Hedgerow oaks and elms were likewise decorated and in the air was that keen spice of frost which made the blood tingle.

The first drive was outside a big oak wood and when we arrived we found about half a dozen guns already assembled, standing about, talking and smoking. A little distance away was a cluster of keepers and loaders, and a knot of cloth-capped rustics carrying white rags tied to sticks. Major Heathcote's head keeper was giving instructions to the beaters as we came up. He touched his hat to my godfather and I thought he regarded me with rather a jaundiced eye; he was the kind of keeper who views all small boys with distrust.

Major Heathcote came bustling up. He wore a rough brown tweed jacket with leather shoulder pads and cuffs, and a deer-stalker.

"Glad to see you, Boy," he said, giving my hand a terrible grip and looking keenly at me with piercing blue eyes. "I hear you are a useful shot; good of you to stand in, I'm sure."

I saw his glance fall upon my new twelve-bore which I carried proudly under my arm. "Nice little weapon; you ought to be able to shoot with a gun like that."

My godfather nodded. "He hasn't really got used to it yet, Major, so don't be too hard on him if he misses a bird or two."

"Quite right, quite right," puffed the Major, "start on a twelve as soon as you can." He took my gun from me and examined it with a professional air. He opened the breech, looked down the barrels, snapped it to, and handed it back with the verdict—"a little beauty; you're a lucky feller; better gun than ever I had when I was a boy." (A remark I did not believe for a moment as it was not a first-class weapon.)

Meanwhile other guns were coming up and exchanging greet-ings. I looked about me, to see if I could spot Hughie Bell. I saw him a little distance away deep in conversation with a keeper. They were discussing Bruce who was submitting to a close examination. Bell's companion had his hand round the dog's muzzle and was looking at his teeth. Other dogs sat about expectantly, all on leads, with their pink tongues hanging. I noticed a fat Clumber which followed Major Heathcote about with an air of anxious weariness, never leaving his heel, and ignoring the other canine guests with an expression of superiority.

By now the sun had come up and rime began to rustle down from the twigs of the trees; blue shadows lay in the shelter of hedges but in the sunlight the frost was melting. I noticed a few pigeons flying over the big oak wood.

All along the cover side, out in the field, were little sticks with white labels stuck in their tops, and I wondered which my stand was to be. Perhaps I should be 'beater's gun', whatever that entailed, and rather hoped I would be. I did not fancy standing out in the open competing with the 'professionals'.

Major Heathcote was now moving energetically about giving orders in a military manner. The beaters and keepers trailed off round the wood and the guns and their loaders began to sort themselves out.

Then the Major came puffing across to my godfather. He had a habit of blowing out his purple cheeks.

"Ah, there you are. I've put you at the top, number seven, the boy's at number ten. Mind my beaters, Boy," he added, turning to me, "and remember—cocks only!"

Bell, with my godfather's second gun under his arm, and carrying a cartridge magazine, came up, and I tagged along after them, wishing myself pottering about with Rollo at home.

My godfather, never a keen shooting man, had not instructed me in the etiquette of shooting parties and the Major's last remark about 'cocks only' was rather mystifying. If I had had more warning I would have confessed my ignorance to Bell who might have enlightened me. As it was I remained mute; there was no chance now to buttonhole him.

I could not for the life of me see how I was to distinguish cocks from hens if they came out of the wood at any height. A pheasant at home, cock or hen, was speedily in the bag. Also I had forgotten my number and pictured myself wandering about trying to find my peg.

I need not have been anxious, however, for when my godfather and Bell reached their position the latter nodded reassuringly to me and said, "You're number ten, Master Denys," and I found my place without difficulty. On my right was a very tall thin man in knickerbocker breeches, white spats, and with a drooping moustache. A dour-faced valet was in respectful attendance. My left-hand gun was a stout little Pickwickian man with a merry rubicund face and glasses which glinted in the sun. He looked as if he couldn't shoot a thing. He had no loader with him and I mildly wondered why. A fat liver-and-white spaniel sat bolt upright behind him looking at the wood.

A silence fell. I looked along the line, saw the expectant figures waiting, and sensed the intense drama of the scene.

Beaters and keepers had vanished. Away to the left a kestrel was poised, its outspread wings quivering a little. Then it tilted, slanting away over the wood. The minutes passed. Then a jay screamed somewhere in the cover. It came slyly out with dipping flight to seek the refuge of a small plantation of fir on the side of a hill behind us.

Still nothing happened. My excitement was mounting. My mouth felt 'dried up', I fervently hoped no bird would come anywhere near me. Quite oblivious of the drama being enacted, a man was ploughing on a far slope. The team moved slowly, sluglike, up the tawny stubble, with rooks and a few white gulls clustering and dipping in attendance. Far away a train whistled on the clear keen air, and a party of starlings moved like shiny beetles out in the field behind us, now and again one or two birds would rise up in a jangling quarrel.

Then the first pheasant came straight out of the wood, climbing steadily, its wings whirring and gliding, the long tail streaming straight out behind. It was well away to my right. I watched with interest mingled with a relief that it was not my bird. Looking down the line I saw one man put up his gun in a hesitant way, lower it, then another slender barrel pointed skywards. I saw it swinging and a faint puff of smoke jetted forth a few inches from the muzzle. A second later came the dry thunderclap of the shot.

The steadily flying bird (it was too far for me to see whether cock or hen) seemed to be arrested in mid-air a fraction before I saw the smoke. It fell far back in the meadow. Muffled sounds now came from the wood, far away uncouth noises, and tapping of sticks.

Two more pheasants appeared, right away at the end of the line where my godfather was. One fell, the other went on, followed by a cluster of shots.

Then a bird came out over 'Mr. Pickwick'. For one moment I thought it was coming over me and my heart thumped painfully. I half put up my gun but when I saw him aiming I lowered it just in time. It was awfully hard to judge range and direction.

I could see quite clearly it was a cock. The sun shone on its burnished golden mail, the long tail quivered and streamed behind it with the exertion of its wings.

Then it staggered, I saw a puff of feathers fly from its breast and it fell like a stone, hitting the ground with a thump thirty yards behind me, and the wood threw back an echo to the shot.

The little man, to my surprise, never turned round. I heard his gun click and saw the empty, smoking case fly out. He darted one sideways glance at me and gave me a wink which was immensely comforting.

Shots now began to crack out all up the line and the air was fragrant with powder. The pheasants came out now every moment, all high birds. Some fell like stones, one or two slanted down in a steep glide, a few passed steadily on, ignoring the cannonade. Then I saw *my* pheasant coming. There was no doubt about whose bird it was. With two nervous sidelong glances I reassured myself on this point, for the fat little man simply sat on his shooting stick and watched it through his glinting glasses, and the tall aloof person on my right remained standing like a gaunt old heron and took no notice.

I waited as calmly as I could, hoping the bird would swing off either right or left, but it seemed determined to come for me and with an inaudible prayer I lifted my little gun.

It was the easiest of shots, I had many a more difficult one at home when I was shooting on my own, where they usually rose half-screened by bushes in front of the hunting dog.

This pheasant looked as big as a turkey and flew as straight as a bombing plane. I fired. Its tail seemed to disintegrate, its legs dangled, and the bird dropped a foot or so, but still carried on, gradually losing height, in the direction of the fir plantation.

"Too far behind, my boy," called the fat little man, as I broke the breech and tossed the empty case away. I felt ready to sink into the ground, tears of mortification were in my eyes. I had 'tailored' my bird, and imagined everyone in the line had seen it. I heard the tall aloof man mutter something to his loader.

Then I was horrified to see *two* more pheasants, a cock and a hen, coming dead on the same line. Determined to make amends I swung on to the cock as he came up over me and pulled the trigger. To my horror nothing happened, there was a faint 'click' and I realized I had never re-loaded!

Luckily I thought of my other barrel and after a slight falter I pulled the back trigger. The old cock jerked back, threw his head up, and slumped to the grass behind me. I was so elated I ejacu-lated "got him!" and just stopped myself from rushing across and gathering it. After a successful shot at home I invariably pelted headlong to retrieve my game with wild whoops of triumph. But I had not deserved success.

From my left I heard the 'Mr. Pickwick' exclaim "Well done, my boy," and those four words filled me with pride and gratitude. Assuming an air of having shot high pheasants every day of the week, I looked behind me and saw the still body of my bird half-hidden by the frosted grass, the wind faintly stirring its plumage. I felt immensely gratified. I longed for another chance now. Shots were ringing all along the line in a regular fusillade. Then there was a lull.

The clamour of the beaters was distinctly audible now, rustlings sounded in the underwood. I remembered the Major's words, "Mind the beaters".

Then a faint shout of "Mark!" on my right. I heard a few shots go off but could see nothing in the air and was quite mystified for a moment. Then the tall aloof gentleman faced half-right and I saw him getting ready, his loader crouching down. Still I could see nothing.

Then I spied a little brown round-winger bird coming at a great pace along the line of guns. Everyone was banging off at it. Just before it reached the tall man it jinked outwards behind us and the tall man's shots went bang! bang! without effect.

Instinctively I lifted my gun, it was just the sort of snap shot which I delighted in. I forgot I was at a shooting party, on my best behaviour, the early blunders were forgotten; for one precious moment I was quite unselfconscious. As soon as I pressed the trigger I knew he was mine. The woodcock hit the ground.

The tall man called out in a grudging porty voice, "Good shot!" 'Mr. Pickwick' turned his glinting glasses my way and beamed a wide smile of satisfaction. It was a glorious moment! Then the beaters appeared on the fringe of the wood and I knew the drive was over. I hadn't done too badly despite the shocking start, and

I was puffed with pride when Major Heathcote came up to me and clapped me on the back with a "Well done, young feller, wiped our eyes, eh? you young rascal," and I saw Hughie Bell grinning at me behind my godfather's back.

Nobody mentioned the 'tailored' bird.

I do not remember the next two drives very well save that I never had another shot that morning and all the birds went over the left-hand end of the line. Soon everyone was moving off towards a farmhouse, following a rutty track which led by a large square duck pond where a troop of runners marched off quacking, all their smirking bills turned in one direction as they watched us with their beady anxious eyes.

In the farmhouse kitchen was a welcome sight, a long table spread with a white cloth, loaded with succulent hams, steaming pies and all manner of good things. In the background Major Heathcote's butler was busy over a massive sideboard, with bottles, glasses, and tankards.

"Glad about the woodcock, Denys," said my godfather, helping himself to steak and kidney pudding, and then added in an undertone, "Old Major Heathcote's quite impressed!"

The frosty morning had given everybody good appetites. From time to time I caught glimpses of the Major at the head of the table taking a long pull at an enormous tankard. Others might choose fine wines, "jolly good ale and old" was enough for him, and "jolly good ale" it was, for I was permitted half a glass on the strength of the woodcock.

I like to summon up that picture of our host: the whole scene is faintly reminiscent of Cecil Alden's painting *The Hunt Breakfast*, even to the serving men, with blobby red noses, hurrying to and fro. The buzz of talk grew louder. I found I had on my right the tall lean gentleman who had the next stand to me at the morning drive. I do not think he approved of small boys because he addressed no word to me throughout the whole of luncheon but talked in a loud domineering voice to his companion. From the conversation I understood he was a hunting man.

Soon the expensive smell of cigar smoke was wafted about (Major Heathcote was certainly a good host) and people began to push back their chairs and gather in groups near the door.

When we emerged into the open air I noticed the sun had gone and a faint mist was gathering in the hollows.

The first drive of the afternoon was to be from another smaller wood beyond the farmhouse, with a gorse cover almost adjoining it. I heard Major Heathcote saying that he had a lot of birds there "but the damned beggars would get into the gorse", and if it wasn't for his fox-hunting neighbours he would have it burnt.

The beaters were assembled in the yard and by the good humour prevailing I understood that they too had been 'done well' by the Major in the matter of beer.

Again there was a council of war with the head keeper and the beaters trooped away. I was still basking in the warmth of my morning's triumph (my head was affected by the Major's Stingo) and went to collect my gun which, by rights, I should have given into the charge of Bell, who was looking after our gear.

However, I had propped it against the wall by the door of the farm, copying the example of another guest who should have known better. There were one or two dogs with their keepers waiting for their masters close by and as I went to retrieve my weapon two of the dogs started to scrap. At that moment also Major Heathcote emerged and bawled to the keepers to "mind those damned dogs". Then the most frightful thing happened. I go hot all over when I think of it, even now. One of the quarrelsome dogs, a big black retriever, bumped my gun with its stern. I saw it slide sideways and the next moment there was a terrific report.

I felt as if truly the end of the world had come.

For a moment I did not realize what had happened. I was numb with horror. There followed a shocked silence. I saw Major Heathcote's eyes bulging and his face going very red, his cheeks puffing in and out. Then he let drive with his parade ground voice.

"Who the *something something* left that *blankety blank* gun against the wall there—loaded too, by Gad!" One of the keepers walked forward and picked it up without a word, and, in a hesitant way, handed it to the irate Major. Other guns were now gathering round. I felt a mad cowardly desire to bolt and leave my beloved weapon unclaimed. Then Bell stepped forward and I knew in a moment my awful guilt would be made known and the identity of the culprit revealed. It was one of those periods in my life when I have wished the ground to open silently and swallow me without trace. I will draw a merciful veil over the ensuing minutes . . .

I still seem to feel my godfather's grip on my arm holding me like a vice as he led me away and then there was the ignominious journey home, for, of course, I was sent back at once in disgrace.

I never uttered a word the whole journey even though Bell tried to comfort me in his clumsy fashion by giving me a sly wink when I miserably glanced his way. I went straight up to my room and threw myself on the bed where I sobbed and sobbed until some interfering female came knocking at the door.

Looking back on this incident I could think myself lucky that nobody had been harmed by this gross piece of carelessness, and the sentence of not being allowed to carry a gun for twelve months afterwards (an edict which was communicated to my parents and fully endorsed) was well deserved.

Such are the meagre delights of the inland fowler but they are poor substitutes for that magic land of saltings and creeks. And though I enjoy my winter rambles in my favourite woods, with the chance of a pheasant and a rabbit and an occasional woodcock, it is small beer compared to that other sport which I love above all others.

You can have your finest partridge manor or pheasant shoot, I prefer the dawn or moonlight ambush, and those fleeting chances which come so seldom, which, when they come, test all your skill and vigilance to the uttermost.

I feel, therefore, it is time that we once again followed the trail of the wild grey geese and that we have dallied long enough among the inland fields and woods.

20. *Wildfowling in Ireland*

THE Ultima Thule of the longshore gunner is surely Ireland. Long after all our English localities are ruined by shore-poppers, bombing ranges, and flying fields, there will be the wild bogs and bays of the rugged west coast which will be safe havens for duck and geese, places where roads are non-existent, bogs are deep, and above all no accommodation can be obtained by the most enthusiastic and hardy fowler. From Horn Head to Slieve League, from Sligo Bay to Bartragh Island, from Killala to Achill Sound here, as that knowledgeable writer 'Paddy Flynn' has said, are vast tracts of country, untamed, unspoilt, where the geese and duck are teeming. Kilkieran, Cashel, Renvyle, the vast flats near Dugort and north of Achill Head, there is great 'goose country' for you, there is adventure and privation awaiting the enterprising gunner and bird watcher, for the man who does not mind bog tramping, black mire, and wet clothes.

I can claim no experiences of goose hunting in Ireland, I have yet to visit that emerald land in winter time; I only know the south, in early autumn, with its fuschia hedges and cloud-patched green mountains, its still deep lakes and islands innumerable.

For a few memorable weeks I stayed in a little village near a large lough noted for its trout and salmon. I went to Ireland to fish but also took my gun. I was glad I did so.

The trout and salmon would have none of me. For several days Teehan, my gillie, rowed me about the lake until his arms must have ached as much as mine did from perpetual casting. Perhaps my mind was not on my job. After all, how could it be? I, by nature no great fisher but a longshore gunner! It was not in the grey wastes of mid-loch where I found interest, it was around the wooded islands, the fringes of the green bogs, and most of all, in a vast willow-girt bottomless bog at the northern end of the lake. For there in the evenings, as the boat glided along in the shallows, team after team of gleaming mallard sprang up, some in easy shot. It was there, if you landed on the peaty banks, that every step rose a snipe—how could I think of fishing with the gun ready to my hand?

So I forsook the Greenheart and Teehan rejoiced for he also was a shooter by nature, and liked the gun better than the rod; more-over, he had a lovely red setter which, he said, was a paragon among dogs, and which he offered to sell me for ten pounds on my return to England. Henceforth, for the rest of the time, I shot to my heart's content.

I have never been a keen snipe hunter, but in the south that year I almost became one. At first I missed bird after bird because I was unused to the game.

My experience of snipe was of the odd bird springing from the dyke at home, from the little winter ditches and horse ponds of the midlands, and the occasional one which jumped under my feet as I was walking out to flight by Curlew Bay.

At first I shot too late, and then too soon, I shot too high, too low, and I felt a fool. But soon I got the knack, firing with number eight shot as soon as the snipe jumped, taking that snap shot which is instinctive, when there is no time to think of 'follow throughs' or forward allowances.

I was shooting at a disadvantage because I had my three-inch goose gun, somehow I had forgotten to bring my game gun, but even so, after a day or so I was bringing my bird down. It was the first time I had shot over a setter, and I thought it wonderful sport.

The ranging setter would come to a stop and gently we would steal up behind. Now and again the dog would look over its shoulder at us as though to say, 'Hurry up, you idiot' and every second I found myself waiting with taut nerves for that sudden tearing sound as the snipe jumped.

There was that wonderful day when Teehan told me we would try for a grouse. The grouse, he said, were way up on the mountain tops at the head of the lake, and it took us two hours to row down, past the wooded island where the wild goats lived, past the long stony island where the hermit's cell is still to be seen (a curious haunted island peopled by innumerable rabbits). One day we had landed there to eat our lunch while we were fishing and within the bramble-grown ruin, in a little niche in the wall, was a yellow skull which some said was the hermit's skull.

Teehan, superstitious Irishman that he was, would not go near the ruin, but he told me I should find the skull there, and I did. Once, so he told me, a visiting fisherman (I regret to say he came from the U.S.A.) removed the skull, intending to take it home with him. But his boatman refused to row him ashore, and would not allow him near the boat until he had replaced the skull in its niche in the wall. When the story got around the native disapproval was so strong that the fisherman had to depart.

On we went, then, to the head of the bog, following a narrow and deep winding river and beaching the boat on a shingly shore. We climbed away from the lake until it lay below us like a blue harp, we climbed up to the misty heights until the clouds came down and shut out all the valleys, and I was transported from a sunlit smiling world of summer green to a clammy November fog through which there suddenly loomed at intervals huge jagged pinnacles of rock gleaming wet with moisture, and where a silence closed around us, broken only by the squelch of our boots in the spongy peat.

It was a naked primeval world above the clouds, even Teehan was not sure of his ground until we had called at a cabin in a glen where dwelt a friend of his, a farmer, who went with us over the mountain.

I do not know how many miles we walked that day, I do know that all I saw of a grouse was the tail bird of a pack which I glimpsed whipping over the crest of a low boggy hill. Grouse had been about there in plenty for we came upon their piles of drop-pings, but from midday to five o'clock I never pressed a trigger, and so the day was a failure.

We went back to the cabin where the farmer's mother sat over a peat fire, an ancient leather-bound Bible on her lap. I remember the face of that old lady now, so calm and serene, like that of Rembrandt's mother.

We were ravenous after our climb and fed heartily on home-baked bread, multitudes of eggs, and thick slices of tender beetroot. When, on parting, I tried to press a token of gratitude into the hand of our host, I realized that I had been guilty of a breach of good manners.

I remember the long climb down to the boat, it was twilight before we reached it.

Teams of duck and trips of teal were heading away from the bog against the yellow western sky, and as we rowed quietly past the wooded island a wild goat was outlined on a crag, staring down at us.

There was a small very deep lake to the north of the main lough which was a great haunt of teal. The water was a deep, deep brown, almost black, and there was no cover, no screening vegeta-tion which made an easy approach possible. But one afternoon, by crawling and creeping through the soft bog, I gained a rock upon its verge, and peeping over surprised a spring of teal. I had a right and left, though the second bird gave me a lot of trouble before I found him hiding under a tuft of rush.

There was another place which was a favourite haunt of mallard, a quiet backwater of the lake screened by reeds and high smooth boulders. Every time we went that way we jumped a party of mallard, and I do not think we ever stalked this bay without accounting for a duck. I felt more at home with these bog mallard than the snipe, and I did not miss many that rose in range. In any case, a rising mallard is a fairly easy shot, perhaps the easiest of all shots with the exception of a grouse. I can usually account for a grouse if it gets up in range.

Another good place was a peaty islet in the lake itself which lay in a remote arm on the west side. There was a large and very deep pool on this islet ringed round with smooth domes of rock, an easy enough place to stalk.

One afternoon Teehan landed me on the shore and I stalked through the heather to the foot of a large boulder which was on the edge of this pool. Peeping over I could see nothing, and raising myself a little higher I suddenly glimpsed the bottle-green head of a drake mallard directly below me. He saw me the instant I saw him and up he got with a great quacking, two ducks with him. I fired at the drake and missed, for I was half-kneeling on the rock, but my second shot crumpled him belly up on the black water, where his brilliant orange paddles kicked once or twice and then were still.

The body slowly drifted in to the foot of the rock just below me. Meanwhile Teehan was rowing up the deep arm which connected the pool with the main lake and just as I began to descend the rock, he brought the boat alongside. The high wind, however, drifted the boat past the bird, and I thought I could easily reach it.

I took another cautious, downward step, with my heel against the rock, when I felt myself slipping. Under me was thirty feet of black water and I had my gutty boots on. I slid gracefully downwards, spread-eagled against the rock, desperately digging in my heels.

The icy water gently crept upwards to my arm pits when my heel lodged on an underwater ledge which could not have been more than an inch in width but it was enough to halt my progress.

There I remained, flat against the rock, the icy water lapping my chest and the body of the mallard almost bobbing against my mouth.

Teehan, seeing what had happened, tried to bring the boat about, but the wind was so strong he could not make it. Somehow, after a pause to weigh up the situation, I managed to jitter along the ledge with my heels until I found a better purchase, when I turned about and scrambled up to safety, Teehan retrieving the bird a few minutes later. Had I gone right off the rock I do not know if I could have kept my head above water, as my big boots would have filled, and I should have had a terrible job to kick them off. Also I am a very indifferent swimmer.

I asked Teehan once about the wild geese which came in the winter. He called them 'Scotch geese', by which I gathered that they were greylags. They would certainly not be pinks as the pinks are rare in Ireland, and from his description I do not think they could have been whitefronts.

Though they came in some numbers to the bogs about the lake, Teehan told me they were hard to come to terms with.

This is often so in wild broken country, as the birds have no set flight lines (as they are more inclined to have on an estuary) and Teehan himself never bothered about them very much, in any case; snipe were more in his line.

So much for my brief experiences of Irish shooting and I shall not forget Teehan's last words to me. "Come again, Sorr; come in the winter when the woodcock are in, and the Scotch geese are here. You can't walk a yard, but you kick against a snipe. Come again, Sorr, and you'll have some *real* shooting."

And one day I am going back.

21. *Lone Lindisfarne*

A LOT of sentimental rubbish has been written about Holy Island, or Lindisfarne, and I shall have to be careful not to err in this respect. Of late years, since the coming of the charabanc (hateful vehicle) and the car, much of its romance and mystery has been dispelled. If that Grandfather of all wild-fowlers, Abel Chapman, whose favourite haunt it was, could return to-day, in summer, to watch his beloved 'globe spanners', he would, I think, get a nasty shock. It is becoming tripper-ridden, a fate which befalls many of the beautiful wild places where forty years ago one never met a soul.

I did not, of course, know Holy Island in Abel Chapman's time, but since boyhood I had been familiar with it from his books, particularly from those chapters in *The Borders and Beyond* and *Bird Life of the Borders*. And as Abel Chapman had always been a sort of hero to me it gave me a great thrill to meet old Selby, his punts-man, when I visited the district in 1929. Selby was then a great age, well over eighty, but seemed very hale and hearty, and appeared little different from his photographs which I had seen in Chapman's books.

It was on the slob lands of Fenham Flats that Chapman collected so much of his interesting data concerning the passage migrants, the waders, and the geese. Up till then nobody had really studied the subject at first hand. Chapman possessed deep knowledge, not only of birds, be it said, but of butterflies and animals as well, in fact he was a very great naturalist in every sense of the word and no mean artist.

He drew the birds he saw and though some are quaint and some-what 'wooden' he did, at times, bring off some excellent studies. His eye was searching and very little escaped him.

His knowledge of fish was extensive, too, especially of salmon, for Chapman was a keen fisherman as well as a 'shot'.

His literary style is somewhat verbose, and at times heavy on the hand, well larded with Latin tags and with copious footnotes. But despite this he gets into his writing a wonderful sense of the long-shore gunner's delight in his sport (and the puntsman's also) and through it all shines the man's boundless enthusiasm for his subject. This makes his books very readable.

I went to Holy Island, or rather to the district, several times. I was not drawn thither by the sport, which is poor from the shoulder gunner's point of view, unless he is a keen duck hunter; it was the wonderful teeming bird life which fascinated me and the strange bleakness of that part of the Northumberland coast.

I stayed at a farm, or rather an old mill, Fenham Mill, which was situated right on the edge of the mainland opposite Lindis-farne, and what comfortable quarters they were! Wonderful food, home-cured hams, and good 'farmhouse fare', most excellently cooked by the lady who looked after us. From our window we could look directly on to the slob lands, and at night wigeon whistled all round the house.

Fenham Slakes, or the slob, as it is called, is a vast mud-filled tidal dish, one extensive 'plickplack', but unlike the latter, you can-not walk on it. There is, of course, plenty of sand far out, but near the shore it is black odoriferous mud, and it cannot be traversed save with mud pattens. I have a horror of mud (as I have of quicksands) and I did not employ a local fowler, which I might well have done. Consequently I did most of my shooting along the edge of the slakes, and a certain amount of wigeon flighting from the stone butts a little way out from the land. Also, I was lucky enough to get an introduction to the owner of the Ross Links, a tract of arable land and sandhills lying on the south side of the slakes.

Strange to say, Lindisfarne is the only place where I have seen Brent geese (I am not familiar with their great stronghold, the Essex marshes) and the chances of bagging a Brent with a shoulder gun from the shore at Holy Island are very remote (as indeed they are elsewhere), unless one goes out to the Beacons on the Ross Links when a gale of wind is blowing.

The Brent do not usually frequent Holy Island in very great numbers, though in hard weather Chapman tells of many thousands. But that is exceptional: in an open winter I doubt whether there is a resident pack of more than six or seven hundred Brents. I may be corrected in this statement by those who know Holy Island better than myself: I am only giving my own observations, made during several winters from 1929 onwards. And in all fairness I must admit that while I was there we had no arctic weather, it was for the most part open, with a week or so of fairly hard frost.

My usual procedure was to walk up the shore from Fenham Mill to the Ross Links, spend the afternoon and early evening there, and return at dusk along the shore; and if it was moonlight, go out to the stone 'pulpits' for the wigeon.

I found the wigeon wary, though I believe much better sport may be had from the Beacons. I never went there, but recently I had a letter from an Eton boy who has been on one or two occasions and, he tells me, he had great sport with wigeon.

An amusing thing happened one night when I was sitting in one of the stone pulpits. It was moonlight, with an overcast sky. Wigeon had been flying about but none in shot when, without any warning, one came in from behind me and actually settled on my

head! I was astonished (not to say alarmed) for the sudden, rush‚
ing apparition appeared so suddenly, plumping down right on
top of my balaclava. To this day it is a puzzle to me why the bird
did this, as wigeon rarely settle on rocks.

I suppose there is not another place in Britain where so many
waders congregate, at least within view of the glasses, than on these
slob lands by Lindisfarne. When the tide begins to flow they
crowd the edge of the advancing water, knots by the thousand,
redshanks, dunlins, curlews and whimbrels: it is a paradise for the
bird watcher.

At about eleven o'clock each morning I would hear the far
trumpetings of the Brents coming in to feed, and away over the
Castle I would see a bundle of black specks approaching from the
open sea. The only chance I had of bagging a Brent occurred at
high water. I had walked with a friend up to the Ross Links, and
was on my way home when we separated. I went to a stone butt
on the shore for the chance of a duck and my companion went on
down towards the Mill.

After about an hour I heard two distant shots and saw two
Brent flying along on the edge of the tide towards me. They had
come from the direction of the Mill and at first I thought I was
going to get a shot. But as they came nearer they saw me and
swerved aside, going out to the slob.

Afterwards my friend told me that he had seen these two geese
sitting on the shore in quite a stalkable position as they were
below a bank. He had no gun with him (he was a bird watcher,
not a shooter) but seeing two fowlers not far off he went across and
told them of the birds. They made a clumsy and unsuccessful
stalk. It was their shot which I had heard. If only he had come
back for me I might have been more successful.

The farmer at the Mill told me that many times, in bad weather
and at high tides, the Brents would swim within easy range of the
stone wall by the Mill and he had often shot them.

The Brent are kingly little geese. Though small, like the barn-acle, they are worth-while game and are true geese. Their beautiful black heads and necks, and the white ring around them, give them a distinguished appearance. Their heads are more 'reptilian' than those of the other geese, reminding me rather of the heads of whooper swans.

Though I was unsuccessful on the shore, bagging only an occasional mallard or wigeon under the moon, I fared better on the Ross Links, as besides some excellent rough shooting—snipe, hare, etc.—there was always the chance of geese.

Grey geese are regular visitors to this district: pink-footed geese mostly, and occasional greylags and whitefronts have been recorded. They feed mostly on the arable lands behind the Ross Links. Some winters they are more plentiful than others, and when I was at Lindisfarne there appeared to be a resident party of pinks numbering about thirty birds. I was lucky enough to bag one of these, as I have described in a former chapter.

But I had several exciting stalks at the geese on the fields without, however, achieving any results. Goose stalking is a tiresome, messy business and, though exciting enough, success only comes occasionally.

I remember one late winter afternoon, with a fiery sunset glowing behind the Cheviots, stalking a party of pinks which had settled on a small grass field behind some hay stacks. I spent a long time over my stalk and reached the stacks. Then I saw that among these birds was a lovely albino pink.

My companion that year walked round the geese to try to drive them over me, but, of course, they all went wide of the stacks and the last I saw of them was an undulating line, the white goose amongst them, disappearing over the dunes in the direction of Budle Bay.

It is at night that the romance of Lindisfarne makes itself felt.

Sitting out alone in one of the stone pulpits, the dancing winking stars from the houses on the island are reflected in the slob lands, wavering lines of light which reach almost to one's feet. Far away can be heard the dull continuous roar of the surf breaking on the sand bars beyond the island, and from every hand come the 'wheeos' of the wigeon.

Many thousands of these lovely little ducks infest the muds during the hours of darkness, and ever and again one can hear the rush of the big packs passing high overhead.

Perhaps a punt gun booms out across the slobs, followed by the yodelling of the curlews and the cheetering and teetering of the dunlin and knot. Knot are particularly abundant on Fenham Slakes; I have seen more there than anywhere else in my wanderings, and it amused me to stalk them at night under the moon. They make a miniature buzzing similar to that made by feeding geese.

It always seems a shame to shoot these dumpy, little, trusting waders, though it must be admitted that they are very toothsome, and I fear that fact carries some weight with your true longshore gunner.

To get good sport at Lindisfarne you must have no fear of mud, you must be able to walk in pattens (which to me is as difficult as skiing) and you must be content to lie out all night in some creek or hide on a mussel bed and take what comes. On favourable nights, as Chapman tells, very good and varied bags may be obtained, but I prefer the firmer ground for my shooting, the greygreen salting or the hard high sands.

I heard several grisly stories of people trapped in the mud and Chapman and Selby were nearly drowned on several occasions, the most notable being when their punt capsized in a rough sea. It was to Fenham Mill that Chapman managed to struggle, but only after a grim battle with tide, mud, and wind.

I can well understand the fascination this district had on Chapman; he seemed to prefer it to any other in the British Isles. He does not appear to have done much fowling farther north, at least he does not give any accounts of his shooting beyond the Border. No doubt the varied wader life drew him, as he enjoyed watching fowl as much as shooting them, which every true longshore gunner should do, but it is a pity we have no descriptions of days and nights, say, on the Solway, or Beauly and Dornoch Firths.

One day I shall go back to Lindisfarne, if only to see once more the twisted hedgerow trees, visible reminders of the force of wild winter gales: the dark silhouette of the Castle rising up in the moon-light over the slakes: and to hear once again the sound of the surf beating on the rocky shores by Bamburgh and Budle Bay.

It is all good country and possesses a wildness and loneliness (out of the tripper season) which appeals to the heart and mind of the longshore gunner.

22. *The Wild Grey Geese of Kirkconnon*

THERE is an estuary on the coast of Scotland which is unlike any other I know. It is small and the marshes are not extensive, but it is remote and not overshot. The wild scenery and romantic surroundings make it a most attractive locality. I will call it Kirkconnon. This is not its real name, but for obvious reasons I am not going to give its map reference because I hope to go there again one day.

Two things are imprinted on my mind when I think of Kirkconnon. Oddly enough, they have nothing to do with wildfowling. One, a grey gaunt building, like a convent, on the right of the lane as you come up the hill. Each night when I came home from flighting, weary and sweating with the long tramp and the steep hill, I saw this dour building rise up before me, and one room was always lighted. Through the window I could see, festooned across the ceiling, the Hogmanay decorations not yet taken down, green and scarlet paper wreaths, with here and there a brightly coloured bell suspended. I never saw anyone moving in the room (after all, I could only see the ceiling) but no doubt bairns dwelt there. Yet it seemed a house of the dead. Even in daylight when I passed it by I neither saw nor heard life within—mysterious house!

The other thing I remember about the village is its population of jackdaws. Now these jackdaws were no ordinary jackdaws. They were true inhabitants of Kirkconnon, as much as the people who dwelt in the low whitewashed houses (one-storied). The birds, in a sense, lived in the houses too, for they roosted in the 'lums' or chimneys *and* nested in them. These surprising birds were always visible, sitting on the chimney-pots during the day, or circling and playing about the tower of the kirk. One woman told me that in the nesting season they were a perfect nuisance, filling the 'lums' with sticks and blocking up the flues. Yet the jackdaws of Kirk-connon have always been there, and I should imagine they always will be, for as long as the stones stand one upon the other, for as long as there are 'lums' to nest and sleep in.

The bairns of the village are well behaved, much more mannerly than those in an average English village. When they see a wild-fowling stranger pass by in his absurd get-up—balaclava helmet, muffler, leather coat, and thigh or 'gutty' boots, with bag on back and with nose a rosy red—they hardly notice him. Perhaps they are used to such sights.

But it is not of the village and its people I would speak, it is of the green marshes which ring it round and where I have had so many happy, albeit chilly, hours.

The grass upon those saltings is fine, almost lawn-like. Here and there are shallow pans or flashes. Some are not shallow. You cannot tell. Tramping back from Portsollon Marsh at night you have to jump them, it is better so. In broad day you may observe that the majority are not more than three inches deep, but some will be over the tops of your 'gutty' boots.

There are creeks, of course, but not so many as on other marshes which I know—the Wash, for instance. But they form fine hidey-holes for gunners on dawn and evening flight, especially near the sea, where they are deep and not too wide.

And across these marshes the greylags flight at dawn, and very often, during the midday hours, you may see the grey geese at feed, some six or seven hundred of them, on that part of the marsh known as the Kirk Moss, just below the harbour.

These geese are treated fairly by the local gunners. They are not harried all day long (and all night too) as they are in other places. It is not 'done' at Kirkconnon to disturb them when they are resting on the sands. This would be an easy thing to do, and a deadly attack could be planned, for numerous branching creeks intersect their sleeping sands. But they are left alone. The geese take a sporting view of this agreement too, and incidentally provide fair shots for bankward gunners on the morning flight. It is an excellent arrangement. Only visiting gunners, mostly in ignorance, and with a mild wonder at the trustful geese, break the unwritten law. They soon hear about it from the 'boys'.

Large-bore guns, such as eights, are frowned upon, they make too much noise, though this view is mostly expressed by the punts-men. When you point out that a punt-gun causes far greater disturbance, there is a shaking of heads.

However, I always prefer an eight-bore for geese; it kills more surely and one does not lose so many wounded birds. I sometimes use a single eight and thereby miss a good many geese through lack of a second barrel, but as I do not wish to kill very many geese, this does not worry me.

Come with Angus and me, then, this January night, to try for a wigeon on Portsollon. It will be a long tramp, for we have no car to take us. Hired cycles will help, but we shall still have a weary bog-jumping tramp to reach the place I have in mind. The fire is blazing high in the grate and we are sleepy for we have been out at dawn for the geese, we have also eaten well, for these are good quarters in Kirkconnon, so much so that (dare I whisper it?) we even find hot bottles in our beds, an unheard-of thing for wild-fowlers!

I looked at my watch. It was half-past ten. Angus lay sleeping, head aslant, mouth agape, on the other side of the warm fire. I went to the window and drew aside the curtain.

At first the night seemed dark and then the square became

visible, faintly lit by a three-quarter moon. Stars were shining and there were a few clouds. This was not a good night, not yet, but I hoped that, later, clouds would come.

Angus roused, we dressed; first the muffler, cartridge belt, leather coat, and then the 'gutty' boots. I checked up on flashlight (useful this for seeking a fallen bird), cartridge extractor, 'sit' bag, which contained an air cushion (and will hold four greylag geese should the happy event require it), mittens and gloves, and we were ready.

Clad, then, like deep-sea divers, we clumped down the stairs, and out into the cobbled yard to the shed where we housed our rickety cycles. Neither had brakes and there were one or two steep hills to negotiate. Be that as it may, off we started, and soon the village and haunts of man were left behind.

It was not a very cold night. The hedges and ditches were sweet to the nostrils, a warm and leafy smell, oddly reminding me of woods at home. The moon lighted our way, there was barely need for lamps.

We reached the lane-head, hid our cycles behind the hedge, and tramped down the green lane flanked by trees.

Soon we saw the marsh, grey-green, pitted with bog holes and runnels. A hundred little burnlets run down from the ditches to Portsollon, and where they spew on to the marsh itself the ground is boggy and green, in the dark you will sink above your 'gutty' boots in places (if you are unwary).

I decided to go to the old fallen tree cast up on Portsollon edge; Angus was going to a pet hidey-hole of his own on Portsollon tip. Like birds, wildfowlers have their favoured places which they regard as their own by right of discovery.

For a while, however, our ways lay together. Soon the sweat was beginning to run into my eyebrows. It was hard work tramping the marsh, dodging the holes, balancing from tussock to tussock, jumping the flashes. We came to the sheep bridge. Seven feet under, the Bogle Burn gurgled. At high water, on a biggish tide, the planks of the bridge are awash; to look at it now you would never have guessed it could ever rise so high. In truth, Portsollon is a dangerous marsh to the unwary. Once over the bridge you have the Bogle Burn between you and the high land, so you must be cautious of the tide.

But there was no high water to-night to threaten, to steal, like a murderous assassin, behind us and cut us off. It would barely reach the edge of the 'green'.

Beyond the bridge I said good-bye to Angus with the usual "good luck, good shooting", and heard him splashing away until his dim figure melted into his surroundings.

I now struck across the marsh on an easterly course. Now and again I thought I heard the whistle of a wigeon, but I did not stop. I wished to reach the tree before shooting.

The 'flashes' became more continuous, snaking about like a jig-saw puzzle. I jumped and jumped. The sweat ran down.

And then I saw the moonlight shining on the knotted branches of the water-worn tree. Impervious as a boat to the boring of the tides it lay there, deeply grounded in white—pure white—shingle, and anchored securely by two pointed arms driven deep into the marsh.

Beyond it the 'green' ended abruptly in a mass of tumbled turves, a patch or two of pure white sand, a little shingle, and the sea itself. The tide was dropping back, I could hear its low rustle and murmur. The clear yodelling whistles of many curlews sounded. I saw their dim shapes passing up the tide edge.

Behind the tree was a cavity in the sand, made by the action of the tides, a sort of oblong empty bath. In the centre stood a clean-looking tide-washed wooden box. Empty cartridge cases were strewn around. Obviously this was the favourite perch of a moon-light wigeon-shooter.

I sat down, sweating, on the box. I took off my woollen helmet and felt the cold night air about my wet hair. It was delicious. What of the night?

As I thought, clouds were forming, banking up high above the mountains at the throat of the bay. They covered the very tops with a deep and forbidding pall. Already filmy masses were very slowly drifting up towards the clean-edged pale moon which rode high on my left, casting dark shadows from the tree and throwing my own shadow in weird and distorted form upon the white sand.

I have never known such a sense of complete peace as I experienced that night on Portsollon. No wind stirred the grasses of the marsh or fanned the cheek, and the only sound was the faint and far-off talk of geese out on the sands to seaward, and now and again a curlew's call or wigeon's 'wheeo'.

This marsh is a favourite feeding-ground of the wigeon. But this little duck (the cock is the most beautiful of all our British ducks) is rather a bird of mystery. One never knows where or when they will feed. One night they may be here, on Portsollon, another, they will be way beyond the harbour, or the Kirriemoss. Even Robert MacCrae, the local fowler, cannot tell you where they will be. Would they favour me to-night? Would Angus be lucky?

Kirkconnon was now beginning to put out its lights. Like the embers of a dying fire they vanished one by one until a single light remained, burning in a farmhouse window a mile away beyond Kirriemoss.

At half-past one of the clock that light still burned; I sat and wondered why. Some farmer, maybe, poring over a tangle of accounts and red tape; sickness perhaps, a child tossing on its little bed; a good book? An argument? A lad and a lassie? How should I know?

Were the wigeon waiting for that last light to snuff out before daring the green and sinister gloom of Portsollon? They had safety on the sea, but food they *must* have, the marshes must be dared *somewhere* along their length.

I have often thought how the wildfowl must dread this nightly approach to the marshes, their feeding ground. I have talked with Robert MacCrae, the fowler in Kirkconnon, and he has told me how he has sometimes hidden himself in a seaward creek and seen the greylag geese walk in for sleep. They are led by one old gander whose neck is like a poker. He comes with stately carriage, his quick and cunning eye turns hither and thither, now and again he stops and utters a warning croak of danger. Behind him come his clan, trusting to his watchfulness, pecking from side to side but stopping when the leader stops.

They come on, clearly visible now to the man whose face is within an inch of the broken sea shells in the dyke. He can hear the sticky 'plickplack' of their paddles on the mud.

So they have come, so has the leader come, until Robert could have stretched forth his hand and touched that noble fowl. But the gun is left alone in awe of their loveliness. Robert respects the geese, though he likes shooting them, shooting them fairly, that is, on the morning flight. He is not an assassin stabbing them in the back as they sleep upon the merse edge. Nor does Robert enjoy making huge bags of geese. It sometimes happens that big bags are made.

Only a day or so before the night I am attempting to describe, two gunners shot thirteen geese on Portsollon tip on the morning flight. They were using decoys. But the sight of a bundle of big orange bills and brown heads tied together by the neck, the limp, plump bodies with wings awry, piled on the stone floor of our fowling quarters, filled me with sorrow. Most wildfowlers want one good day at the geese, I have done so myself, but once you have shot more than eight geese at one flight the joy has gone.

The shadows from creek and gully were forbidding and weird. Was not there a ship lost with all hands in the mouth of the bay three days ago when the gale blew with such fury? (The morning I shot two greylags on Kirriemoss.)

What was that whitish object on the shore over there, oblong, horrible? Had not Robert told me of how (two nights ago) he lay out here with Wullie Bell, the laddie who has just come back from the wars?

Robert and he were waiting, as I was this night, for the wigeon. And Robert saw an object lying in a creek-mouth a few yards away. "Wullie, it's a mon, a dead mon, I'm tellin' ye, one o' the puir fellows lost on the ship out yonder. Go you and see, Wullie."

"Na! Na!" says Wullie. "I'm na goin' to see!"

"An' you a soldier!" Robert tells him.

But Wullie starts up. "I'm awa' hame," says he, "I'll no like the marsh the nicht, I'll awa' hame!"

And 'hame' he went. Robert gets up from his seat and walks over. It was no corpse but something, indeed, from the wreck— a lifebelt. And an oar was there as well!

This object that I glimpsed so fearfully proved to be an empty ammunition box. Like the belt that Robert found, it was from the wreck, and I knew that two bodies had, the day before, been washed up on the other side of the bay. Five were still missing.

Yet why should a poor drowned body seem so fearful? No different, surely, than the body of the greylag I passed coming over the marsh!

Now I looked behind me. The clouds about the mountains were thickening, pouring down a wide corrie like smoke in a bottleneck. And the bright moonlight dimmed. It was as though I were in some darkened chamber, and an invisible hand had stretched forth and drawn-to a curtain.

Looking up at the moon I saw it veiled with filmy cloud, slowly drifting cloud. The 'flashes' in the marsh grew dim. There was a rustling of wings, and then the cheeping elfin squeaks which a wigeon pack makes when in flight. They passed somewhere close by me, I heard the sudden growing *russsh* of their wings, but I could not see them. They sped towards Portsollon tip where

I knew Angus was awaiting them. Sure enough, the quiet of the night was broken by two ringing shots. Then silence.

Now my straining ears caught a continual whisper of wings. I had a glimpse or two of speeding shapes, half seen, low over the marsh, but no chance of a shot.

"Wheeo! Wheeo!" the fluting whistles were sounding, now here, now there. Then against the filmy moonlight ceiling high above I saw three swiftly moving objects like beer bottles. The wings were invisible. The gun swings up, and at the report I hear an answering thump.

The wigeon, a lovely cock, was clearly discovered lying, breast up, on the dark marsh. There was no need of the torch to find him. I retired again to my soap-box beside the tree.

A big pack of wigeon were now on the move somewhere, again and again I heard the *russsh*, the cheeping squeaks, pass and repass. But not another shot did I have for a full hour.

I looked towards the line of trees which marked the land. The farmhouse light had gone at last, the love-making was done, the book was closed, the feverish child slept.

It was now that small chill hour when the heart of man (so they tell us) beats most feebly, that hour when the ill and aged break adrift from their moorings and go out into the dark, unknown sea which must one day receive us all.

Yet though man slept the birds were full awake, throbbing with the warm fire of life. Far away I heard the clear thin crow of a farmyard cock. And, listening carefully, I heard another answer it from across the bay.

Darker grew the moonlight. The moon itself was tilting and dipping. The shadows from the creeks stretched long; just as the evening sun casts shadows across the meads, so does the sinking moon.

Something dropped straight out of the sky on to a flash not ten yards from where I sat. Clearly, for one second, I saw the outline of a wigeon sitting framed against the bright water. The gun moved, the wigeon sprang up, to be instantly invisible. Yet I fired instinctively, and I heard it drop with a splash. It was a wigeon duck.

Minute by minute the moon sank lower, the shadows grew longer. This was a queer little-known world, at this small dim hour when other men slept. Somehow or another the wigeon knew that all was not well on the marsh. Perhaps they had heard the solitary shots, perhaps some sharp-eyed scout, used to this time of deepest night, had seen a dark and baleful shadow by the tree, or the white-faced Angus peering upwards from the creek at Portsollon tip. At any rate they did not come.

My body became a nuisance, complaining at being kept awake instead of being wrapped up in a warm bed and within walls. A sudden shiver took me through the small of my back. I rose from the soap-box. I wanted to stay. My mind was keen and alive, wanting me to stay. My body was irritated.

But it was no use. The wigeon were not coming, they would await moonsetting, they knew perhaps that the eyes that aim the deadly barrel must have light to do so. And so I set off on the long tramp to the sheep bridge, my body happy now in movement after so long a period of inaction.

But before I had traversed half the marsh, the moon, tilting ever more absurdly, as though tumbling backwards, sank into the dark black shadows of the Moss of Connon, and it was by starlight only that I continued on my way. I lost sense of direction and was brought up by the Bogle Burn, rushing merrily with daytime talk (despite this secret hour) between its sloping cushions of mud.

I was far above the sheep bridge, it would be quicker to strike left and follow the burn along to Kirriemoss. There I could rejoin the road without crossing the burn, and no doubt I should meet Angus at the head of the lane.

The way was not so easy as I had imagined. Yawning pits

opened up under my feet, other gulleys which led into the banks of the burn. Down into them I slipped and slithered, hauling myself up by the tufts of wiry grass, panting with the exertion, sweating with the effort.

But at long last I hit the road, and with only pinpricks of stars showing between the topmost branches of the bare hedgerow trees I at length reached the head of the lane and saw the dim glimmer of my cycle awaiting me in the hedge. Angus's cycle was not there—so he had gone on before and was now, in all probability, well tucked up in his warm bed, oblivious of the world.

Tired though my body was, I stood there in that dark and lonely place listening to and smelling the beauty of the night. How soundless was this secret hour!

Above my head, in an oak-tree, I could make out the dim mass of a crow's nest, built in the merry bustling days of spring when the sun shone and the buds were breaking. The architects—where were they? Had their plans reached fruition? Had the family flown unharmed?

I have been abroad at dead of night in a great city and felt its sorrow and its sin. But here man played no part. I had less business to be there than the hunting owl, whose trembling, mournful cry I heard at that moment, as he quartered the heathery swamps and birch thickets of the Moss of Connon.

23. *The Life and Habits of Wildfowl*

THERE is a new moon in its first quarter. The tide is beginning to flood up the gutters. The time is near 1 a.m. on a wild January night.

Out of the nor'east comes a roaring wind, driving the snow in madly whirling flakes, jagged crystals which sting the cheek, a wind which pierces through and through like a sword.

In the warm stacks on the flat fields (they are weighed down with massive stones suspended from ropes, each stack 'wrapped about with bandage stout' like the Dong's nose of Lear's poem) the little finches and sparrows cuddle cosily, buntings with them.

About them is the smell of summer, of lazy days in the hayfields when the linnets and greenfinches sing; they scarcely hear the boom of the gale without, no man sleeps more sound or as snug as they.

In the ivy on the leeward side of trees wrens huddle close in family parties, tiny mites who strive so gallantly to keep the spark of life burning in these bitter days of midwinter. No rabbit ventures abroad, they are well below ground; so are the badgers in their ancestral setts. Sheep find shelter behind stone walls or barns, cattle are safely housed. In farmhouse and cottage the lights have been put out; men, women and children lie under that same magic spell of sleep, cosy, safe, and warm, tucked away from the icy storm outside. The mice, too, are full-fed, warming themselves by ruined kitchen fires.

What in Heaven's name do the wild grey geese do on such a night as this? The ducks, the mallards, even the wigeons cannot face this bellowing icy darkness; they left before dusk and are away in sheltered bays and tree-girt ponds well known to them as refuges. The curlews, also, are looking after themselves, they are crouching in the rough tussocks beyond the 'plickplack', like the big fieldfares, who seldom roost in hedges.

Out on the sand banks, half a mile or more from shore, with not a stick nor stone for shelter, are the geese, the whole grand army, over a thousand strong. The snow settles on their breasts and backs, and along the creases of their necks (heads are tucked into backs, eyes only are covered, those little brown windows through which they look so fearfully out at life).

Most are sitting down, every bird head to wind, or rather, breast to wind, a little conical pile of droppings under each tail. They can sleep secure. No punt can steal upon them on such a night, no boat could live in such a sea. The wind raves and whines, sinks a little as if to gather strength, then roars anew. The sand particles fly and mingle with the cutting snow flakes. Clots of foam are caught up and whirl through the darkness. Yet the geese sleep.

As a background to their dreams (and surely birds dream if dogs and men do so) the thunder and turmoil of the surf, breaking on the outer edge of the sand bars, beats a steady thunderous tattoo. As the tide rises, backed by the wind, the tumult grows and shakes the sand banks under them.

Then over the flats the tide comes racing, on and on towards the sleeping geese.

The snow clouds thin, the quarter moon gleams out, like the half-closed eye of God looking down upon His charges. And at that moment the outermost geese feel the water swill about their paddles. Heads are untucked on the instant and the wind whips their complaint away.

Those birds on the outermost fringes of the gaggle stand up, one after another, and flap their wings, and so strong is the tide racing, and so deep, they gently kick with their paddles and are afloat.

But once the water has covered the sand, small waves run side-ways in vicious darts, bigger weightier waves follow through with a burst and boom of foam.

The outermost ranks of geese rise, calling wildly, and scores of heads are jerked forth from snow-covered backs. Bird after bird gets up and beats its wings to shake away the frozen snow. The rest of the gaggle do not wait to feel the icy onslaught. A mass of wings are spread, those precious, precious vanes which bear their owners so securely from danger and which bring them so surely to the pastures of peace. The thunder of the rising gaggle for a moment masters the roar of the storm.

For a few beats they head into the wind then, turning, the gale whips them round, it almost blows their short tail coverts up on end. Away go the big birds like so many puffs of thistle down, over a thousand pounds' weight of goose flesh, carried away as if they weighed no more than thistle down, or the spume which is whipped from the curling crests of the churning waves!

In a matter of minutes the sand-banks are covered, hidden by an angry white smother of breakers, which come slamming in from all directions, pounding the big banks until the sand particles turn the water a muddy hue, like a burn in spate.

But where are the geese to go? There is barely a glimmer of moon and now, again, the snow is flying. They cannot venture inland in this pitch blackness for geese can see little better than a man when there is no moon. If they are borne inland they may perhaps, by instinct, find some open field they know of, but foxes, their old arctic enemies, are there and can steal on them in the blackness. The only refuge that remains is the 'plickplack' or the saltings.

No gunner will be out on such a night as this, not because of the wind and snow, for such things are prayed for by the longshore gunner, but because he could not see to guide his deadly tubes of death. There is seven hours yet to daylight and the coldest part of the night yet to come.

We do not realize the difference in the length of a winter's night compared to the brief four or five hours of half-darkness at midsummer. A night of fifteen hours' duration, that is the lot of our winter birds. Small wonder the rooks have to work so hard, and continuously in December and January, they have to stoke up the fires to last them all that time! And the same applies to all our wintering diurnal birds.

In one wildly flying mass the geese beat round again into the wind and settle on the sea. If it had been calm they would have swum slowly in to the shore, but now the ochre rollers (full of sand particles) are running. Each bird rises and falls into the troughs of the waves like a miniature fishing smack, each head to wind. But they dislike the boisterous wind, spinning and tossing them in the air.

This cannot be borne so they flog forwards up wind in unison and take the air again. In a moment or so they see below them the edge of the marsh whitened with the snow. Inland fields also show now, white even in the darkness, but there is no shelter there.

Down they come in a cloud among the short reeds of the shore; instantly they feel the shelter of the two-foot-high growth. The wind can no longer reach them. It spitefully yet so vainly flutters the reed tips above their heads as they settle down. Here they are snug and warm, as snug (comparatively speaking) as the fieldfares or the sparrows in the straw stack. It must be a blessed relief to feel at peace, no waves buffeting them, no wind ruffling their feathers the wrong way.

And so they sleep on towards the dawn, the whole vast company. Now and again a wakeful watchful gander will call 'wink! quink!' but the main mass is asleep, sound, sound asleep. Wildfowl, once they have dropped right off, slumber very soundly. I have stalked sleeping geese at dawn, even when the light is quite strong, and they have never heard or seen me; each bird would be sitting down with intucked head, one or two perhaps standing on one leg, for a goose can rest almost as well in that position.

The roar of the tide grows louder and soon after five o'clock, when it is still dark and snowing hard, and the wind still booms over the white-capped waves, it begins to wash and slap among the reeds. The outermost geese wake, retreating into the inner marsh. The gaggles are pushed slowly back into the higher, warmer reeds where the growth is thick.

That is the limit of the tide this morning, and soon after 6 a.m. it begins to drop back, the signal being a redoubled roar of surf a little way from shore. This roar of the turn of the tide is very noticeable on the sand flats, even on a dead calm day. It is the tide turning back on itself. An ancient sound, we cannot say how long this eternal movement has been going on—millions of years.

A wan grey light appears in the east. The snow has stopped now, save for a few lone questing flakes. The wind drops a little. The awful night, like the tide, is almost spent.

And as the light grows the geese wake up and talk grows to a babel, the babel to a roar, bird answering bird. After the long, black, icy night their bellies are very empty; soon they begin to walk about in the 'plickplack' and tear at the reed roots, throwing back their chins as they gobble the nut-like tubers.

Hundreds of sharp eyes scan the gloom of the shoreward reed beds but they do not, as yet, spy the creeping slug-like form of a gunner, squirming along the bottom of a shallow gutter.

He rolls himself along on his elbows. The icy water has soaked him above the waist, it has half-filled his waders, yet the man is warm, warm with anticipation, the exertion, and the excitement of his stalk. Only his hands are half-frozen, and every now and then he has to put each hand in turn under his armpit to keep it warm.

But this growing grey light is a danger signal to the geese. This is no place to be at eight-thirty on a January morning! Yet hunger is still a driving force and each bird tears and gulps at the reeds as though anxious to make the most of its last few moments. Some fight together, old enemies in the gaggles.

A little apart is the old gander, one of the leaders of the skeins. He has won that position like the master-dog of a sleigh team. I have seen a skein of geese in flight led by an old bird, and a youngster (he must have had force of character and would one day, if he were spared, be a leader of the skein himself) move up from a position astern of the old bird and try to take the lead. But the old bird turned on him in the air and forced him back to his proper station.

Now this old bird, who has come to this estuary for fifteen seasons, spies a black round object bob up and down among the reeds a hundred yards away.

It is a sight he has seen many times in his long career. In his experience it has been followed, on at least two occasions, by the whistle of death-dealing lead, humming like bees about him, some smashing through his broad vanes, breaking precious quills.

In a moment he is up, the whole gaggle with him. The thunder of wings fills the air as the man rises quickly to his knee, his gun half-raised. But the birds are too far away and no whistling hail comes after them. The great company fly low ('clawing' along like a centipede) over the muds which are now bare, and away they go into the dim distances of mid-river.

The man curses and then smiles to himself. His hands are masked with icy mire, he is soaked and shivering now. No warmth in him. The sickness of disappointment dies slowly but he cannot help admiring the sagacity of these grey birds. All pretence at concealment is cast aside and he rises to his full height, looking out over the river where the dawn is now coming quickly. Beaten again! So have I seen an old dog fox, when baulked of his prey, gaze wistfully after a departing partridge.

If there had been no 'plickplack', and no cover in the short reeds, those geese would have come down on the bare saltings. But danger threatens there also from winding creeks. If there were no creeks the geese would be as safe on the merse as on their mid-sea sands; that is why open saltings with no gutters are so favoured by the gaggles.

I never fail to admire the hardihood of these birds who seem so impervious to the worst the weather can do. The only thing they cannot stand for long is hard continued frost, but the answer is they do *not* stand it; with their wide pinions they go elsewhere, to the warm green bogs of the west coast; there is always some place where they can find food and gentler conditions.

Wigeon, more than any other wildfowl, appear to be able to see well on the darkest night and this has always puzzled me. Their eyes are no different in appearance from any other ducks, they certainly are not 'night eyes' like those of the owl.

Yet wigeon find their way about the marshes when there is barely a glim of moon, and do not flight in from their daytime resting places until it is too dark to see.

Sometimes one may find their feeding grounds on the saltings, those areas of fine grass which they delight in. The piles of droppings are scattered everywhere and round the 'flashes' delicately pencilled feathers flutter from grass tips.

You think that this is the place. The birds were here in force last night, they will come to-night! You sally hopefully forth at dusk with the cartridge belt heavy around your waist, fully expecting a weighty bag.

Yet darkness comes, the moon rises, and not a wigeon comes near you. You may hear them whistling in the distance, the 'wheeo' of the drakes, the deep purr of the ducks, but not a single bird passes by, still less circles to land. One can never tell *what* the wigeon are going to do. But on another night, perhaps, when you are out on the merse they will come thick and fast, pack after pack, and they seem to ignore the continuous cannonade.

The fact is, I think, that wigeon have very many feeding grounds on their 'visiting list', that they will not use the same one night after night. Long experience has told them it is dangerous to do so.

Though we can lay down rough and ready rules for wild-fowling, the birds never fall into the dangerous habit of sticking to one place. Those rules might be mentioned here, though I have tried to avoid in this book the technical side.

Rule 1. No moon.

Geese will feed by day and sleep on the sands at night, coming in at dawn. Therefore, moonless periods are best for flight shooting on the shore.

Rule 2. Half-moon, waxing.

If the sky is clear geese will lift from the sand banks or the sea as soon as there is enough light. Some may remain on the sleeping ground all night and flight out at dawn in the usual way.

Rule 3. Full moon.

Geese feed inland at night returning at dawn, invariably far out of shot. They will sleep through the day but *some* will go inland to feed. In fact, one might say there are always small parties shuttling back and forth at all hours of day and night. But there is no 'grand army' coming in at dawn.

Rule 4. Hard weather (continued frost over several weeks).

Geese will go away, returning the day before the thaw begins. In some way they know when a thaw is imminent.

The above remarks apply, remember, to *grey geese*. *Black geese* or Brent will, for the most part, always feed by day when there is no full moon, but in some districts where they are harried by punters they will also feed under a half-moon on the slobs. On dark nights they very rarely feed near the shore unless they have been kept off the 'zos' beds by gales during the daylight hours.

Barnacle geese are, for the most part, night feeders and seem to be able to see as well as wigeon.

These rough-and-ready rules apply, though less rigidly, to the *mallard*. The mallard I have always found the most unpredictable quarry, one never knows where they will flight in (or out) or when they will do so. Their feeding grounds, such as potato fields, or barley stubble, are changed from night to night, but it is safe to say that by far the greatest number of mallard are shot inland on the fields, mostly soon after harvest. I never remember bagging more than seven mallard on one flight on the marshes. I sometimes think that the wild sea-going mallard is harder to shoot than the geese.

Wind and tide, of course, affect all these rules. It may be said that high water and wild weather, combined with dusk or dawn (the two coinciding), will produce some sport, either with geese or duck.

But as I say, we cannot form hard and fast rules, and it is this uncertainty which makes wildfowling such a fascinating game.

Whether or not grey geese, especially pink-footed geese, have visited Britain in greater numbers than they did half a century ago, I am not expert enough to say. But from all accounts there does seem to have been an increase in numbers during the last thirty years, and that larger numbers visit the Lincolnshire potato fields. They appear to benefit from extensive agriculture, one of the few species that do so. I do not think, however, that we have seen so many during the last five years. It must be remembered that in Lincolnshire the geese have a great measure of protection. At first the farmers were dismayed when the grey legions descended on their winter wheat fields, eating down the crops, and boys were employed to drive them away. Now it is found the geese actually benefit the crop, eating it back and so making it strong, and well manuring the ground.

Nor do the Lincolnshire farmers allow gunners to disturb the birds, and on some big farms they are protected. A great deal of this reluctance on the part of the farmers to give permission to strangers is most understandable. Each year they are pestered to death by people begging permission. At first this was granted, until the 'fowlers' began to help themselves to pheasants and part-ridges. Lincolnshire is crawling with game; pheasants and partridges may be seen in dozens on the roads and just over the hedges, and the 'cad gunner' has no scruples about helping himself.

Were I a Lincolnshire farmer I would be just as adamant. The sporting farmer does occasionally shoot up the geese on his land with a party of friends, twice or thrice a year, and big bags are sometimes made, usually at night under the moon when the geese are coming to 'taty bottoms' and winter wheat. But as a rule they take little interest in wildfowling. The vast majority are hard-working, and very rich men, for the black fenland soil is some of the finest in Britain.

I have not visited the Wash district at the time the geese are making ready to return to their arctic homes. But I believe that most of the birds do not start the return journey from there but go north to the hereditary tribal 'airports' or 'jumping' places. I only know this from hearsay and cannot be sure of this statement. I do not think that one sees on the east-coast saltings the vast gatherings one sees, say, on Loch Leven, or the northern firths.

It is very strange that the species keep more or less to their own winter territories. Whitefronts at Wells, pinks on the Wash (with a few greys and bean geese), whitefronts on the Severn, Anglesey, and Ireland, barnacles on the Solway and the Western Isles.

What the effect will be of the reclaiming of the Wash is not yet known; it is too early to say. But I doubt whether it will affect the geese very much as in any case they have never resorted to the saltings in the numbers that frequented the inland feeding grounds. (From recent reports I hear the wigeon have increased.) Geese do sometimes pitch on the Wash saltings and even feed there, but this is rare and now it is very noticeable that they fly far out of gunshot when they come over the marshes. When I first shot the Wash one could often get a shot from the gutters.

Some years ago an acquaintance asked me where he could shoot a goose. He had never done any goose hunting before, he told me, all his sport was inland at driven game, but he wished to try his hand at wildfowling, and that is why he came to me.

Contrary to my usual procedure, I told him where to go, I even drew a map and marked in all the dykes and gutters and showed him the exact spot—as near as I could judge—where I shot my first goose.

Accordingly he went and when next I saw him I asked how he had fared.

"I got a goose," he said, "got it from the very gutter you told me about! I followed the directions on your map and the geese came over, just where you said they would! But wildfowling is a silly game," he told me, "you get beastly cold, wet, and muddy, the idiotic birds fly far too high and I'm not going again. It's a silly sort of game. Why, you hardly let your gun off! But I shot several gulls."

Evidently this man was not a born fowler and what riled me was the fact he shot a goose!

Even that did not please him. "Nasty tough brutes with no taste at all," was his verdict.

But occasionally I have put friends wise to the game. Two ex-Service men, good sound fellows, and keen wildfowlers, who once asked me if they could accompany me on one of my fowling trips, had the time of their lives. One wild morning on a western estuary, when they were with me, they shot fourteen greylags at morning flight, using borrowed decoys.

After that slaughter, I think they had a sneaking idea that wild goose hunting was a 'piece of cake', but I doubt whether they ever shot so many again in a single morning and one of them, I know, was rather sickened by the slaughter of so many of these lovely birds.

Five or six geese in one trip is enough for any one gun, and you will be lucky if you get a single goose on unpreserved ground. Private goose shoots are a different matter. Then, on a well-keepered goose marsh, you may kill as many as you like. But that is not wildfowling, and it ranks with shooting hand-reared mallard.

It is far better fun to work hard for your game, and have three or four real chances in a week, than to kill a cartload in a single drive.

The wild goose soon becomes most trusting when he is protected. On the Solway, after the season is over, they may be seen feeding within gunshot of the high road, and this applies to the Lincolnshire geese, not only after the season has ended on the last day of January, be it said, but all through the winter season.

Of the two geese the greylags are more trusting and will fly at a lower altitude, especially at dusk when they have been feeding a few fields back from the shore.

But the pinks will never 'flop in' like the greys and, in any case, they rarely feed close to their sleeping grounds but voyage ten or a dozen miles to feed, sometimes a good deal farther. They have a much better idea of how to look after themselves.

What does anger me on the estuaries is to meet some so-called 'fowler' armed with a small bore rifle.

To shoot a goose with a rifle is most unsporting. The wild goose has come to gauge the range of a scatter gun and plans accordingly. But to send bullets whistling about the gaggles as they rest on the high sands only serves to put them right off the district. They are as nervous of a rifle as they are of a hawk, and geese, like elephants, have long memories.

The pink-footed goose has strange breeding habits. It nests in Spitzbergen in June, so that the birds leave these shores in April, but sometimes linger until early May. In that country it makes its nest on the ledges of cliffs, and it uses the same hollow year after year, lining it with grass and a mass of feathers. The nest is large. It will also breed on islands and on the open tundra, but the risk from the arctic foxes is great and very many nests built on the ground are ravaged.

It has been the subject of much speculation how the goslings are transferred from the breeding ledges to the water below, as some nests are lofty.

The most likely way is for the gosling to 'parachute' down, for they leave the nest almost as soon as hatched. It is amazing how goslings, and even ducklings, can descend from a considerable height without taking harm, but it must be remembered that they are very light, and as they go down flippers are spread and the impact of landing is small.

The pinkfoot also breeds in Greenland and Iceland, and there may be other breeding grounds as yet undiscovered.

The greylag is the only wild goose which breeds with us, in the far north of Scotland, and some of the outer islands. The nest is always on the ground and, like that of the pinkfoot, is a fairly large affair. It also breeds in Iceland, Finland, and the Baltic States and sparingly on the Continent.

The breeding grounds of the barnacle goose were for a long time unknown until A. Koenig discovered it nesting in Spitzbergen: again, like the pinkfoot, it breeds on the rocky ledges. But there must be other breeding grounds so far undiscovered.

The Brent, however, does not breed on the ledges but makes its nest on the marshes and tundra, in Spitzbergen and elsewhere. For some reason Spitzbergen seems to be the true home of most of the geese which visit our shores. Much useful information on their breeding stations was collected by such explorer-naturalists as

S. W. P. Freme, Trevor Battaye, Congreve, and others. Peter Scott has also done some very useful research; indeed it might be said that he, more than any other, has made a very close study of wild geese of all species which visit these islands, and has been able to pass on his knowledge by means of his fine paintings and entertaining writing. When he was at school at Oundle he was able to study the whitefronts in the field, for in those days they frequented the flooded pastures every winter. Now the Nene Catchment Board has got busy, these floods no longer come out in the rainy seasons or, if they do, never remain for more than a day or so. The whitefronts are gradually ceasing to visit the district, and in time they will be a rarity in the valley of the Nene.

24. Butterfly Weather

ONCE Christmas is past, and as soon as December is out, one begins to feel the turn of the year. Even in January, which is the prime month for the longshore gunner, there comes an odd day or so when the sun shines brightly, and even the geese feeding out in the centre of the lowland fields sit about lazily, sleeping and preening. Such days, I have noticed, occur very frequently in the north during the first fortnight of January. There is a great truth in the old country saying that as the days get longer the cold gets stronger, and the countryside never looks so bare and naked as in March, for instance, when the winter growth has completely died down and all fallen leaves have been eaten by the worms or blown away. But when fine days do come, there is a perceptible increase of warmth in the sun. The fowler, waiting on the shore at evening, notes that the sun has begun its forward journey, and is setting just that much farther along the mountains, and he smells a new smell down among the reed paths.

In these fine, still days when one hears a thrush or two trying a few tentative staves, flighting on the shore is useless. Our old friend Colonel Hawker hated these tranquil times of midwinter because they so often coincided with his arrival at his fowling quarters at Keyhaven, when the fair-weather fowlers, the Milford Snobs (all boots and breeches), emerged like flies after winter's cold and banged away to their hearts' content.

Yet for me these days have wondrous beauty. It does not worry me that for once the gun remains silent. I rejoice with the geese that a truce has been declared by men and weather, that no hateful winds vex those majestic grey birds stalking on the furrow. I believe that on such days the thoughts of the geese turn to the flowering mosses and tundras of their birth-land and certainly sexual desires are awakened. One may see many a little act of sly love-making among the lazy, resting gaggles.

These are the times that rejoice their hearts and the gladness and happiness is noticeable when the geese gather on the sand-banks after sun up. There is much chatter, much coming and going, much bathing and preening, much flapping of wings.

The flight-out is unhurried. They pass in chiming chevrons and orderly lines, far up in the cloudless sky, the early sun shining upon them so that even their paddles may be seen. As you walk back along the sea wall they pass over. In the bright light the berries in the hedges gleam a brilliant scarlet, wet as yet with the dew. Among the branches of the straggling bushes on the bank the fieldfares and redwings sit and preen, they too love this sun, as much as the geese. Sometimes I have heard the fieldfares sing; their thoughts are turn-ing to the northern pine forests over the sea—perhaps they see shadowy mind pictures of the breeding colonies, and smell the scent of the pines. We do not know what goes on in the mind of a bird.

Down on the saltings a stand of plover are massed, their white underparts shining out against the grey-green background. Red-shanks flicker along the dykes, their white wing bars flick, flicking; their clear 'pew! pew! pews!' carry far on the still crystal air.

I like the redshank. It is a delicately built wader with simple plumage, but its orange legs and black and white flash of wings is most attractive.

What a yodelling of curlew comes this morning from the sands! Even the tide seems to be basking out there in the river, and acres of gleaming mud are peopled with tiny dots as dunlin and knot run hither and thither. The curlews are all along the tide edge, so far you can hardly see them in the glasses.

They are strung like small beads along the fringe of the bright winking water, each with a reflection which makes them look as big as geese. Now and again one or two lift and come wavering in low across the sands—'curlee! curlee!' As they near the shore they rise a little and pass in towards the green fields.

Hundreds of curlew are stalking about on the grass behind the sea wall, golden and green plover with them. The little crested green plover are not shy of man, and as you climb the sea wall and scan the fields, several are within twenty yards of you, standing upright, their crests so trim and jaunty, looking at you. Then one runs on twinkling feet a little way, stops, and pecks at an imaginary object. This is an amusing trick of plover when they know they are being watched; it is a sort of vanity, I fancy. "See!" they seem to say, "am I not a fine bird with my blue-green back shot with purple, my snow-white flanks and cheeky crest? And notice my under-tail coverts! What other bird has such a sunset-orange tint under its tail!"

The golden plover, despite their high-sounding name, are drab mouse-like birds in winter kit; they are not so friendly, they keep their distance. Their eyes are on you as you stand with lifted bin-oculars. Now and again the whole stand rises and flies in unison like dunlin, twisting and turning to drop again on the sward.

The bright morning sky is full of gulls coming in and their snow-white forms dot the fields. They do not feed near the sea wall but keep well out, like the geese, which is strange, as they are not persecuted.

A white curtain hovers behind the tractor over there in the far field, it stoops to the newly turned furrow, as it does to the surface of the sea. The gulls pick up a worm, their white wings fan, and on they go with hanging legs, eagerly scanning the bright plough-share and its dark stirring wake.

Running in and out, almost hidden by the larger tufts of the meadow grass, the starlings are busy, their bodies gleaming like those of beetles. Now and again they rise up in the air, two birds at a time, fighting and jangling over some morsel. They are greedy, quarrelsome birds but the quarrels are soon made up.

Far out in the centre of a level green field (and it looks a spring green this morning) a party of thirty-three pink-footed geese are sitting. About a quarter of their number is standing very still with their heads up. The others are walking about in a leisurely manner, cropping the grass with graceful plucks, their necks curled close to their bodies like swans. They seem a pale buff, like short-eared owls, in the bright light, but their necks are dark in contrast.

As the sun climbs higher and its warmth increases the geese settle down, all save three who stand sentinel. I love to watch them on these serene sunny mornings. One by one their heads are tucked into backs, and through my powerful glasses I can see their eyes are closed. The sentries begin to walk about, stopping now and again to take a very careful scrutiny of their surroundings. It makes me smile to watch the sentries when they are scanning for danger. Through the glass I look directly into their cunning little brown eyes, but they cannot see me.

Occasionally they will pluck uneasily for a minute at the grass, ten or eleven plucks, then up goes the head again, and for a full two minutes they will stand motionless, turning their heads in every direction.

You would think that geese would be quite unshootable out on that open field, with not a dip or gully, not a piece of dead ground behind which one could stalk. But Jim Jagoe shoots them on mornings like this, and he shoots them on these same flat fields. How he does it I know very well, and would like to describe his method, but in the interests of my feathered heroes I will keep silent lest others, reading these pages, follow his example. I have tried his method myself, and found it deadly. But it is not true fowling.

The stutter of the tractor stops. The driver, I see, is climbing down from his seat, and is plodding away to the farm by the tall bare poplars for his luncheon.

The sentries catch sight of him, though the man is five hundred yards away, and the low warning 'quick! quick!' brings every head from every back. But the resting geese know that no imminent danger threatens, and, after watching the sentries for a moment or two, tuck their heads in again.

Now come away to the high mountain crests which line the immediate horizon. Climb with me up the long winding road among the beech and pine woods, smell the clean sweet air and feel its growing chill.

A wonderful view is soon revealed, the far gleaming river and the mountains on the far side. You can see now (but not without some effort of geography) all the favourite spots of yours, Smith's Post away there on the right, the line of oaks by Jim Jagoe's cottage, the Long Breakwater and the Castle towering over its buttressing woods.

To the left is Bight Point and Curlew Bay; Curlew Rock you can see, even at this great distance, for your stalker's telescope is powerful and the light is good.

There is Leaning Buoy and Goose's Graveyard, there is the farm and the long neat row of conical stacks where you leave your cycle at morning flight.

You turn and climb higher still towards the summit, and at once the summer feeling is forgotten for King Winter reigns up here. There is white hoar frost on the road, the burn on the right, plunging down its wooded chasm, is fringed with ice, but it sends up to you a merry music on the keen air. It is like stepping from April into December.

Here is an upland country of sloping fields and trim farms and, higher still, grim jagged peaks of rock, red bracken and heather. We will not climb to the very top, for with every step our dreams of spring and summer are dispelled, but, resting by the bole of this giant beech (the tits are ringing their tit bells in the graceful branches), will scan the whole expanse of the level land below with its pattern of green fields and dark earth.

Soon you will spy a skein of geese coming off the estuary. They are heading this way, and no doubt intend to cross the mountain range.

You are looking down on them, on their grey backs and slow flapping wings. It seems to take them a very long time to come. Now and then you lose them against the sombre tones of wood and field, but then you pick them up again and at last, very faintly, you hear their music. It is a big skein of six or seven hundred birds. They wheel now and then and go parallel to the mountain, as though they are searching for a quiet field where they may alight. But the leader is adamant. "Over the hills, my boys," he seems to say, "stop this circling round", and so on they come, still in our direction.

Now you can put the glasses down, for the birds are near enough to be seen clearly with the naked eye, and you notice you are no longer looking down *on* them, you are on a level with the skein, and this makes them harder to pick out. Now they are rising and you are looking at their bellies, and here at last they come, right overhead. Instinctively you shrink back under the cover of the beechen boughs, and through that delicate twig tracery you see the skein pass directly over in grand display. You can see with the naked eye the paddles tucked under the white sterns. And look at that old leading gander! He is a quarter bigger than any of the others; he must be an eight pounder, maybe even more!

They have passed, they have gone, and you come out from under the beech for a last glimpse. There they go, over the far ridge between two jagged peaks of rock.

I have talked with men who have tried to ambush the geese from the ridge top and sometimes they have been successful, but it can be imagined how hard it is to judge just *where* the skeins will pass.

Now the birds appear to be dropping. One by one they sink behind the range and now their wings are set. They have gained the summit, and can now begin a long glide to the valley fields by the famous salmon river beloved of kings.

There, the last 'Arse-end Charlie' has vanished from view, and you will not see that skein again until evening comes and the stars are lit. Then, in the last glimmer of day, that same skein will return to the sea and maybe, as you sit beside your cosy fire in your fowling digs, you will hear them pass right over the village.

Now, as you see the last bird out of sight over the ridge, you wish them well, and may they have five hours of peaceful feeding with no alarums or disturbance.

Already, as you reach the lowland road, the sun is setting behind the Castle woods. There is a chill in the air which hints at frost.

But though it has been a 'butterfly day', it has been enjoyable. Not all the fun of wildfowling consists of pulling a trigger.

25. Dull but Necessary

I WAS afraid I should find myself writing this chapter before I reached the end of my book! But I am well aware that many people do not know very much about wildfowl or how, if they are sportsmen, they may be shot.

In writing (as in broadcasting) one has to remember that what interests you, the author, does not necessarily interest everybody else. You will hold the attention of those who 'speak the same language' as yourself, but if one writes entirely of the habits and mannerisms of ducks and geese, and lets oneself go on descriptive matter, although such matter is based on actual experience (as mine is), then some people will complain and cast the book aside as mere twaddle.

There will even be people who will feel an anger within them that I, who profess to love wild birds so much, specially wildfowl, seek to slay them. With these people I cannot enter into argument. I only know that, like Richard Jefferies, I enjoy birds and nature more if I have a gun under my arm.

Then there will be practical level-headed fellows who have no use for moonshine, who are not stirred, as I am, by the cries of wild-fowl in the night and the majesty of the starlit saltings. They will want to know something of ballistics, what are the best guns to use, what size shot is the most useful, and so forth.

What I do want to make plain is that this chapter is not included for 'padding'. It is necessary for those who will demand it, and if you are not interested in guns or gear then skip the following pages!

First, let us discuss gear, by which I mean clothing and cartridge carriers, etc.

It is a curious thing that those who first take up wildfowling invariably dress in the most unsuitable manner, usually rubber knee boots—sometimes not even those—a flapping mackintosh, and hatless, or if they do wear headgear, it is a cap. (I have seen pipit poppers in Homburgs!)

In very bad weather, driving wind and rain, the cap is not a good head covering. The water soon soaks it through and the peak is inadequate. Eventually the cap becomes a sodden pudding on one's head and water begins to trickle slowly down one's neck, which is cooling to one's ardour.

A balaclava is an excellent fowling headgear. It keeps the ears warm, and if made of windproof felt, as mine is, it will take a very long time to reach saturation point. Its only disadvantage is that it shields the ears. Ears are as useful as eyes to the longshore gunner.

Also, when it does at last become sodden, it will take a very long time to dry. My balaclava has several large holes burnt in it, the reason being that I am an absent-minded person, and I have frequently put it in the hearth to dry and forgotten all about it. I have also used it as an oven cloth when cooking Oystercock Pie.

My wife patiently darns these holes, but others appear in the fullness of time, so that it now presents a somewhat dilapidated appearance. I found that when I wore a cap, and my ears were uncovered, the latter appendages became almost frostbitten on several occasions. The average sportsman has no idea of the rigours of dawn and night shooting in the far north in the depth of winter, especially if there is an icy wind blowing.

Two years ago I discovered the best possible headgear for fowl-ing, the old-fashioned deerstalker. It is waterproof, and is so cunningly designed that one's head is protected by a miniature roof which sheds the water clear of the neck, and it is beautifully warm, indeed too warm at times, for the head sweats with bodily exertion, and there is no ventilation in a waterproof hat. The eaves of the deerstalker come low enough to deflect both water and wind from the ears, and it is also the colour of the reeds and winter mosses. They are not easy to purchase.

The only advantage a balaclava has over the deerstalker is that with the former the face is partly covered. This is of great impor-tance to the goose hunter. Wildfowl detect the pale flesh tones of the face very easily as one is usually against a dark-toned back-ground. But this drawback can be overcome by rubbing the face with the mud of the district (the complexion benefits too).

A word of warning. Wear a deerstalker south of the Border, and small boys will openly remark upon it, and adults will smile to themselves as they pass by, they will also turn round and stare. Over the Border the deerstalker is looked upon as perfectly normal, shepherds and farmers wear them, keepers and stalkers swear by them.

Woollen underwear, long pants, a muffler for the neck, a leather waistcoat, topped by a dark-toned raincoat of the best quality, or, better still, an American 'hunting jacket', which has a big collar which you can turn up, and a belt round the waist, are the best garments.

The hunting jacket has long skirts (with big deep pockets) which come below the tops of your thigh waders. This is a most impor-tant point. If your raincoat is too short it will guide the water down inside your boots.

Your rubber 'gutty' boots should be those that deep-sea fishermen wear. The tops should be high, protecting the thighs (these can be rolled down if you wish to appear 'tough'), and they should need no strap to attach to one's braces. Inside these, long fishermen's stockings are ideal, failing that, ordinary long stockings, but they must be thick. A sock worn the wrong way round, with the heel uppermost, will prevent that annoying 'potato' heel which is such a bugbear, and which so soon causes a blister on the heel. One does not take one's wife wildfowling, remember.

For straightforward walking on the saltings, where there is no deep mud or large gutters to be waded, shepherds' waterproof trousers are the best. These are worn over knee-high waders and the legs are completely protected. But no clothing, other than that of a 'frogman', will keep you dry if you have to get down in the mud and crawl. That is the only time you should have an excuse for getting wet. One more point, which I have mentioned before, always have a thick paper sole inside your thigh boots as this absorbs the perspiration. 'Gutty' boots will soon become soaking wet inside if the sweat is not absorbed, and will be quite unfit to wear after a day's creek jumping.

To dry such boots, fill with rolled-up balls of newspaper right up to the tops (you will need many copies of *The Times* for this) and stand the boots in the grate, but not too near the fire. They will be fit to wear in the morning.

The best possible arrangement is to have *two* pairs of 'gutty' boots and wear them on alternate days.

For hand covering I prefer leather gloves to mittens. Not stiff thick leather, but pliable skin. They will get wet in time but can soon be dried. Waterproof gauntlet gloves can be worn if you have much mud crawling to do.

The reader may wonder why I have devoted so much space to clothing but it is of the greatest importance to keep dry and warm. Fowlers who neglect to look after themselves suffer later in life.

Some suffer at the time and valuable fowling days are spent in bed, usually at not-so-comfortable digs.

Cartridges are best carried in a clip belt under your hunting coat so that they are out of the wet. I suggest a belt because you can then separate your cartridges, *sevens* for snipe, *fives* for duck, and *BBs* or *ones* for geese. All these can be clipped in at appropriate distances round the belt, and it is wise to memorize the position, otherwise in a hot corner you will be shooting at geese with *number eights*, and be wondering why the birds treat you with such disdain. (They will do that anyway unless you are a good shot and they are well in range.)

I have tried all sizes of shot for geese from Home Guard SSG issue to *number fives*. I have brought off some spectacular shots with SSG at very high skeins, but this is not a thing to boast about, rather it is something to be ashamed of as no sky-high geese should ever be fired at.

I must confess, however, that sometimes in desperation I have shot at high geese with SSG. Once I remember firing from the sea wall in the north of England: I killed a pink, the leader of the skein, at a hundred yards. It fell stone dead in a ploughed field half a mile away and split itself in half. When I examined it I found one SSG had passed obliquely through its head from the underside of the chin.

BB and number one shot are the best for geese. With anything larger than BB you get a very open pattern. One ounce of SSG contains only 15 pellets, BB 70 pellets, and number one 100 pellets. Some goose shooters swear by threes, and in one ounce of three you get 140 pellets, which is going to give you a respectable pattern out of a 3-inch twelve (which will carry more than an ounce). My 3-inch case Magnum twelve is proved for $1\frac{1}{2}$ ounces of shot, and Belching Bess $2\frac{1}{8}$ ounces in a $3\frac{1}{2}$-inch case, more than double that of the twelve.

The recoil of these big guns is considerable, and after a good flight, when a dozen or more shots may be fired, you will suffer from a hangover. In my case my nose invariably bleeds. However, a little bloodletting is judged by many longshore fowlers as a certain relief from 'goose fever'.

On the whole the 3-inch case Magnum is the best gun; it is lighter, and if you hold it straight will more than equal an eight. Start with an eight if you wish for some encouragement for, to an indifferent shot, the increased pattern is, of course, more deadly, but later, when you have got to know the ropes, take to the 3-inch Magnum.

I do not think the length of barrels matters very much.

Always have a canvas cover for the gun and, when stalking in mud, cork the end. Remove the cork before you fire, because if it happens to be a long cork which fits well down the barrel it may be the last time you will ever shoot at a goose.

Needless to say, clean the gun after use and never leave it dirty overnight. Sea-water plays havoc with a gun however well you look after it, and that is why it is inadvisable to use a really high-class gun for this type of shooting.

The game (if you shoot any) can be carried in a goose bag. These are ample bags with an outside net and within you can place your air cushion which you will inflate when you wish to 'sit up' in a creek.

I once knew a fowler who took with him on to the marsh one of those rubber rings, or 'invalid' air cushions. When he sat down all was well until the ring began to sink, and soon he found he was sitting in a little ornamental pool in which goldfish could have swum quite contentedly.

On strange saltings carry a compass. Fog can be dangerous; a whistle, too, is useful. If you are shooting with a companion a timely blast may warn him of approaching geese.

And one or two last words on the actual shooting. Fowlers sometimes go to extraordinary lengths when they are just beginning to shoot and carry to the marsh all manner of strange devices for their comfort, massive flasks filled with rum, special 'sit boards', and once I seem to remember a chicken-hearted fowler who, dreading a night out on frozen muds, tied a hot water bottle under his coat. This was moved about as various parts of his anatomy felt the grip of the frost. It was a cumbersome way of keeping warm but effective. I know, because that chicken-heart was myself. It is an awful confession to make, but that night there was a truly grim frost, and I was lying for hours on the open muds. Remember, I was very young and callow, so do not be too hard on me. I need not have said anything about it.

If you wish to know more about weapons and ballistics I advise a study of Sir G. Burrard's learned words on the subject, and there is an excellent chapter in the late Terence Horsley's book on wild-fowling which was published in 1947, an entertaining book by one who knew the game.

That is all I am going to say about guns and ammunition, and the practical reader must be satisfied with what I have written.

I do not know a lot about guns, nor do I take the care I should of my own guns. Some fowlers have an immense pride in their weapons, and quite rightly too. But with me the wildfowl interest me more than the gun.

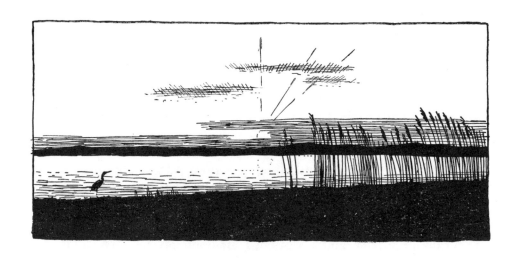

26. The First Star

THE brief winter's afternoon is drawing to its close. It has been one of those calm frosty days we so often get in the north in January; there has been no cloud in the sky since dawn, then there was mist. Now those mists are gathering again, lying in level veils close to the surface of the marsh. Later, when the moon has risen, it may be thick. Jim Jagoe thinks so. As we came past his cottage on the bank he was standing looking at the sky, his dog by his side. At the foot of the bank, tied to the rickety ladder which serves him as a jetty, was his gunning punt, trim and ship-shape, a long sinister craft painted white from stem to stern, a man-o'-war in miniature.

"Och aye, it'll be frosty the nicht, some fog maybe." Jim does not want to gossip and I can see he wishes us elsewhere.

Opposite, on the bank top, the oak tree twigs are madder black against a salmon-tinted sky; a few gulls pass silently across, the advance guards of the evening flocks which will soon be coming out from the fields. The atmosphere is so still the rattle of a dredger far out in mid-channel can be heard, even the voices of the crew come clearly over the water.

We leave Jim Jagoe standing by his cottage, a dark sulky

silhouette against the reflected glow of the evening sky in the burn, and walk away along the bank top.

The straggling hedge is, even in this late month, laden with berries, and from them the fieldfares rise up while we are yet eighty yards distant. This estuary is one of their first 'landfalls' after their journey over the sea. On days when the big migrations are on, you will see countless thousands feeding on these thorns. They are hungry after their journey, but they will not tarry long. The wander pain is still working within them, they will scatter far and wide, ever journeying south. Though a bird of the cold lands, like the redwings, they are not so hardy as our native thrushes, and a prolonged frost will reduce them to skeletons while our native birds are fat and well.

The bank top is rough to walk upon, but it is better going now because it is frozen hard; in mild weather it is a real labour to plough through the slippery mud in rubber waders. There is a keen, sharp smell in the air which tells more than anything it will be a hard frost as soon as the sun is down.

How clear are the mountain tops to-night! Their edges are so keen against the sky and you can see the blue-white tint of snow on those high crests.

Here is the path down the bank by the ancient rowan tree, and at the bottom of the bank is a spring. The grass is a bright green even in the frost and, no matter how hard the weather, it is always soft just there for the water, welling up imperceptibly from below, is warmed by the earth's inner body.

A snipe rises as we scramble down the bank—always a little startling, this 'jump' of a snipe; it seems to spring out of the ground, to be quite invisible until it is in the air. Even when you see a snipe alight (with that same suddenness), as soon as it touches the earth it seems to 'snuff out', so cunningly does it harmonize with its surroundings. The 'jazz' pattern on its back is responsible.

Had we a number eight cartridge in the breech we might have had a shot, yet somehow, this evening, it would seem sacrilege to break this stillness which has fallen over shore and estuary. The little zig‑zagging bird goes away over the dead, buff reed beds.

How strange it is to think we have seen these same reed beds in high summer when they are green, when each slender wand is tipped with a dark plume, soft and feathery! Yet how beautiful they are now in winter when seen against the sun—how the acres of feathery plumes seem to shimmer with a sheen!

Though it is barely roosting time, the starlings are beginning their evening exercises, rushing back and forth over the tops of the beds and settling now and again in a cloud upon the branches of an ash yonder, until the tree seems weighed down with a strange fruit, medlars perhaps, or blackened figs—or blood‑sucking bats.

As soon as they settle they begin to sing in unison a cascade of silvery, jangling notes which is like a mighty rushing wind, or the stridulations of a host of insects. But, as suddenly, the cataract of sound is cut short and away they go again in a madly whirling throng.

Why do they do this? Surely the explanation is that all through the short winter's day they have been busy winning their feed, bustling about on the low‑lying fields. Now they feel the need for wing exercise, just as a man, chained to an office stool, feels the need to walk, or even to run. So do the rooks in my midland meadows. They, too, must have their evening exercise, though in their case it is much later, when it is almost dark. The rook stays longer on the fields than any other inland bird. The pigeons go in first, then the jackdaws, and lastly the rooks, and they caw and wheel over their roosting woods long after other diurnal birds are tucked up to roost.

The estuary seems empty of wildfowl to‑night. The tide is far out, so far it is but a silver streak beyond the sand‑banks where those mists are gathering. Yes, Jim Jagoe was right, it will be thick out there as the tide floods, and it will not be long before the low slender punt steals to sea. The calamitous detonation of the big gun will set the echoes tumbling and rolling across the bay, and the stags up in the corries will lift their heads and cock their big ears. On such a night as this I have heard the rumbling echoes of a punt gun tossed back and forth for as long as sixty seconds.

Now we are down among the reeds, with our feet on the wind-ing path, the vista of saltings, mountain, and water is shut away. On all sides rise the slender wands, little birds flutter up as we pass along. There is a dank, marshy smell down here on a level with the river, as exciting a smell as that of leafy winter woods, or of park ponds.

The reeds thin, glimpses of water gleam forth, and the black tones of the 'plickplack'.

We cannot walk noiselessly now, for it is unfrozen down below, and in places the dead reeds have fallen, making a level roof through which a way must be broken. The foot must be lifted high and placed with care, for there are hidden gutters. Frost lies white on top of these horizontal reeds and here and there a whole mass is frozen solid. Many times I have used these frozen palisades to form the walls of a hide, for they are not attached to the dead reeds underneath. The tide breaks up the dead growth and pushes it all together into large sugary 'rafts' or cakes.

Right ahead is my favourite gully where the short reeds are some three feet high and act as a screen. I must, in my time, have shot a score of geese from this spot. With my feet in the gutter I sit on the goose bag and settle down to wait.

We cannot expect much to happen on a night like this; I can count on one hand the geese I have slain at evening flight. Had a wind been blowing we might have stood a chance, but to-night they will be heavens high. But an incautious mallard may come our way, or even a party of late greys which have been feeding on the fields behind the sea wall. Fortune holds many a surprise for the patient longshore gunner. Geese rarely gabble when feeding inland on the fields, they remain quite silent, very different from their habits when feeding on the marshes.

The starlings have ceased their evening exercises. A hush descends. Westwards the crimson sun has burnt down like a fiery coal behind the oaks, leaving a few streamers of pink cloud against a background of palest daffodil. Now we must wait.

There is a brief interval between the setting of the sun and flighting time. To the impatient shore-shooter this period seems an eternity.

The gulls have gone to the sand-banks (they began to drift out before the sun had touched the hills), their flight is as regular as that of homing rooks but far more leisurely and less vociferous; for the most part they are silent, though a few will utter a thread-like 'Keeeweeeze, keeeweeeze' as they pass over. If the evening is still they will twitch and turn in the air as though fly-catching, but this mannerism is merely a spasm of exuberance, of delight, at seeing the open water after the graceless seaward fields. Curlews will do the same thing; so will the wild geese.

When the gulls have gone out the geese follow. They come from distant pastures, possibly thirty miles or more inland, in long lines, rarely in arrow-heads, nearly always in a slanting line or, in other words, one 'leg' of a 'V'. On a calm evening such as this they are very high, so high they might even be plover or starlings. Sometimes they arrive with impressive music, unearthly, strangely moving; sometimes they are silent until they, like the gulls, first catch sight of the sea below them. Then they scatter and spread, each bird peeling off independently and descending in a swift, slide-slipping motion, wonderful to watch. They may be a mile from you, but even at that distance you will hear the indescribable sound of the rush of air through their broad vanes.

And as each bird comes to rest the whole skein will shout aloud, a triumphant glad outcry which, I fancy (but it is only fancy), has a hint of defiance in it.

Then there comes the lull I have described. A peaceful hush settles on the estuary. The clamour of the geese is stilled. I believe that after long hours in the fields they sink to sleep very quickly, even when day still lingers in the western sky. Their watch, for a while, is over, even their sentries sleep.

An occasional curlew will come in, low and late, and small bunches of green plover. These birds, with restless nervous beat of rounded wing, call one to another, 'Keer weet! Keer weet!'

They, too, are bound for the high sands.

You may scan the sky around, but no star shows. The turquoise tint above the hills is fading, the few faint golden streamers of cloud which mark the going of the sun fade also and dissolve away. Keep your eye fixed now upon that part of the sky where Jupiter is due to light his lamp. You see nothing. Man-made stars begin to wink across the water. From farmhouse and cottage, village and harbour, twinkle, twinkle, they spring out, and their reflections dance in the tranquil and sleeping tide.

You look again for Jupiter, and lo, he is there! It was as if he waited for that moment for you to turn your eyes away! Wink, blink, a holy spiritual light he sheds as he blinks his eye in the persistent glow of the sunset.

Now you shift your gaze to other points of the sky behind you where the gloom of night is advancing apace, to where other stars are pricking through. They come thick and fast, but somehow you miss their coming.

The silence has ended. The distant 'popping' of shots rouses your bewitched senses. Secret muttering quacks are heard, the thumb slides the roughened edge of the safety-catch forward, the spaniel gives a quiver, and stares with solemn eye and listens with ready ear. First he glances at your face and then at the vault above. The night is profoundly still, no breeze moves in the reeds, the gnarled oaks upon the dyke-top are sharp-etched, motionless. Faint and far-off whisperings come and pass. Sometimes you glimpse, against the pale flush in the west, a cluster of black bodies, apparently wingless and headless, speeding purposefully straight inshore. Nearer birds you may see, too, if you look hard enough, passing high overhead, far out of shot.

And this whispering of invisible wings and muffled duck-talk goes on for half an hour, you hear it when there is nothing above you but bright-diamond stars glittering in the deep blue immensity of space.

You may see the coming of the ducks—you will never see the coming of the first star.